Livin' the Dream

Life inside Britain's most successful *MXGP* team

Livin' the Dream

Life inside Britain's most successful *MXGP* team

ANDY GEE

BROWN
DOG
BOOKS

Published under licence by Brown Dog Books and
The Self-Publishing Partnership, 7 Green Park Station, Bath BA1 1JB

www.selfpublishingpartnership.co.uk

ISBN printed book: 978-1-78545-328-1
ISBN e-book: 978-1-78545-329-8

Cover design by Kevin Rylands
Internal design by Andrew Easton

Printed and bound in the UK

All photos by ace moto photographer Ray Archer unless otherwise stated.

Front cover
Graeme Irwin's Hitachi/ASA KTM 450 with his British championship number 1 plate
Back cover
The team picture, taken at the first round in Argentina.
L to R, Bryan Connolly (BC), Ian Browne, Graeme Irwin, Conrad Mewse,
Vaclav Lavicka (Vas), Paul Keates

Contents

Foreword

The life of an MXGP team is an on-going cycle that refreshes every year as one season finishes, and a new season begins. If the team had good results it's a time to build and make progress, if the results were below expectations then it's a time to wipe the slate clean and start over, but either way the work goes on with one caveat: that sufficient sponsors and funding can be gathered to let the cycle continue, otherwise it's the end for the team, at least in that iteration.

It's not uncommon for teams to fold, shutting their doors as the funding stream has run dry. But just as in nature, as one team dies a new one springs up, fresh with optimism and new ambition, sometimes buying up the remnants of the defunct team such as the transporter or employing the mechanics and other staff.

The subject of this book, Hitachi/ASA KTM UK, have been around for thirteen years, although not always in their current guise as sponsors, bike manufacturers and personnel have changed over the years.

With eleven British championships in that time, they're <u>the</u> most successful British teams in the paddock and one of only two full time grand prix teams that regularly compete in Britain.

My involvement with the team started years ago as a fan, but also as an old friend of some of the team riders and staff at that time. I worked for the Husqvarna importers back in the '80's and got to know a lot of the top riders of the day before my career took me elsewhere. In 2016 I was back on the grand prix trail and in 2017 I started working as a freelance journalist covering some of the MXGP's, providing reports and interviews for dirtbikerider.com which led to spending more time with my old friends on the team.

Seeing what it takes to be part of the MXGP paddock has been an education. The sport has progressed and grown so much since I was first involved in the early 1980's and whether or not you agree with the vision of the current promoters Youthstream, it's now a global operation with races around the world, a growing television audience and the relentless appetite of the internet and social media to sustain. I've worked with team owner Roger Magee and the rest of the crew to bring you a factual, 'warts-and-all' account of life in the team, the history and growth, the business side of running the team and the ups and downs of the 2018 season. I've included quotes and interviews from the people who have been instrumental in the team becoming what it is today as well as reports, interviews and examples from other teams and industry insiders looking at all aspects of life in the MXGP paddock. I didn't want to write a book that was just another politically correct press release, painting a picture that it's all group hugs and nothing ever goes wrong, so I hope you find my story interesting, informative and entertaining.

Introduction

Before we go any further it's worth pointing out a few home-truths so there's no misunderstandings as you read this book.

Number 1. This is a business not a sport. Obviously, motocross is a sport, but running a team to compete at the highest level, that is MXGP, is a business. Fundamentally, it's a marketing business where the teams represent and promote their sponsors' products and the sponsors or partners use their association with the sport and teams as promotional tools and/or corporate hospitality for their clients. For the manufacturers of the bikes and aftermarket parts there may also be some research and development work done with the teams but essentially it's still about marketing a product and what better endorsement than 'as used by XXX team. Hitachi/ASA KTM has worked its way up from a relatively small 'privateer' outfit, to become a factory supported team with direct links to the motorcycle manufacturer, in this case KTM in Austria, as well as a host of sponsors that have been cultivated over the years as both the profile and success of the team has increased.

The manufacturers' teams are known as the 'factory teams' and their budget, resources and equipment are the top of the tree, with budgets running into the millions if not tens of millions per year and high-performance parts that aren't available to the public.

The next level is 'factory supported' teams. They may receive bikes and/or parts from the factory but have to buy much of their equipment. They are funded by their sponsors with only a small amount of revenue coming from the factory, which could be in the form of special race engines, performance parts and technical assistance. They generally act as a "B" team, with riders that will one day move to the factory team. Hitachi/ASA KTM sit in this group.

The privately funded or privateer teams are generally supplied with bikes and parts by the country's importer or distributor for that brand and depending on the success of the team they may get additional special parts and/or support from the factory. Private teams' budgets are usually smaller, relying on cash and products from sponsors to pay the bills. And even for a small team the bills can be considerable, certainly hundreds of thousands of pounds a year. With a workshop and race truck to run, mechanics, riders, a truck driver and team manager to pay, plus flights, hotels, air freight, entry fees and fuel, it's a small to medium sized business. More on this in the coming chapters.

Number 2. Each team is like a family, and just like the families you know, some are tight-knit and stick together through thick and thin, whilst at the other extreme some are so dysfunctional that it's hard to believe that they work at all, with all the human foibles, quarrels, money problems, relationship issues and insecurities that could be found in any group of people. The GP paddock is like a village that has every type of family, and despite the façade of corporate shininess that they all portray, when you scratch the surface they're not all as shiny as you may think. You'll also meet a wide variety of people from virtually every nationality. It would be easy to stereotype some of them with national traits but that would be both lazy and wrong; some people are just odd, wherever they come from! But that multicultural mix is also one of the great strengths of the paddock; despite language barriers, team affiliations or the politics of the real world everyone seems to rub along using the international language of hand gestures, broken English and beer.

Number 3. Almost everyone is there because of a shared love of the sport and a desire to do as well as possible. They certainly aren't in it for the money. Sure, a few people earn a very good living, but the window of opportunity is very short if you're a rider, and if you're a mechanic I would suggest that many are working for less than the minimum wage if you include all the travelling, long days in the workshop and even longer days at the track. It can be a relentless grind; as soon as the last race is over they are packing up to get back to the workshop and start preparing for the next race. With twenty MXGP races in 2018 and 8 British championships, there only a couple of free weekends between March and October. It's no different for the reporters, journalists and photographers that follow the circuit. It's a labour of love with probably only 10% making a living from their work and with magazine circulations around the world decreasing and the abundance of free websites and social media pages giving real time information, it's only going to get harder.

Chapter 1

HUMBLE BEGINNINGS &

TEAM PRINCIPAL ROGER MAGEE.

The team started in 2005 as the Lizard Honda team. Set up by Roger Magee, a business man from Northern Ireland with a passion for motocross and a desire to compete after his own racing days had ended. A long-time friend of Willie Simpson, who was a GP racer from the late '70s until the early '90s, Willie's son Shaun was just starting to make a name in racing having finished in the top 15 in MX2 world championship and scoring points in every race in the British MX2 championship. Roger's family had business interests in running bars and with support from SOBE energy drinks and a few other sponsors, the start-up team was born.

Honda Britain wanted to support Simpson and came on board Roger's new team, supplying reduced rate bikes and spares for Shaun Simpson and local rider Adam McKee racing MX2 in the British and world championships. The RTT team had folded and Roger purchased their HGV race truck and with Willie Simpson enlisted as truck driver and mechanic, he and Shaun set off to Belgium. They would operate out of commercial premises in Ternat, west of Brussels, living in the race truck. Simpson would break his collar bone during practice at Hawkstone Park, before the season had even started so it wasn't all plain sailing.

Honda would increase their support in 2006 with Irishman Gordon Crockard enlisted for MX1, and Scott Probert joining Simpson and McKee in MX2 in the renamed Wulfsport Honda team as Wulf clothing joined the team, paying Shaun and Gordon bonus money for points scored.

" Team Principal Roger Magee

Life in Belfast in the '70's was a lot different than today, the height of 'the troubles' with British troops on the street. A young Roger met a road racer called Jim Rogers and started going to watch. Buying the ultimate starter bike, a step-through Honda, it was used around the garden until his dad bought him a 197 Sprite trials bike for Christmas in 1972. The following year schoolboy scrambling started in Northern Ireland and Roger entered on the sprite against a host of converted TS Suzukis but he saved up and soon graduated to a TM125, the third one in the country. At a schoolboy meeting in England Roger finished the first race in thirty-second place then lent his bike to his mate Lawrence Spence who was having bike problems. Spence rode it to second place and would go on to become a factory Kawasaki GP rider, but Roger's talents on a bike were more limited. By 1976 Roger was in the adult class on an RM370 ("the throttle would stick wide open if it rained") racing against the likes of Spence, Dave Watson and Stephen Russell, all later becoming professional racers, and still friend with Roger today.

In 1986 and now Honda mounted, Roger had a slow speed tip-over that damaged his right shoulder affecting the nerves. After nine month of physio he regained most of the function, but it was the end of his racing. Already part of the Killinchy and District Motorcycle Club, he would become the secretary of the meeting for their John Donnelly International, a bit like the Hawkstone International today. Held in July around the time of the Orange parades, some riders thought all the bunting was part of the race.

In 1986 they ran the first 125GP in Northern Ireland, running GP's until 1993. That experience established relationships with some of the movers and shakers still in the paddock today, Jacky Martens, Sylvain Geboers, Joel Smets, Michelle Rinaldi and more. He recalls a story of a well known British rider at that time bringing his passport because he didn't know that Northern Ireland was part of the UK.

The Magee family own a bar but also have a business repairing street lights. The work ethic instilled by their granny still guides Roger today; if you're going to do it, do it right. Roger's dad is 85 but still works six days a week.

2007, saw a bike switch to become Wulfsport Kawasaki and additional support from 7-up and Magners cider, with Simpson still their main rider in MX2 saw the young Scot begin to show his potential with a maiden British championship win at Canada Heights and some consistent top ten finishes in the GPs although a broken collar bone in Italy disrupted his progress. Mark Jones replaced Crockard in MX1 but a pre-season ACL injury meant he didn't race until August. The difficulty was that the production Kawasaki was slow. The Simpsons met a Dutch engine tuner called John Volleberg who would become instrumental in the team's and Simpson's success. The workshop in Ternat wasn't ideally situated, being too far away from the tracks that everyone used. The team would relocate to Holland, near to Volleberg's engineering workshop and when Shaun's younger brother Stefan finished school he would join his dad and brother on the team, learning the ropes as a mechanic. Said Roger "It was the first year we started to get recognition in the British Championships".

2008 would be a water-shed year. Roger had been in touch with KTM UK for a couple of years and '08 would be the start of a very long and successful partnership, changing to the RedBull KTM UK Team, becoming their premier UK team and become a factory satellite team for GPs.

◀ *Roger Magee –
Team Principal*

Shaun Simpson – 2007, ▶
Wulfsport Kawasaki

◀ *Shaun Simpson –
2008, first year
as a KTM team*

Simpson immediately felt at home on the orange bikes, winning his and the team's first British championship and finishing 4th overall in the MX2 world championships. Alex Snow also won the British under 21 championship and James Noble was runner up in the MX1 British Championship. The success was bitter-sweet as Simpson's success led to an offer to join the Factory KTM team. Roger had always said he wouldn't stand in the way of Shaun's progress, but it was a loss to the team and a wrench personally. "I had mixed emotions, and I'm not afraid to say I shed a few tears but you can't turn down an offer from a factory", said Roger. Willie Simpson would also leave to team to support his son Shaun and didn't feel he could do that properly if he was working for a different team.

There was some good fortune as the MJ Church Kawasaki team had ended, so their top rider Stephen Sword was hired by the RedBull KTM UK team along with Jake Nicholls to race in MX2 for 2009 with Graeme Irwin to race in the under 21's with Alex Snow retained in MX1. Sword and Nicholls would finish first and second in the British MX2 championship both scoring well in the GPs, and Irwin third-overall in the under 21 championships. Roger remembers Sword well, "he was a good fit for the team and one of the most professional riders I've ever worked with. He knew from factory Kawasaki how to present himself, always turned up on time and always ready".

HM Plant joined as title sponsor to form the HM Plant/KTM UK Team where Jake Nicholls would be the main MX2 rider for 2010, again finishing 2nd in the British championship with Irwin also improving at British and world level. New signing Natalie Kane won the British ladies championship for the team.

2011 would be a frustrating year for the team, marred by injuries. An early season injury for Jake Nicholls put him out, and Irwin's season ended in France with a serious neck injury that he thankfully made a full recovery from. Jordan Booker score points in MX2 but the highlight was another British lady's' title for Kane. "It was our worst year" remembers Roger, "It's frustrating when you have everything in place and it's hard to keep sponsors, we knew we had to do something different".

2012 was another water-shed year for the HM Plant/KTM UK team, taking them to new heights with a double British championship and becoming the only team to achieve this to date. Belgium Kevin Strijbos was signed with direct support from the factory in Austria and dominated the British MX1 championship aboard his 350 (with factory engines), also getting 3 GP podiums and finishing 6th in the world championship, results that rejuvenated his career. Roger said "Kevin Strijbos was very good, he knew what to do. He was coached by Harry Everts who was very hard on him but got him back up there, together we extended his career".

Elliott Banks-Brown snatched victory in the final race at Little Silver to take the MX2 British championship (it's the video Roger has watched the most) and Natalie Kane finished a career best 2nd in the women's world championship, marking an incredible year for the team although there was some controversy at the last round of the WMX. Kane had crashed and was 'required' to go to hospital or she would be excluded. The race was started before she could return, and Kiara Fontanesi won.

Strijbos moved on to a factory ride at Suzuki for 2013 leaving the team to concentrate on the MX2 class with Banks-Browne and James Dunn, and the Watson brothers, Nathan and Ben in the European 250 championships. Banks-Browne was British MX2 champion again with Nathan Watson 6th and Natalie Kane finishing 4th in the women's world championship. James Dunn had beaten Tim Gajser on a 125 but just couldn't get going on a 250f. The team also moved to a new workshop in Wuustwezel, providing their continental base.

2014 saw Shaun Simpson return to the team as their MXGP and British championships with Mel Pocock in MX2. James Dunn, Ben Watson and James Cottrell would complete in EMX250 and British MX2 with Natalie Kane again in the WMX. Simpson would deliver another British MX1 title and finish 7th in MXGP, while a new sponsor came on board in the shape of Mark Yates and his Revo tuning business. Yates had some strong ideas about the direction the team should take and wasn't shy in expressing them. The team, now Hitachi/Revo KTM had also leased a brand-new race truck from long time sponsor and associate Shaun Osmond, the owner of S.O. Rentals. Osmond would drive the truck to the MXGP' and British championships but a clash of personalities with Yates would ultimately lead to another step up in the team's history. They also moved to their current workshop in Lommel. On the same sight as Jacky Martens Rockstar Husqvarna team the unit backs on to the Lommel track. With most of the European motocross industry within a few miles it is the epicentre of motocross and the ideal base for a grand prix operation.

For 2015 the team purchased an articulated race transporter. Formerly used by Swift Suzuki, it had been stood up for a few years but would be refreshed and take the Hitachi/Revo team's paddock presence to the next level. Simpson would again lead the team, delivering a stunning double race victory in Lommel at the Belgium MXGP (which we will look at in more detail later in the book) and winning again in Assen to finish 4th in the world and win the British MX1 championship for the second time. It was the team's most successful year, but more drama would unfold as the season wound down. KTM had been slow to commit to supporting the team for the next year. Without bikes and a parts budget Roger was stuck and couldn't commit to signing riders. The delay meant that Shaun Simpson would again be leaving, unable to wait for Roger to make a firm offer as delay followed delay. Roger is still quite bitter about the events that transpired. Simpson had been approached by STR with a firm offer that included a practice mechanic and other expenses and didn't feel that Roger could match the deal. Roger has his suspicions that STR not only poached his rider but also his deal with KTM as suddenly he was without support for the next year.

2016 loomed and eventually it was agreed that Hitachi/Revo team would switch to Husqvarna and would sign Jake Nichols for MXGP and retain Ben Watson in MX2. The bike switch was very much a last-minute deal that was for bikes and a small parts budget. Bel-ray would replace Motorex as lubricant sponsor and Contract Furniture would also join the team to enable Ben Watson to do the whole series including the fly-aways. Nichols had his best year in the British championships, finishing third behind eventual winner Tommy Searle and runner up Shaun Simpson.

Watson would start the season with a few steady rides but at the fourth GP in Argentina disaster struck when he injured his ankle. The injury was a lot worse than first thought and Watson would not race again that year.

It would also be a watershed year for Roger in his personal life as health problems came to the fore. He had inherited kidney disease, and knew since 2003, in fact it was one of the reasons for starting the team. In 2007 it had got worse to the point of kidney failure and by 2016 he only had 5% kidney function and would need to start dialysis. With no energy, he was just going through the motions in his business and day-to-day life, feeling lethargic and going for dialysis three times a week. The doctors would not put him on the transplant list because he was so over weight, so knowing that he needed to do something drastic or face a future with a diminishing quality of life he lost over fifty kilograms and would be put on the kidney transplant list.

Whilst it's obviously sad that someone will need to die to provide a kidney, the act of being a donor will improve Roger's (and anyone else who receives a transplanted organ) life immeasurably. While Roger waits, he continues to need dialysis three times a week but with the weight lost he felt much better and regained both his energy and concentration. Because of dialysis which takes place on Monday, Wednesday and Friday, he is limited with his ability to travel to the MXGPs as he can't leave until Friday lunch time and must be back for Monday. Fortunately, the team structure means that he doesn't need to be at every event so he is able to pick the races that fit with his hospital appointments.

Chapter 2

THE SEASON REVIEWED FOR BRITAIN'S PREMIER MOTOCROSS TEAM & TEAM CO-ORDINATOR IAN BROWNE.

By now the team had grown from a small privateer outfit to become the most successful team in Britain with GP victories and British championship titles, a 40-tonne race truck and workshop in Belgium. Returning to KTM machinery, 2017 started full of promise for the Hitachi/Contract Furniture/ KTM UK team, with both riders, Jake Nicholls on the 450 and Ben Watson on the 250 going well in pre-season training. Both had suffered injuries and setbacks and had spent the previous season just trying to recover and get back up to speed, so with both showing good pace and confidence as they trained in Spain hopes were high for a double British championship and top ten MXGP performances. KTM also had a young New Zealander under contract, Josiah Natzke. After showing promise in the EMX125 class, he then underachieved on a 250f but was contracted to KTM and it looks bad if they drop riders part way through an agreement. Natzke was placed with Hitachi who would facilitate his EMX250 challenge by hosting him at European rounds and British championships.

The MXGP season started on Qatar, the first of four 'fly-away' races that saw teams working out of air freight crates in Qatar, Indonesia, Argentina and Mexico before the European leg kicked off over Easter weekend in Italy.

Those races are very expensive to get to; it costs around £40,000 plus with bikes and tools away for about seven weeks it means additional race bikes are needed for the British championship races that fall in between and for the race in Trentino, Italy. If the results go your way it's all worth it but for the Hitachi riders it was a slow and disappointing start to the MXGPs.

Watson was still struggling with the damage to his foot and ankle sustained the previous year. It had been OK in training, but race conditions always raise the intensity and have a way of teasing out any underlying weakness. Nichols was also off to a poor start, it would transpire that at times he had privately been reduced to tears as his desperation got the better of him. Relief came at the first British championship round at Culham, where Watson and Nicholls won, to lead both the 250 and 450 championships.

The joy was short lived for Nicholls as he would catch his foot in a Trentino rut, dislocating his hip without even crashing. Air lifted to hospital, he was out for the season with a very serious and potentially life-threatening injury. With time to contemplate his future, Nicholls wrote a moving, open letter on social media half way through the season announcing his retirement from GP racing at just twenty-seven-years-old, no longer able to motivate himself to put in the necessary sacrifices for the limited success he had in the 450 class. It was a bitter pill to swallow for Nicholls but also meant the team had no 450 rider and with no viable candidate as a fill-in, the 450 berth was left empty.

This is Jake's letter.

As many of you know, I had a big set back in the middle of April, where without crashing I dislocated my hip. My mind was a mess at the time of the crash but once I was stabilised that evening, I said to my Mum who was at my bedside, that I'm done with racing GP's. 2017 is my tenth year racing the Grand Prix series, it's been a rollercoaster at times but overall a great 10 years in my life. From the day I started racing I always dreamed and believed that one day I could be a world champion. The hardest part of this decision is giving up on that dream, something I've always prided myself on not doing.

A big part of my career was the move to Belgium, some people saw it as a sacrifice, leaving a nice home, family and a perfect practice track behind, I never saw it like that, it was a dream come true, living there for 3 years made me the racer and the person I am today. But after signing with a British team for 2014 I was determined to prove that I could be just as good if not better in GP's by living at home and practicing on one of the best tracks in the world at my parents house along with all the other professionally built private tracks in our area, rather than the subpar practice tracks in Belgium where you regularly have to share tracks with Quads, sidecars and 85cc, and deal with the fact that there is no marshals.

But I realised, these days you cant be competitive in GP's unless you're based in mainland Europe. And I'm not prepared to do that anymore, last season I enjoyed 2/3rds of the season with the Hitachi Revo Husqvarna team and we had some good results after 2 years of injury. The last couple of races I fell out of love with the travelling and racing, I didn't realise, I worked harder than ever this winter and I was feeling really good before the first GP, I enjoyed my preseason race at Hawkstone, but as soon as got to the first GP that some feeling hit me, no enjoyment and the risks being taken for a mere point. I was so lost in it, not knowing why I felt like this.

I went through the first 4 flyaway Gp's having not rode very well and having even less fun, not enjoying the tracks and the travelling at all, it had caught up on me. I got to Trento, and my head was all over the place, I was taking big risks to get 21st in timed practice. I was so down on Saturday night, I cried over the phone to my wife not knowing what's going on. Feeling like I was maybe putting too much pressure on myself I approached the Sunday with a different attitude, just wanting to ride well and enjoy it, forgetting about the results. Next minute I'm sat on the track with my leg facing the wrong way, thinking why!

I've become heavily involved in my father's business since I've been injured which ultimately is my future and I'm excited about it. But I love racing so, so much and I'm only 27. Right now I'm talking to some teams to race in GB only and concentrate on winning the British titles, which will also allow me to stay involved in the business during the week, and mainly to enjoy my racing again.

I leave with no regrets, I'm eternally grateful for all the experiences I've had, I have some great supporters around Europe and I thank them for always backing me.
Thank you dearly to all that have helped me on this 10 year journey!

Sincerely,
Jake Nicholls

Watson's season started slowly on the GP scene but gradually picked up with some flashes of speed in Portugal and Sweden, and some low points and retirements. To me, the team seemed quietly frustrated with Watson and in turn, Watson also seemed unhappy, frustrated with the bike issues; you could see the relationship breaking down. After the French GP, Watson's dad launched a furious verbal attack on the mechanic and team manager which resulted in him being banned from the team's awning under threat of a substantial fine for Ben; not the best atmosphere to nurture a young talent. At the time, I could understand both sides point of view, both sides frustrated with the other. The incident erupted when Watson pulled out of the second race with a few laps to go saying that the bike had something wrong with the engine, and there was a further issue with the back tire and mousse. The whole incident rapidly became very heated and emotional with things said in the heat of the moment that would have been better kept for a calmer debate, and when disagreement turns to a hostile shouting match it's hard to rebuild relationships. For the record, Dunlop checked the tire and mousse afterwards and found nothing wrong and the team checked the engine on the dyno after and also found nothing wrong. I didn't speak to Watson at the time but the steep hills of Ernee and slippery conditions may well have caused him to think there was a problem, it just didn't get expressed very well.

With other teams keen to sign Watson for the following years, Hitachi/Contract Furniture/KTM UK had the option of first refusal provided they could match any offer for his services but it became apparent during August that Watson would be leaving to ride for the rival Kemea Yamaha team. With the fly-away race to the US GP in Jacksonville fast approaching he was offered the option to go but he would have to pay the costs, despite being fourteenth in the championship. He had been sixteenth in the championship earlier in the season when the team sent him to Russia with fifteenth being the cut off so it was quid-pro-quo. Ben's personal sponsor wanted Ben to go to the states, but with the delay in making the decision it became too late to air freight bikes over or borrow bikes from an American team.

There was also a social media frenzy round this time over the MXoN team that included Tommy Searle on a 250, despite being injured all year and not riding a 250 for four years. Watson had just clinched the British MX2 championship and many felt he should be the automatic choice for the 250 spot. Team owner Roger Magee's comments in support of Watson on Facebook really poured petrol on the flames with thousands of comments on both sides of the debate. Watson kept a dignified silence but it's hard to imagine that the furore didn't add to his stress levels at the last few GP's.

Whilst all of this was going on, young Natzke was mostly under performing and was not really making much impact with the team, or much effort to engage, at least that was their perception. It's easy to criticise, but it can't be easy living half way around the world, on your own and still only eighteen years old. Natzke had won in Latvia but otherwise there was little to shout about. Picking up an injury mid-season, he wasn't expected back so with a bike and some spares budget available, the team offered an "extended interview" to Todd Kellett, supporting him at the last couple of British and European races. Todd won his first British championship on his team debut and did enough to arouse the interest of a few other teams in the paddock. Natzke managed to come back from injury sooner than expected, but with an agreement to ride for Buildbase Honda in 2018 there was little interest in him from the team. Yes, they continued to provide bikes and support, but the atmosphere was apathetic at best. His mechanic, Minty, did his best to support his young rider but there didn't seem to be any real bond between them. If you think of it as a normal work place, then it's understandable that you're not always going to be BFF (Best Friends Forever) with everyone but I think it's quite important in a race team!

Natzke decided to try his luck at a couple of MX2 rounds as any chance of success in the European championship was long since gone. In Switzerland a rock in the face ended his weekend and the long trip to Sweden also ended without a point. Without the funding to enter any more GPs, he just rode out his contract at the last EMX250 race in France, then represented New Zealand at the MXON.

Another problem faced by the team in '17 was staff turnover. Getting a truck driver who was prepared to live away, drive the truck and help with general duties such as erecting the awning, cleaning and sorting the hospitality was harder than you would think, largely due to the wages and living conditions being offered. Four drivers were used during the season, one actually took his bag and walked off at a GP!

> " ### Ian Browne – team co-ordinator.
> When I sat down with 'Brother Browne' for this section the first question was what's your job title? "I don't know, Roger's never actually said, I just run things". (I asked Roger, and its Team Co-ordinator.)
>
> His resume is impressive, at fifty-four years old he's 'been there and got the T-shirt' many times. Hanging out in Gordon Farthing's motorcycle shop when he was thirteen, it turned into an apprenticeship, working on road bikes. Gordon compete in world championship trials, so Ian saw what went into preparing for that. In 1987 he started work as a grand prix mechanic for Mark Banks, then moved to spells at factory Suzuki, Action workshops and factory Kawasaki with a

'who's who' of top rider that include Jeremy Whatley, Rob Herring and Billy Liles. In 1995 he moved to RWJ Honda where he would stay for eleven years working with Joachim Carlsson, Justin Morris and James Noble among others, until the team folded, then to Swift Suzuki, L.P.E Kawasaki and D.B. Honda before joining Roger in 2012. Through all the teams he worked as a mechanic before becoming the team co-ordinator for Roger in 2013. Short of a mechanic, he went 'back on the tools', finally returning to his current role in 2016.

Whatever the job title, it's a catch-all role that means he's responsible for the day-to-day running of the team. It's a full-time role with a salary so there's no over-time, you just do what it takes to get the job done. Ordering spares, technical liaison with factory KTM (Roger manages the business side of the deal with KTM), speaking to sponsors about products and updates, as well as technical partners like Steve Payne at Multi-tek who is 'the ECU guy'.

Ian is also the engine builder, working closely with John Volleberg on the 450 this year and rebuilding the semi-factory engines for Mewse, although this year BC builds the 450 engines for Graeme's bike.

Then there's the paper-work and admin, booking flights, hotels and hire cars for the European races (Roger arranges the fly-aways with S.E.L.), carnet documents, fuel and the aforementioned Russia visas. Co-ordinating the mechanics, the truck driver and Minty to make sure the bikes and people are where they need to be plus sorting out anything that breaks, for example the tail-lift on the race truck broke last year at Assen, stranding the truck until it was repaired.

Ian's year started in January when the team de-camped to Spain for a month of testing. With twenty GP's and eight British championships, plus Hawkstone International and the MXON, there's three weeks off throughout the season, only getting home after a grand prix when there's a British championship the following week.

> The season ends in October but planning for the next season will mean that Ian's job just rolls on.
>
> He also works with Roger to advise on team members and with the team struggling to get a driver for the race track what do you need to work for a race team?
>
> *"It's a lifestyle. It's not a job, you need to have a passion for it, you could never do it as just a job. The money isn't great for the hours, you've got to be prepared to work long hours and have good times and bad times. You need experience but then someone's got to give you a chance. You need a certain amount of technical skill and knowledge, and be able to fit in. We thought Steve was the perfect man for the job, but you can't force somebody if they don't enjoy it; I'm surprised but we'll have to find a replacement. You can't just take on a truck driver though, they need to be part of the team, be involved and know the job, it's a lot of work to keep everything tidy".*

Likewise, with the mechanics. The team have a workshop in Lommel, Belgium, but it means living in the race truck parked outside during the week, in effect you never leave the work place. With little opportunity to have any personal time it's no wonder people can get on each other's nerves at times, and with all the travelling involved, finding experienced mechanics who will work for the money on offer proved nigh on impossible. Natzke told me he had had six different mechanics. He ended up with Paul Whitehead, aka Minty, who had previously worked at L.P.E. Kawasaki. Jake Nicholls mechanic quit after Jake's injury and the only permanent mechanic was Steve 'Hendo' Henderson. Hendo has been around for years, previously working for Pro Circuit in America and factory Suzuki among others and certainly knows how to prepare a grand prix bike, but when it comes to his inter-personal skills there's work to do. Best described as a grumpy old man, I think much of his grumpiness is born of frustration with his environment

◀ *Jake Nicholls –*
2009, MX2

▲ *Jake Nicholls –*
2009, MX2

▲ Jake Nicholls –
2017, MXGP

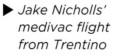

▶ *Jake Nicholls'*
medivac flight
from Trentino

but as a result, he can be very difficult to work with. I did say that the teams were like families, and this one had a dysfunctional uncle living in the house! The problem was that Hendo's complete inability to be sociable, especially in the morning meant there was often a horrible atmosphere in the workshop as everyone was 'treading on egg-shells'. In the evening if we went out for a meal he could be good fun, but this split personality can be very wearing. It was Hendo's second year on the team and he was adamant it would be his last as a grand prix mechanic. Fed up with the travelling, he wanted to stay in England, do the British championships and prepare the practice bikes; time would tell if that would pan out.

At the dirt bike show, the team go out with many of their sponsors for a celebration meal. Watson was there and made sure me shook hands with everyone and thanked them for everything they had done. There was also a warm embrace with his mechanic Hendo. Despite the turbulent year there was a genuine warmth between them, hard to believe that grumpy old Hendo cared as much as he did. It was a good way to end the season, and the right way for Watson to go, no hard feelings and the door left open for a return at some point in the future.

Chapter 3

PREPARING FOR THE NEXT YEAR & 'SILLY SEASON'.

Like any business, you've got to plan ahead and as anyone who follows motocross knows, 'silly season' starts around June. Silly season is the term given to the time when riders and teams start to position themselves for the following year. If you already have a deal in place you're OK (unless the team is folding, in which case your contract could be worthless e.g. team CLS Kawasaki riders, or from a teams' point of view, if your rider is seriously injured and unlikely to come back, i.e. Jake Nicholls).

Roger probably knew that Jake Nicholls was finished as soon as the reports came back from the hospital. In June, Graeme Irwin was spectating at the Ottobiano MXGP in Italy, searching for a grand prix ride for 2018. He was leading the British championship but riding for the Buildbase Honda team meant there was no opportunity to race a GP as they were only interested in racing in Britain, and Honda had other teams that they supported for GP racing. Irwin is from Northern Ireland, his brother Glenn is a top-level BSB racer, and younger brother Andrew an up-and-coming road racer in World super sport, meaning the Irwin family are something of a motorcycling dynasty in the making.

It was like the perfect marriage waiting to happen. When interviewed by Geoff Meyer for the MXGP website in November, Magee said *"Graeme rode for us in 2010 and 2011. He was young and inexperienced, and he moved onto some other teams. We feel he has improved a lot and matured a lot. The previous teams he rode for didn't do GP and he deserved that opportunity. He is also from my country, so that is a bonus for the team. He can also pull in some Northern Ireland sponsors and also retain the British championship and top ten in MXGP. That will be difficult at first, but I think he showed at the Motocross of Nations, that he can compete with those guys. We will try and nurture him and give him some good advice, keep him calm for the first half of the season.*

I asked Roger how they pick the riders for the team.

"We try to get the best riders for the budget available. A, up-and-coming, B, from the UK and Ireland as that fits with KTM UK and C, foreign riders if that's who is available. We did have one who got away, Marvin Musquin. In 2008 he approached us, he was a top ten supercross rider and I thought that's all he was, obviously I was wrong" he says with a chuckle.

"The team make suggestions about riders, but I have the final say. We don't want any prima donnas. We measure success with championships, but you can only ask that a rider gives you their best. We can try to encourage them and get them to the next level. We've done well picking riders that are dedicated and talented, the only thing is that you don't always get their loyalty in return." He wouldn't be drawn on who he meant by that last remark.

"We have a few Irish boys that we help. Conor Mullan on a 125 and Ryan Mawhinney and Cain McElveen on 85's, it's important to keep the young riders coming through. We also Help Oli Benton and his dad helps us with the M.A.N. and Dunlop deals. Mechanics too, after M.J. Church finished we picked up Wayne Banks and Jeremy Long. Banks now works for Herlings and Long was also at Factory KTM, so it proves we're picking dedicated people".

The bonus for Roger comes in the form of ASA scaffolding. Owner Lee Tolan is Graeme Irwin's personal backer and had money to spend on making his young friend's dream success come true and a big vision for elevating the professionalism of British motocross. Lee had already signed his young protégé to a deal to ride in the British championships for him, but they were looking for a way to get him into MXGP. A deal was struck whereby Roger's Hitachi KTM team would provide bikes and support to Graeme for both MXGP and the British championship, with the team being renamed Hitachi/ASA KTM. Lee was spending big bucks and wanted to have some input and influence. A brash, confident Londoner and passionate about motocross, it was understandable that he would want to be involved, but too many bosses are never a good thing, and the team already had a co-ordinator in Ian Browne who ran the day-to-day operation. Roger's solution was simple; Ian Browne would manage the MXGP's and Lee Tolan would manage the British Championship effort, providing the race truck and hosting the team in the UK as per his agreement with Irwin. There's a saying that goes "if it seems too good to be true, it probably is". I predict conflict ahead.

The potential MX2 riders were also starting to come together with three riders on the shopping list. Being a British based team with a preference for British riders to race in the ACU British championship and generally represent the mostly British sponsors, they were looking at Ben Watson, Conrad Mewse and Adam Sterry. The three British youngsters all showed promise, and all had been affected by injuries or other issues, but the consensus was that any two would be a good fit for the team. As keeping Watson became more unlikely, Conrad Mewse became the target as he had been released by factory Husqvarna but still had a contract with KTM (owners of Husqvarna) who wanted to keep him on one of their teams. Without any fuss of hoopla, he agreed terms in July although it was kept secret, pending final clarification of support from KTM and really just as a curtesy to his current team.

Adam Sterry was on the road to the top, finishing third in the EMX250s in '15 and '16, and winning the British MX2 title in '16. Signed to a long-term deal with CLS Kawasaki his future looked assured, but a clash with Calvin Vlaanderen in Valkenswaard left him with a torn ACL and out for the season. To add insult to injury (literally) the team would fold at the end of '17 and he was released mid-season as they knew that Kawasaki was pulling the plug.

This is where it gets complicated for everyone. Sponsors want to know who the riders are before they commit to supporting the team and teams need to know how much support they're likely to get before they can commit to riders, particularly the expensive ones. The key player here is the manufacturer, in this case KTM and/or their British importer. There's a bit of a poker game here as teams and riders try to negotiate the best deals and hopefully with everything agreed in principle, contracts can be signed. Those contracts will stipulate everything a rider is obligated to do. As the saying goes, "the devil is in the detail".

Josiah Natzke had already agreed to race for another team for '18 and Todd Kellett was hoping to snag the vacant berth to compete in EMX250

For up-and-coming riders like Todd this means that the other pieces of the jigsaw must fall into place before there's a firm deal on offer from a team like Hitachi KTM. Although he'd had some good results for the team and had a reputation as a real grafter, the team had doubts about his potential, specifically, had he already peaked or was there more to come? I thought there was still potential for improvement and that he would be a good fit for the team but at twenty years old Kellett was a few years older than some of his rivals and the harsh truth is that he wasn't a high priority signing for KTM so would have to wait until the other riders were in place, then if budget and resources permitted they could offer him a deal.

Roger Magee travelled to the Assen MXGP in early September to meet with the KTM bosses, hoping to agree an increase in the level of their support for the following season and perhaps benefitting from the budget allocated to HSF Logistics when a curve ball was thrown. It turns out the hot MX2 prospect Davy Pootjes had a contract with KTM and with HSF, both keen to retain his services. KTM wanted to place him at Hitachi but HSF wanted to make sure the young Dutchman had a suitable team to support him. The contract issue would need to be resolved but it meant any decision on riders would be on hold, leaving Sterry and Kellett in limbo for a while longer, and with riders like Hunter Lawrence and Bas Vassen now also looking for a home following the collapse of Suzuki, the market forces of supply and demand were working in the favour of team owners rather than the riders.

Silly season.

This is the time of year when riders start trying to secure a home for the next year. It may be a contract extension with their current team or a new home elsewhere. It's very much a market economy' driven by supply and demand, that is the availability of riders and teams wanting their services. Results are the rider's bargaining chip; the quality of material is the team's chip. The time of year isn't fixed, but it usually starts about mid-year. While the 'silly season' was in full swing, it became apparent that there would be some big changes in the paddock for 2018. As well as CLS Kawasaki closing, Suzuki would not be running a team in MX2 as the budget from Japan was cut, and HSF Logistics KTM would also be shutting their doors. The HSF money was going to HRC Honda along with Brian Bogers, but for the other riders from the three teams, as well as mechanics, truck drivers and other staff, the scrabble to find employment was on.

In the MXGP paddock the on-going uncertainty of riders and teams was starting to become clearer as Valentin Guillod and Kevin Strijbos agreed terms with the returning Standing Construct KTM team and Ken DeDycker announced his retirement. Max Nagl was just one of the 'big names' without a deal. The German had been a top ten rider for the last eight years, finishing second in 2009 and third in 2016 but was also blighted with injuries. At the age of thirty he was being viewed as a rider unlikely to contend in the future, and with younger, cheaper talent coming up from MX2 it was proving to be a tough time for Max. His only hope was a berth at TM, but with no budget for wages he would need to bring a personal sponsor to cover his expenses and wages, something that he felt unable to do. Max told me "I have a house, a family, things I must pay for. I have no sponsorship from Germany or from outside motocross. This is my job and I must make a living from racing".

Nagl's situation is one that would appear to be coming more common as teams feel the economic strain. In sports like Formula 1 and MotoGP its normal practice to have a paid driver and a paying driver, i.e. a driver who brings sponsorship to the team, in effect buying his ride. At the very least he may drive/ride for free with a personal backer covering his wages and expenses. This is particularly the case with the poorer teams who will accept a less talented driver with cash over a more gifted one without a backer, for example teams like Jordan and Minardi who's survival often hinges on a driver's cheque book. Nagl would agree terms with TM in late October, with a positive press release announcing the deal but some websites predicting the downslope for Nagl's career. By the start of the season it was clear that Nagl had been hired primarily to develop a new 450, with expectations set suitably modestly.

When silly season was in its early stages there were confident predictions of MX2 riders moving up and securing MXGP factory rides for 2018 only for them to be gazumped as their wealthier counterparts moved in with their sponsor's money, for example Brian Bogers move to HRC Honda with HSF Logistics money and Julien Lieber's move to Factory Kawasaki, allegedly funded by private sponsors, after Benoit Paturel and a few other names had been linked to those teams. The vacant seats also came at the expense of Evgeny Bobryshev and Jordi Tixier respectively, although you could also see that both MXGP riders had underachieved by factory teams' standards, so it was understandable that their teams would look for fresh talent, and with the established stars such as Herlings, Gajser and Febvre already under contract, gambling on a new arrival from MX2 is the best and cheapest option. Bobryshev had spent seven years under the HRC awning with only a couple of victories but had survived because of the marketing potential the big Russian brought for Honda in Russia, and because he was a solid 'number 2' rider, backing up their main man (most recently Tim Gajser) and also a good test rider. In the same situation as Nagl, (in so far as no outside sponsor on board to offset his wages,) Bobryshev found a home riding for Neil Prince's Lombard Express/Suzuki team in the British championships which would have a late twist before the season started.

Jordi Tixier was the 2014 MX2 World Champion, winning the title when Jeffrey Herlings broke his leg. Tixier was Herlings' teammate at the time but had already been told by KTM that he would not be kept on for 2015. When Herlings got injured Tixier came alive, clawing back a one hundred and fifty-one-point deficit to claim the title, however his time in MXGP has been less fruitful. Not all riders are able to make the jump to racing a 450. The extra power and weight just doesn't suit everyone, and the extra depth of talent in the MXGP class means any weakness is soon exposed. It doesn't help that Tixier has a reputation (allegedly) in the paddock of being somewhat arrogant with an equally arrogant father; maybe it's just them being French (apologies for the racial stereotyping) and misunderstood, I've never met them so I can't say but in the small village that is the MXGP paddock, sometimes a difficult reputation can be as much of a deterrent for teams as poor results. The old saying that 'you're only as good as your last ride' has perhaps never been truer, unless you've got a pocket full of cash. Tixier would eventually find a home in a brand-new team, Bos Suspension, riding a KTM that the team would purchase without any support from the manufacturer. Bos Suspension products are widely used in other motor sports such as

WRC and the plan is to develop their own suspension products for motocross. As KTM also own WP suspension it was understandable that they would not support a rival suspension manufacturer. Benoit Paturel signed in November in a late deal after being passed over at Kawasaki, but there was trouble ahead!

Suzuki dropped a bombshell at the end of the season, announcing that they were pulling out of both MX2 and MXGP racing, leaving Stefan Everts high and dry, and the contracted riders and staff scrabbling to find a home. The contents of the workshop in Belgium were sold off along with vans and tools. In late November a very deflated Everts was advertising the team transporter for sale on Facebook and saying that he would take a year off to support his son Liam's racing dreams. It was a bitter blow for Everts personally but also for the world of Grand Prix motocross. Suzuki had been one of the pioneers of the two-stroke era that started in the 1970's winning titles with Roger DeCoster and Sylvain Geboers. Without a factory presence in the paddock it was as if a piece of history was lost.

None of this had any effect on the Hitachi KTM team as their riders, Graeme Irwin and Conrad Mewse, were already signed, although Roger did receive a number of enquiries from riders, mechanics and other team personnel seeking employment. It does illustrate the harsh side of the business that is involved in running a team, both for team managers as budgets or support vanish and for all the staff who are often on short term contracts, although even a long-term contract is worthless if the team folds, as was illustrated by Adam Sterry's situation. As the season wound down, the fate of some top riders generated plenty of debate and speculation, bench racing the relative merits of the new arrivals from MX2 versus the existing riders ousted to make way.

At the MXoN, the Hitachi/Contract Furniture KTM truck would play host to the New Zealand team and the Israeli team. Both teams were paying for the privilege, renting the logistical support necessary to compete at the biggest race of the year. Davy Pootjes was also at the race with his adviser and met with Roger to discuss terms for joining the team. It seemed like a deal was done; he would be getting factory support for engines and suspension, and along with Conrad Mewse, Hitachi KTM would have two of the hottest young riders in the paddock with extra material ('material' is the word used to describe bikes and parts) from the factory. It didn't exactly fit with their all British model but was too good an opportunity to pass up. As Team GB finished on the podium and Max Anstie did the impossible, winning both races in front of the home fans, it was a great weekend in Hampshire.... until Monday.

"What happened on Monday?" you ask. Pootjes decided he would be better off staying in Europe and signed for the Leiber Racing Team despite agreeing terms with Magee the previous day. This didn't go down well with anyone but as I've said previously, it's business! I can fully understand the frustration and disappointment felt by Roger after he had reached a deal with Pootjes, but I also understand that a year is a long time in a rider's career so if he (Pootjes) felt he would be better served at LRT then it's understandable that he would renege on the agreement. I don't know the details of the LRT offer but results in 2018 would show if it was the right decision.

Whilst the negotiations with Pootjes were going on, talks with Adam Sterry were put on hold. Unsurprisingly, the Merseyside man decided to accept a deal with F&H Kawasaki rather than wait for KTM to make up their minds. Already familiar with the Kawasaki, and with a deal on the table, plus all the uncertainty with teams cutting budgets or closing completely it was the right deal for him. I think there was also some pride at stake, after all who wants to be second choice?

Todd Kellett also missed out. Despite winning the Weston Beach race and getting plenty of attention in magazines and moto websites there just wasn't the support from KTM for an EMX250 rider on the team. Unfortunately for Kellett, winning a round of the Maxxis, and the beach race wasn't enough to raise his stock sufficiently; a couple of top 5 results in Europe may have made the difference. I spoke to him at the MXoN and he was still upbeat and philosophical. It had been his best year in the Maxxis British Championship, finishing fifth and he had exceeded his expectations in the EMX250's. There were some other offers on the table and so one way or another he would be racing, but he was rapidly learning the importance of mental resilience where silly season was concerned. That resilience would be tested to the limit when a big high-side crash in December whilst putting in laps at Fatcats moto parc resulted in a broken back and a ride to hospital in the air ambulance. Although he had broken several vertebrae he was very fortunate not to be paralysed, and even a broken back couldn't dampen his spirits, the ever up-beat Kellett announced his new deal with Verde KTM with a picture wearing a medical neck brace and a big smile. 'Little Ando' would team up with Brad 'Ando' Anderson for a full season of European and British championships.

Chapter 4

'SUCCESS BREEDS SUCCESS'; SPONSORS & CONTRACT FURNITURE.

I said earlier that teams rely on the revenue and support from sponsors to keep going, and sponsors decision to commit to a team is often dependant on several factors. Results are the most obvious factor. Everyone wants to be associated with success, so whether its winning races, or more importantly championships, results do matter. Brand presentation and reputation is also important. The teams in the MXGP paddock go to great expense to run big race trucks with huge awnings to present the most professional image possible. Vehicle livery, printed back-drops, embroidered mats, matching tool cabinets and strategically placed sponsors' products all help promote the brand, whilst the hospitality area offers refreshment and shelter to the invited guests but more importantly a sense of exclusivity to the chosen ones lucky enough to be 'on the inside'. The size of the team and where they race is also important. By competing in the world championship, a team will offer global exposure with TV coverage to potential sponsors, and by competing in a national championship (in Hitachi KTM's case the Maxxis British championship) there's the chance of national exposure, both come with all the attendant magazines, websites and social media. For a sponsor like Monster Energy or RedBull, this global presence and association with a dynamic and glamourous action sport with the right demographic of fans is vital in their choosing to invest in MX rather than other sports. Conversely, there would be little point a local business spending a fortune to promote their business globally, better to spend a few quid supporting a rider who races locally and can represent the business in their catchment area.

The first sponsor to get lined up is usually the bike manufacturer as without bikes and a spare parts budget it's nearly impossible to go racing at grand prix level unless the team has a very wealthy backer. For teams like Hitachi this is from the national importer/distributor in the form of discounted bikes on a deferred payment i.e. the team gets allocated a number of bikes, maybe 8 per rider, and pays for them at the end of the year at a discounted price. Spares budgets will be in the tens of thousands of pounds/euros for the main rider with discounts for support riders. Although the support for Hitachi is via the UK importer, it still has to be sanctioned by the bosses in Austria, but with Conrad Mewse on board Roger had been promised additional support direct from the factory in the form of engines and suspension. Mewse would get semi-factory engines to start but if the results were there the material would improve. The KTM support also comes with support from Motorex lubricants in the form of budget and product as they have a world-wide agreement with KTM.

With all the manufacturers cutting back, deals were getting harder to find. As HSF logistics were shutting their doors the sharks were circling, hoping to benefit from some reallocated budget, but Standing Construct had already pounced and been promised support. The meeting in Assen was supposed to iron out the details of KTM's support going forward but with the rider line-up still uncertain the deal on bikes wouldn't be done until after the motocross of nations. Roger has a long association with KTM, going back to 2008 (although they did run as a Husqvarna team in 2016) and is KTM's premier UK team. British championship success is more important for them (KTM UK) than MXGP results, hence the team usually have British riders and compete in the ACU Maxxis British championship although Conrad Mewse is expected to graduate to the Red Bull factory KTM team as he matures so they do take an interest in his development and GP results.

For some sponsors, the decision to go with a particular team may be because of a personal relationship, and this is where Roger excels. Beneath his gentle Irish brogue, like a genial, smiling Terry Wogan, he cultivates relationships with fellow businessmen with the savvy of a city banker, and never misses a trick when it comes to potential new sponsors.

Hitachi are the joint title sponsor and according to Roger they are a dream to work with. They contribute financially and for their investment the team entertain a lot of their guests and employees at British championships and MXGPs with rider meetings and hospitality. Originally supporting a team in BSB, they moved to motocross and through a contact with Howard Smith, one of Roger's friends and a long-time team associate, the deal was made.

Milwaukee tools have been a long-time supporter of British Super Bikes much like Hitachi but were looking to get into motocross. An employee comes from Northern Ireland and through a friendship with Roger they became a financial and product sponsor for the team. Hitachi/ASA KTM offered the perfect partner, with a good chance to win the British championship Milwaukee send 'Big Red', their promotional display truck to every British championship while the team also promote the brand on the world stage. They are set to become a substantial sponsor in 2019 and with plans in the pipeline to become part of the KTM official parts catalogue, an instant dealer network will be created for the Milwaukee brand. With both brands looking for a multi-year partnership everyone's a winner and it's especially satisfying to get sponsors from outside the motorcycle industry on board.

" Contract Furniture.

Contract Furniture would stay on board. Originally a personal sponsor of Ben Watson in 2016 before becoming a joint title sponsor of the Hitachi/Contract Furniture KTM team as it was known in 2017, MD Riece Bellamy has a long history with the Watsons. A childhood friend of their dad and their uncle, Riece originally started sponsoring Nathan Watson in world enduro, then supporting Ben with expenses to facilitate the fly-away MXGPs. After a successful season with the team which included Ben winning the British championship, the only question was whether he would go with Ben (to the Kemea Yamaha team) or remain with Hitachi KTM as a joint title sponsor. In the November issue of Dirt Bike Rider magazine an interview with Irwin referred to the ASA Hitachi KTM team. Was this the 'team within a team' scenario or had Contract furniture pulled out? It took me until February to catch up with the Riece Bellamy and ask what his plans were. He confirmed that he would be staying on board as a team sponsor but no longer as a tile sponsor because he was putting less money into the team in order to support some other riders within the same total budget. Contract furniture would get their name and logo on the team transporter, and on the bikes in three places, both mudguards and the front number plate as well as some corporate hospitality throughout the year. Having two outside sponsors like Hitachi Construction Machinery and Contract Furniture on board is quite a coup for the team as most sponsors tend to be industry sponsors, that is they have a direct link to motocross as a supplier or manufacturer. Contract Furniture is a furniture supplier to the leisure industry (hotels, clubs, restaurants etc) so what does Riece get out of his involvement with the team?

"Clients like to be entertained. They like to go out, see a different sport and have an interesting day. Hopefully they remember it,

remember us and come back to us. We take them to a track, show them what goes on and meet the riders then out for a meal, or go to a race and give them hospitality" said Riece.

His involvement with the sport has had some surprising dividends, for example one of his suppliers in Slovenia is a big Tim Gajser fan and a haulage firm they use in Austria are also motocross fans that have recognised the Contract Furniture brand as a sponsor. The Contract Furniture logo will also appear on the shirts of Ben Watson (MXGP), Nathan Watson (World Enduro) and Josiah Natzke (British Championship MX) as Riece will also be a personal sponsor, but in the clearly defined world of rider contracts the logo won't appear on their bikes. Does Riece expect to generate any sales directly from the association with the team and/or riders?

"Not necessarily, but the team and riders all mention us on their social media, Paul Malin often mentions us during his commentary and people recognise our name so its all good for getting our brand known".

Like most people in the sport, I think Riece is a fan first and foremost, who loves to be involved rather than the decision to become a sponsor being a business decision. This isn't unique; I went to the NHRA Winter Nationals Drag Racing in Pomona in February, in between the Oakland and San Diego super-cross races. Whilst I can't adequately explain the noise, vibration, smell and shear violence of Top-fuel dragsters and nitro Funny cars launching down a standing quarter mile run, reaching over three hundred and thirty miles an hour in under four seconds (you need to experience it at least once in your life) there are some parallels to motocross. Walking around the paddock is impressive, seeing lines of race transporters with teams of mechanics rebuilding the engines after each run is like MXGP. I got talking to one of the sponsors of a funny car team who said he just loved the sport and helped support the team because 'they're a real nice family and not a big corporate team'. The budget was immense, well over a million dollars a year for this small, private team with part-time mechanics and multi millions for the big teams with corporate sponsors. 'The car burns about thirteen gallons of fuel in a run (under 4 seconds!) which is about thirty bucks a gallon. The engine gets completely rebuilt each run. Although he owned an engineering company, he didn't supply anything to the drag racing fraternity, and didn't expect to get any business from it, it was purely that he loved being involved. 'The best bit is standing behind the cars when they launch. You can't buy a pass for that!' he said.

M.A.N. trucks were staying on board, providing a tractor unit for the race truck. It's a big expense for the team to lease or buy one so although there's no cash it's one of those deals where the product is worth a lot to the team. S.O. Rentals, a Bristol based van and car leasing company owned by Shaun Osmond provides three vans for the team to use as general run-abouts and for practicing (no teams use their race trucks at the practice tracks). Shaun is a long-time friend of team co-ordinator Ian Browne and has been around motocross all his life, running his own team for a few years before joining forces with Colin Reed at RWJ and now with Roger's team. Not only providing vans, Shaun also goes to almost every race and assists Ian with the practical day-to-day running of the team

Sometimes, products are as valuable to a team as cash, as with the M.A.N. deal above. A raft of sponsors contributes everything from oils and lubricants, plastics, bolts and performance parts, to workshop benches and storage units to get their name on the team truck and bikes. PRO carbon provide carbon fibre guards for the bikes, Twin Air provides air filters, Troy Lee designs provide financial support, team wear and riding gear, with Alpine Stars providing riding boots and trainers, Doc-Wob provides titanium bolt kits and ASA Scaffolding are joint title sponsors, providing financial support and providing the race truck at British championship events; it's all part of the jig-saw that makes the team look professional and allows them to compete at the elite level. The Dirt Bike show at Stoneleigh marked an

◀ *Elliot Banks-Brown - 2012*

▼ *Kevin Strijbos & EBB, double British champions in 2012*

◀ *Natalie Kane at Matterley, 2013*

▲ *Natalie Kane winning in 2013*

◀ *EBB – another MX2 title in 2013*

opportunity to meet many of the industry sponsors, tie up the final deals and get a few early photos out on social media, all topped off with a night out to thank them for their support.

By now, virtually everything was in place to go racing again, with better support from KTM than in previous years largely because KTM still wanted to nurture their star of the future Conrad Mewse. Despite having most of the sponsorship agreements in place, it would still be the middle of February before some deals were finalised which meant the final design for the race truck and bike graphics was delayed. Regarding the truck design, Roger told me it costs about £3000 to re-do the graphics each year. Andy McAlpine does the design for the truck and graphic, and each sponsor wants their logo in certain places. The team also has a good relationship with Enjoy graphics who produce the graphics kits for the race bikes.

While I was researching this book, I read a very interesting interview with Forrest Butler, owner of the Rocky Mountain ATV/MC-KTM-WPS team in America. The team have some remarkable similarities to the Hitachi ASA KTM team in terms of their progression from a small privateer outfit to Factory backed professional team. In the interview, Butler said he has forty-one paying sponsors that form the financial back-bone of the team. Drawing a comparison to the RCH Suzuki team that folded in 2017, they had nine sponsors of which only five paid hard cash according to the interview. Butler said his approach was to ask potential sponsors what they want out of the deal and try to find the fair market value rather than pitch with cocky, overvalued prices. After being unpaid by a major sponsor in 2013 Butler said he learned a big lesson in business; get a contract. You can read the interview by Brett Smith in the February 2018 edition of Racer X magazine.

Roger's way of running the business is that he won't spend any money until it's in the bank. This is good business in many ways but can create some issues, especially at the start of the season when a lot of the big expenses come but the sponsor's cash hasn't arrived. Many teams (and businesses) have floundered on the rocks of bad debt or bad cash-flow so this approach at least safeguards the team financially but can mean they're chasing their tail later on.

Even when a deal is done things can go wrong. Yamaha's American factory team announced a multi-year deal with Knich as a title sponsor with a press release in November, an extract of which is below.

Cypress, CA - *Yamaha Motor Corporation, U.S.A., today announced that its Monster Energy/Yamaha Factory Racing Supercross/Motocross team has signed a multi-year agreement with new sponsor Knich. The official team name is Monster Energy/Knich/Yamaha Factory Racing, and riders include returning member Cooper Webb (#2) and his new teammate Davi Millsaps (#18). Cooper and Davi will both compete aboard the all-new 2018 YZ450F.*

Keith McCarty, Motorsports Racing Division Manager for Yamaha Motor Corporation, U.S.A., commented, "It is our pleasure to welcome Knich to our Monster Energy/Yamaha Factory Racing team. Knich is an exciting, new brand whose message closely aligns with Yamaha's own performance-oriented heritage. We are proud that Knich has partnered with us not only to help support our team, but also to promote their new venture."

Knich is a new action-sports apparel and equipment brand geared towards today's active consumers who demand quality and performance in their daily lives.

Little was known about the new brand, but their logo adorned the race trucks and bikes until mid-February, when a much shorter press released announced that the partnership was over.

"It is with great disappointment that Yamaha Motor Corporation, U.S.A., has terminated Knich's sponsorship agreement with Yamaha Factory Racing, effective immediately. The announcement was made by Keith McCarty, Motorsports Racing Division Manager for Yamaha Motor Corporation, U.S.A."

Transworld motocross elaborated when they reported the news;

"We and many others wondered what exactly Knich is, as it's unusual for a brand-new company to become a major supporter of a factory team. After talking to some people familiar with the company, we were told

that Knich is the side project of an entrepreneur that is highly involved in ammunition and that Knich was created to side-step a restriction against firearm sponsorship. The founder of Knich is a friend to Millsaps, hence the connection to the team.

At the time we were told that aside from the entrepreneur making his initial money in ammunition, there is no direct connection between Knich and firearms"

See the whole report at https://motocross.transworld.net/news/yamaha-factory-racing-terminates-sponsorship-agreement-knich/

The sudden termination of such a high-profile sponsor did raise questions regarding the due diligence by Yamaha but without knowing the actual reason behind the decision to end the agreement it's just speculation. There are international laws banning alcohol and tobacco sponsorship, hence the end of Camel tobacco bibs in motocross GP's and all the other tobacco sponsors on Formula 1, Moto GP, now replaced with energy drinks and other corporate brandings. It would appear there are rules banning firearms sponsorship, and presumably 'shell' companies that get their money from the company manufacturing banned products. Whilst slightly embarrassing for Yamaha it illustrates how difficult it can be even for big companies with substantial support staff to get it right, even more difficult for a small team to get everything lined up and ensure sponsors fulfill their obligations.

Chapter 5

OFF SEASON, TESTING & PRE-SEASON.

By November the last pieces had fallen into place. KTM had agreed support for the team, including semi-factory engines for Mewse, WP would provide a full suspension service and a host of other component suppliers were all in place. Graeme Irwin was fully committed, de-camping to California for a couple of months to train and get used to the new bike. Lee Tolan had a vision of taking the British championship presentation to the next level and had ordered a new race truck for Graeme (and the team) to use in Britain. This would save the team bringing the race truck back across the channel, saving thousands in ferry or tunnel charges. Brian Connolly aka BC would be Graeme Irwin's mechanic, a choice that the other team members were happy with. BC is an experienced mechanic and safe pair of hands, so should add to Irwin's comfort in the new environment.

Conrad was happy to be home in Somerset. His race bike mechanic would be the Vaclav Lavicka or Vas for short. The former Rockstar Husqvarna mechanic for Thomas Covington, comes from the Czech Republic but lives in Lommel and Conrad knew him well as they had lived together at Husqvarna. Before the 2017 season had ended, the first bit of conflict arose when Conrad announced that he was employing a practice bike mechanic to work with him, accompany him to the races and in effect 'babysit' him. It's not unusual for top riders to do this, sometimes the team will provide a practice mechanic as well as a race mechanic as it's too much work for the race mechanic to do practice bikes, race bikes, attend practice with their rider and fit in all the travelling. The issue was that Conrad had given the job to the mechanic who had walked out on the team earlier in the year. Paul Keates was Jake Nicholls' mechanic in 2017 and when Jake got injured at Trentino, ending his season, Keates quit the team stating that he could no longer work with Hendo. The issue was that he didn't give them any notice, he simple quit when they were due to leave for the GP in Latvia but also took ages to return the bike and parts he had previously taken home to work on. Because Conrad could pick his practice mechanic, Roger had agreed to allow it but had not informed team manager Ian Browne. Ian and the others didn't want him back on the team, and although it seemed like a bit of a storm in a tea cup, it was an unnecessary distraction.

I spoke to Paul later in the year to get his version of events. *"I was there as Jake's race mechanic and when he got hurt I ended up with Josiah Natzke for a few weeks. There was talk of me working with Ben, but the team wanted Hendo to stay there. Then Ben wanted me to be his practice mechanic and I didn't know who I was going to be working for. I'd spoken to Ian about leaving and he said if they finished Hendo would I stay. I was good friends with Hendo so I said no and left. Hendo knows that now because at the time he thought I was being funny and didn't want to drive to Latvia but I thought Ian was being a bit disrespectful to Hendo."*

I reminded Paul that there was quite a bad atmosphere sometimes when Hendo was in a bad mood so it wasn't surprising that Ian considered letting him go.

"There's two sides to Hendo, he's a funny one. Away from bikes he's OK but near bikes he's an asshole, that's the easiest way to put it. I thought the team could've handled it better and I wouldn't want someone to lose their job for me to take it. I already had an offer from Steve Dixon so I felt it was better for me to go, then no-one got upset.

When I came back no-one really said anything about it. Shaun was a bit funny in Spain but we spoke about it and he's been fine since then."

The deal with Pootjes fell through at the eleventh hour. After supposedly agreeing terms with Roger at the MXoN, he then changed his mind and signed for the Leiber racing team. Although I think there was some dismay in the team, to me it made more sense for Pootjes to be in a continental team rather than a British team. What interest would he have in racing British championships when he could ride in Holland, Belgium or Germany more easily?

There would be some other changes for 2018 within the team. The truck driver's contract finished at the end of the season, and after a few issues during the year he would not be re-employed next season. Scraping the truck twice hadn't gone down well, (although manoeuvring a 40-tonne rig in and out of the tight paddock confines isn't easy) but more importantly was his attitude and work ethic. In a small team its vital that the team chemistry is right and that everyone 'mucks in', and unfortunately, he had been left wanting a few too many times when there was work to do. The perception was that he just wanted to drive to the track then pose in the team shirt, but the team wanted someone who was far more hands on both at the workshop and the track. There's so much work to be done each week to turn everything around for the next weekend, with endless cleaning especially after a muddy weekend. It doesn't take long for little niggles to turn into big gripes and despite being spoken to on several occasions by Ian, the team co-ordinator, things didn't improve. His last job was to take the truck to its winter storage site after the MXON at Matterly Basin in October. I spoke to him just before Christmas and he was disappointed that he hadn't heard anything official from the team to say whether he was being kept on or released although he had heard it unofficially from somewhere. I can sympathise with his position; it wouldn't have hurt for Roger or Ian to let him know he wasn't going to be used in 2018, at least he could start looking for another job.

His replacement was a perfect fit for the job. Steve Fry had been part of the team for years, albeit as a volunteer. Steve has a plumbing business but is a hard-core motocross fan and friend of the team, coming to as many races as possible and helping with everything from hospitality to fixing things on the truck and keeping the awning tidy. I'm not sure if it was a 'bucket list' thing or just a fortunate quirk of fate but Steve would take a year's sabbatical to join the team full time, driving the truck and doing all the things he had done voluntarily for years but now getting paid. It would be a welcome change of pace for Steve whose main issue would be slowing down (he's a workaholic) instead of constantly working long hours to facilitate going to the GP's.

The race truck also got some TLC through the winter. A new boiler and some internal refurbishment was required after a few issues during the summer. With the constant travelling there simply isn't any time to do any major work during the season so there were a few running repairs just to get to the end of the season such as duct tape holding the sky light on and the boiler which had been on its last legs for months. There's also the need to update the livery, making sure that sponsors logos are correctly displayed, and any old sponsors removed. This used to be a massive undertaking when trucks were sign written by hand but with the wraps and printed graphics available now it's much easier. A new awning had also been ordered complete with new flooring and back drops to divide the mechanic's workspace and hospitality area, and make it look more professional.

Steve 'Hendo' Henderson wouldn't be returning as a mechanic. The self-proclaimed grumpy old man had been saying all year that he intended to retire although as the season drew to a close he had amended that to staying in Britain to act as a practice bike mechanic. As Conrad and Graeme would be working with new mechanics, Hendo was let go. Just as with the riders, mechanics usually work on fixed contracts and Hendo's wasn't being renewed by the team. Chatting to him at the Dirt Bike Show he was like a different man, happy and chirpy rather than the grumpy, sullen Grinch that he usually was in the workshop or at races, it was as if the weight of the long season had been lifted off him. It's a shame he wasn't 'happy Hendo' more often as I had grown to really like him, but more importantly he may have been retained by the team. Unfortunately, they were fed up with treading on eggs shells when he was being a miserable old git. He would end up in Thailand working for another race team. Surprise surprise, he was 'let go' in

April after 'not passing his validation'.

The other mechanic, Paul 'Minty' Whitehead would return as a general assistant. Minty had been Josiah Natzke's mechanic but would now be responsible for duties such as setting up the power washer, getting tires, helping with the awning and anything in the workshop during the week. Hopefully that would ease the workload for the race mechanics a little and provide the extra pair of hands that are needed at the weekend. It's surprising how much needs to be done just keeping the place tidy and sorting out the hospitality area.

The season ends with the last race, which for the MXGP teams was the MXoN on the 1st October. Many of the riders and team personnel take a well-earned break, a chance to lie on the beach for a couple of weeks before the preparation starts for the next year. There are 2 schools of thought here; some like to take a complete break and start afresh in the new year, with injuries healed and fully motivated for the long season (twenty Grand Prix) ahead which would start in Argentina on March 4th, plus a national championship (Hitachi riders will compete in the 8-round Maxxis ACU British Championship). Most teams and riders nowadays simply can't squander the 3 months after the last race, so most take a month off then start again in November.

For Graeme the switch to a new team, a new bike and a move up to MXGP meant he would head to America with his family to get as much riding time as possible on the tracks in Southern California. His wife is from Murrieta in the heart of California motocross country. The beauty of riding for KTM is that they have strong links between their European and US teams, and with Troy Lee Designs being the gear sponsor for Hitachi/ASA, Irwin was able to borrow a bike to get acclimatised to the KTM.

"I'm very lucky that Brooke is from America and we could stay with her parents for a month. Tyler Keefe, the Troy Lee team manager hooked me up with a factory bike, I was really lucky. I had factory suspension and we actually brought our own stuff as well. It was really cool, they gave us everything we needed. Roger sent BC out for me, so we did some testing

with the bike set-up. I rented a truck and it worked out perfectly, you can stick to your program and it's not freezing cold. What I would say though, America is great fun, it's great to go there and ride but it's no good for the GP's. The tracks are so different. It was good to learn the bike".

Conrad would spend his time riding a very stock looking bike in the UK, glad to be back at home after living in Lommel. Although the weather in Britain can be challenging in autumn, the comfort factor of being back with his family made up for that.

With no racing going on through the winter, social media and the internet sites were mostly doing re-caps of the season or showing Instagram clips of various riders 'flying' at the practice track, including Irwin and Mewse. At this time of year any predictions are mostly meaningless, as so much can happen before serious racing begins but more so because anyone can look fast riding around a relatively smooth track on their own. It's very difficult to accurately simulate race conditions at a practice track or learn 'race craft' i.e. the art of actually racing other riders, adapting to changing conditions, switching lines and passing. Still, the aim of riding now is just to get familiar with the bike and get some bike fitness ready for the serious business of 'testing' which starts for most in January.

Testing.

Testing is the process of refining the set-up of the bike for the individual rider to get the maximum performance and 'comfort'. By 'comfort' I mean getting confident on the bike and comfortable in all situations. Without that 'comfort level', it's hard to push to the limit. Even a standard production bike will have numerous clickers and plug-ins available for the rider to adjust the suspension for firmness and damping, plus engine mapping changes to alter power delivery as well as hard parts such as the handlebars, the size of sprockets or the type of tire used, to give just a few examples. It's easy to get confused as a change to one part can affect the characteristics of the bike in unexpected ways, therefore the process requires small, incremental adjustments to one part at a time, with the rider doing a few laps and reporting their feelings to the mechanic who will have timed the laps. A bike can 'feel' fast but the stop watch may not agree, for example because the power delivery is too fierce, so the rear wheel is spinning rather than getting grip and drive, that's why an old 500cc two stroke feels faster than a modern 450 four stroke.

The process begins by setting the handlebars, levers, gear and brake levers, then getting a base line for the suspension that the rider is comfortable with. From there it's a case of trying all the available parts that could alter the power, handling, feel or anything else on the bike, in a methodical way and recording the changes and results. It's important to try to isolate the change that is being tested; easier said than done when you're still trying to focus on putting in consistent laps. The process is laborious but is the only way to ensure the bike is set up as well as possible for each rider, and when tenths of a second can mean five places on the lap chart its vital work. Despite being an incredibly finnicky bunch, not all top riders are good at relaying what they feel on the track, so the team will do the best they can to assist the riders by interpreting their comments, looking at lap times and videoing the laps. At the factory team level, there's increasing use of telemetry to understand what the bike and rider is doing at any point around the track, the data uploaded to a lap-top for comparison. Programable ignitions and electronics in general have been a big part of moto-GP for many years and that technology is now part of motocross. The main difference is the changing track conditions on MX, not just from a sand track to a dirt track, but from lap to lap as bumps and ruts form. Tarmac is much more consistent and therefore easier to predict.

Some changes can be so minute that it's hard to believe they make a difference. For example, when the supercross season started in January in America, there were plenty of pictures and reports online about the bikes. Pro-Circuit drill holes in the top engine support hangers whilst HRC Honda use tapered hangers on Roczen's bike. These small changes are said to alter the flex characteristics of the chassis (frame). I don't think many people would think of an engine stay as a tuning part, or indeed if the average club racer could feel the difference but that's the level of refinement needed by some of the elite racers.

In an interview by Tom Jacobs published on Gatedrop.com, Dennis Dierckx, the mechanic for Wilvo Yamaha's Arnaud Tonus gave an interesting insight when asked about some of his previous riders.

"...younger riders are usually much more prone to outside influence. They still doubt a lot of everything and anything. More experienced riders like to test but as soon as they have found 'their setting', they will almost never deviate from it. Even if something better comes along, they are not willing to give up what they already know. You will also find riders who are very satisfied with their setting because they have too little demand (understanding) of the technical side. While there is still a lot of margin to be gained by refining the setup. Just look at a guy like Chad Reed, he's known for being very precise with his setup. It's a skill that is only improved by experience. I don't think that at the age of 15, 16 you can be an exceptional test rider." (gatedrop.com/dierckx-tonus, 28 December 2017)

Of course, he was not talking about the Hitachi/ASA riders, but I thought it was an interesting observation. Testing is part of the job, and like any job the skills have to be learnt. Mewse should have some good settings already from his Husqvarna days as the KTM is virtually the same bike but after a few years on a Honda, Irwin would need to adapt to his new ride.

As Britain returned to work after the Christmas holidays amid the wet gloom of winter, the team headed to Spain for the start of serious preparations and testing. Half the GP paddock were doing the same thing, searching for some winter sunshine and dry tracks to start the process of dialling in their bikes and riders. Redsand would host the third round of the world championship in April and provided the ideal venue for the team. Initial times looked very good with Irwin on the pace of the GP runners; pretty encouraging for a rider just stepping up to a full time GP effort.

Team manager Ian Browne talked me through the options available to Graeme Irwin.

"We start with a standard bike, and change things like handlebars, grips, even foot rests to get it feeling right. Graeme uses standard foot rests, but we had others to try. We had two engines with mechanical differences, plus ECU's. we had Steve Payne from Multi-tek with us for two days; he's a genius with engine mapping. Then we had three days with WP suspension."

With so many options it must be difficult to isolate each change

"It's easy to get lost with so many things to try," agrees Browne, *"it's not like MotoGP where you can use data. If a bike is 3 mph slower, you will see it in the data. We record each change in a log book and on a lap-top, use lap times and get feedback from the rider, but we also watch them so that you can interpret what they're telling you. The feedback isn't always reliable; if a rider thinks something is better or worse they often try to justify it. Also, a small mistake could ruin the lap time and if you're not watching you could get false information. We also use back-to-back testing to compare changes."*

I asked Browne about the example earlier where engine head supports were changed to alter frame flex.

"Some riders are amazing at feeling minute changes like frame flex, so yes I understand that."

Does the process continue throughout the season or does the team ever double back later just to confirm settings?

"Yes, sometimes we might get new parts from KTM to try. Or sometimes if it feels like we've got a bit lost we can go back to older settings and start again."

I asked about his riders.

"Conrad is easy, his engines come from the factory. We rebuild them but that's it. Once he's happy that's it. Graeme is a good test rider but he over-thinks things."

Testing and riding was just part of the day. Gym sessions, stretching and bicycle rides were all part of the routine to get the necessary strength and cardiovascular fitness to compete at the elite level.

Speaking to long-time team sponsor and supporter Shaun Osmond, he was impressed with the two riders, saying that Graeme had really stepped up his pace since riding in Britain and was extremely fit. The chance to ride in MXGP was clearly motivating the Irishman to do everything possible to maximise his chances.

Conrad Mewse had also been in the gym, filling out and gaining strength. It's easy to forget that he's still a young man, only seventeen and still growing. The move back to Britain had done wonders for his confidence along with a few months spent working with his manager, James Dobb. Dobb was the 125 World Champion in 2001, the last Brit to win a world title on a 'big' bike, although Mewse can also claim his own 85cc World championship in 2013.

Pre-season usually bring unfortunate news of a rider getting injured during training, but January would bring unprecedented news of a different kind.

Teams are usually very guarded about internal issues, so it was perhaps an indication of the frustration felt by BOS Suspension team owner Olivier Bossard when the team announced on social media that they had fallen out with Benoit Paturel, who had apparently refused to test or ride the race bike. After some back-and-forth on social media, the two parties split, a messy airing of their dirty laundry in public that probably didn't show either side in a very good light. Within days a replacement rider had been signed.... Evgeny Bobryshev. Bobby had been in negotiation with the BOS team in the autumn but for some reason couldn't reach an agreement. The twist was that he would continue to ride for the Lombard Express/RFX Suzuki team in the British championships but would ride a Suzuki under the BOS awning in MXGP, alongside Tixier on the KTM. Bossard said in a press release that it would be a bonus for the team as the they were not receiving support from any manufacturer.

"The fact that Evgeny rides a RM-Z450 does not bother us...... it is even better! We will be present at the twenty MXGP rounds to show that our suspension is great, so doing it on a European base and a Japanese base is perfect."

I can't think of a previous example of a top-level team openly running two brands of motorcycle under one awning before. Teams like Bud Racing Kawasaki have been known to shoe-horn a Yamaha or KTM 125 engine into a Kawasaki chassis to allow their rider to compete in a 125 championship, (Kawasaki no longer make a 125 engine) but they go out of their way to conceal the fact with different engine covers. Bobryshev would use BOS suspension on his British bike so there shouldn't be any issues switching between teams as far as bike continuity goes, and it definitely gives the conventional team structure a new slant.

The whole 'incident' was over in a week or so, 'a storm in a tea cup' in many ways but also an interesting insight into rider/team dynamics and the business of running a team. For his part, Paturel would start the season on a privateer Honda.

Back to the business of racing, and the first outing for the team would be the Hawkstone International on February 11th. There are several pre-season races around that time in France and Italy that teams use as a way to bench mark their preparations. In the 1980's, Beaucaire in France was the pre-eminent race used by the top riders of the day, the gate often looking like a GP. Hakan Carlqvist famously described it as 'a lemonade race', meaning that it was nice but unimportant, which pretty much sums up how all the teams and riders rationalise these events; if you win then great, it proves that you're prepared and fast but if you don't get the results you were hoping for then at least you still have time to fix the issues before the points-paying championships begin. Pre-season races really don't count for much as the season progresses and that's why most of the top riders won't push themselves or take too many chances at these events; they want to win but have also got one eye on getting through the race without picking up an injury that could de-rail their season. For the fans, it's the first chance to see their favorite riders' new livery, gear, and bikes.

The wet week leading up to the race meant the track was a bit one-lined and the organisers cut out the famous Hawkstone Hill much to everyone's annoyance, but the Hitachi/ASA riders came away happy and healthy. Conrad was third overall with two fourth places and eighth in the super-final.

In the press release afterwards, he said *"Overall, we had a really good weekend and that's testament to coming off a great off-season. I'm really happy. I've got such a great team around me and they let me work the way that I need to. It's all working perfectly and that shows today with three solid races and a podium to begin the year with."*

Graeme was fifth in the first race and running fifth in the second when he collided with a lapper which dropped him to eighth. *"The first race result wasn't too bad, but the gap to the front was bigger than I wanted. I knew I had more, I just couldn't find that rhythm and speed in the opening laps. The second race was a shame to have the collision with the backmarker. I don't think I saw a blue flag all day. Anyway, he moved aside for one rider but not me and that was that."*

Graeme's pragmatic assessment was perhaps the biggest plus to come out of the day. In race one, he had been over a minute behind the front four; Herlings and Coldenhoff on Factory KTMs, and Anstie and Paulin on Factory Husqvarna. That's not a bad result, but the reality is that ten or fifteen other riders would occupy that gap in an MXGP race so it's important to be realistic about your own and the team's expectations. Leaving the event healthy was also a positive. Tim Gajser had crashed in Mantova, Italy breaking his jaw and Jordi Tixier needed surgery for ligament damage after Hawkstone, causing both to miss the first MXGP in Argentina. Whilst injuries are an occupational hazard, missing a GP and the loss of preparation time on the bike at this stage of the season means you're playing catch-up from the start and any potential championship challenge is over before it starts. HRC Honda start the year with Brian Bogers and Tim Gajser injured in Europe and in America both Ken Roczen (injured at round 6) and Cole Seeley (injured at round eight) out of the supercross championship and possibly the National too; that's got to be a bitter pill to swallow for the once dominant manufacturer not to mention the money invested. In 2016 Hitachi/Contract Furniture KTM felt the pain of injury as Ben Watson suffered a season ending injury at the MXGP in Argentina, and again in 2017 when Jake Nicholls dislocated his pelvis in the Italian MXGP at Trentino, ending his GP career.

The debate about injuries and what can be done to reduce them came to the fore again in 2018 as a slew of American riders were on the 'injured' list following supercross crashes. Some suggested compulsory body armour (note, front and back protection is already mandatory in MXGP although most riders opt for the flimsiest armour they can get away with) but apparently riders don't want to 'look fat' or be restricted in their movement. It's impossible to pin point a single cause of injuries, if it was that simple it would be easy to fix. The personal protective equipment available is the best and most technically advanced that it's ever been. Modern boots, knee brace, wrist braces, neck braces, and helmets are all light, ergonomic and engineered to give maximum protection for the specific application for which they are designed, and the old adage of 'dress for the crash not the ride' is probably still good advice, certainly for club riders, but understand that no piece of kit is going to offer full protection in every situation. Alpine Stars have developed an air-bag system in their road racing leathers that deploys when the suit detects a crash so maybe it will be developed for off-road use in the future but it's not hard to think of multiple problems with the concept in motocross. Track design has also been highlighted as a cause, but Hawkstone has remained largely unchanged for forty years, if anything the famous whoop section at the back has been tamed. In fact, there used to be a huge double jump following the sand pit where Georges Jobe famously jumped over the top of Andre Malherbe at the 1984 500GP. If you haven't seen the picture captured by Nick Haskell, type this link into your search engine, http://robandrewsmx.com/article.php?id=89 and have a look.

Whilst the proliferation of jumps and rhythm sections on outdoor tracks is offered as the cause of crashes and injuries, Jake Nicholls injury was caused by catching his foot in a rutted turn, so it's not just jumps that cause problems. Whilst tracks like Farleigh Castle offer a great setting for evo and twin shock racing with grassy hillsides and natural undulations, I can't imagine many people being impressed if a modern MXGP was held there on a 1980's layout. Modern riding techniques have evolved to enable riders to skim whoops and scrub huge jumps so perhaps it just comes down to the fact that riders are pushing the limits all the time, both their physical limits and the limits of the bikes and when those limits are exceeded it can go wrong quickly with severe consequences. Tim Gajser's crash in Italy wasn't the consequence of missing a huge jump combination, *"I slid with my right leg before going for a jump and that caused me to inadvertently open the throttle and that's why I overjumped. I landed basically at the base of the following jump and hit my face hard on the handlebar"* he explained in a press release the following week.

The MXGP paddock had also been depleted by injury before the season started. Besides Gajser and Bogers, Guillod, Tixier and Tonus would all miss the first GP. Adam Wheeler posted an interesting article on his on track off road on-line magazine after the Patagonia-Argentina MXGP in which he asked if the 450cc bikes are a cause of some injuries. In the article, KTM manager Dirk Gruebel said that the development was now focused on making the bikes more rideable, not making them more powerful, and DRT Kawasaki rider Tommy Searle made the point that the bikes have become so good as chassis design has developed that riders are now hitting obstacles flat out and assuming the suspension will handle it, while Glenn Coldenhoff mentioned the pressure to perform in such a competitive field and the constant fear of losing your spot on a top team if you don't get the results so everyone takes more risks. You can read the full article at ontrackoffroad.com/2018/03/07/the-450-question/

It's ironic that development of 500cc two strokes stopped in the nineties as they had become too powerful for most normal riders and the popularity of the class was dropping off. Although it was environmental issues that finally made Honda and Kawasaki stop production of open class two strokes, Yamaha and Suzuki pulled the plug long before as demand dropped off. It may be a bit Darwinian, but perhaps natural selection will finally lead to the demise of 450 four strokes too if it is simply that they have gotten too powerful or too difficult to ride. I think it's more likely that electronic aids will become more prevalent to smooth out the power as they have done on road bikes.

The debate about injuries will continue as its quite clear there are so many opinions and in reality there will always be risk attached to racing a motorcycle but for now Mewse and Irwin were healthy, fit and eager for the first gate drop in Argentina, just a few weeks away. As temperatures in northern Europe dropped, Irwin headed to Ottobiano in Northern Italy, venue for one of the up-coming GP's but more importantly to keep the training and preparation going. An Instagram post with Antonio Cairoli and Arminas Jasikonis putting laps in around the sandy track with the message 'awesome day doing motos with these two, thanks for letting me join in' illustrated a couple of things. Firstly, all the MXGP runners are in the same boat; they've done their winter training, but they have to keep that going, and secondly, they're all trying to gauge where they are in relation to the competition. I'm sure Cairoli doesn't view Graeme Irwin as a title threat so he's happy to train with him and even help him by doing motos together. That certainly wouldn't be the case if it were Jeffrey Herlings out there with Cairoli. Both riders are vying for the top spot so any time they're together its mind games, testosterone and mutual suspicion. It's one of the ironies of our sport; the person you want to beat the most is your teammate, because they're on the same equipment as you

Chapter 6

ROUND 1, MXGP OF PATAGONIA ARGENTINA, NEUQUEN – THE SEASON BEGINS & CONRAD MEWSE

As Europe was gripped by an icy chill straight from Siberia, the riders and team staff boarded flights to sunnier climes for the first MXGP of the year in Neuquén, Argentina. Fortunately, they all got away just before the 'beast from the east' hit Europe, shutting airports and bringing much of Britain (and Europe) to a standstill for a few days as snow and freezing temperatures wreaked havoc. It's quite a trek to get there, about fourteen hours travelling with long haul flights to Buenos Aires then an internal flight which leaves you with a one-hundred-mile drive to the beautiful Patagonia Race Track. Compared to last year's calendar which started with four fly-away events, a single trip to Argentina is quite easy but still poses some logistical issues for teams. All teams are required to use the Youthstream travel agent, Sport Events and Logistics (which just happens to be owned by Giuseppe Luongo's brother) for shipping bikes. In fairness, this does make things a lot easier as they are dealing with transporting bikes all the time and by shipping everything together it ensures that everything arrives (or none of it arrives!). It cost the Roger about £18,000 for the trip that includes flights, hotels and hire cars for the riders, mechanics and team co-ordinator plus the two bikes and all the spares. "We could probably do it cheaper, but you have to use S.E.L. to get the free 200kg per rider allowance for the bikes" said Roger. Race fuel gets sent separately and goes a few weeks earlier. That costs another £500. You would think that teams could by petrol locally, but the quality, purity and conformity can't be guaranteed so they all send sealed containers of race fuel that meets the required standards.

As it's the first race of the year, the bikes are put into the transport crate in the workshop, along with spare wheels, parts and tools, and collected about two weeks before the race so that they are waiting at the track on the Thursday when the mechanics arrive to re-assemble and put through technical control. Everything in the crate must be listed on a carnet, (this is a customs form that allows vehicles to be moved across international borders at no cost) and there are strict rules about what can be put in there. A few years ago, one of the Italian mechanics put some food (cheese or cooked sausage I believe) in with the bikes. It was detected in customs and caused no end of problems for all concerned (he wasn't working for this team in case you were wondering). Each team has their own crates, with team livery, that get used for all the fly-away races. They're 2 metres long, 1 metre wide and 1.35 metres high, on castors, so they can be rolled around easily. The logistical issue for the teams is that they won't get the bikes back until the next MXGP in Europe which is in Valkenswaard two weeks later. For Hitachi KTM there is a British championship race in between so it means they will have to have three fully prepared race bikes for each rider, one in the transport crate heading back to Europe and two to use at the British championship race (they always have a spare bike in case of a catastrophic incident that can't be repaired between races). Each rider also has a practice bike so already you have at least eight bikes on the go. When your riders are using standard equipment it's not a great problem, but Graeme has chosen to run the optional factory fifty-two-millimetre forks instead of the standard forty-eights. These forks aren't cheap, and they are leased rather than purchased, so there's a judgement call to be made; does the team spend the money on spare forks that in all likely hood will not get used or take a chance and leave the forty-eights in the spare bike? It's not just the forks, with the different diameter legs they require different triple clamps so if the spare bike is needed the mechanic would need to swat the entire front end or make do with the forty eights. In the end, Roger decided that there wasn't sufficient budget to pay for the additional forks, so Irwin would have two sets, one for his race bike and one on his practice bike.

Because it's a fly-away race the pit area is different to usual as none of the teams have their race trucks. In countries such as America, the local race teams will often host the visiting MXGP teams in their trucks, but that sort of infrastructure isn't in place in Argentina. The pit area was a series of small marquee type tents with teams allocated a work area. It seems to work well, as long as you haven't forgotten anything!

Many of the teams have photo shoots and Youthstream make a big deal out of the new season with press events for partners, sponsors, teams and a rider presentation and photograph like the first day at school. Despite not having all the home comforts of a race truck it's quite an event and everyone is generally pleased to start the new season, especially in such a beautiful location. It makes sense to start in the southern hemisphere where it's still summer time (especially as a race in Europe would certainly have been forced to cancel due to the snow) and with bright sunshine, twenty-degree Celsius temperatures and a flowing track with loamy, volcanic soil over a hard base it's a great venue.

Hitachi/ASA team's focus was on getting Graeme and Conrad off to a good start. The old adage is that "you can't win a championship at the first race, but you can certainly lose it", so the aim was to score some points and get home safely. As I said earlier, in 2016 Ben Watson badly broke his ankle at the Argentinian race, costing him all that year and much of 2017 before he was properly recovered so they have some experience of what can go wrong. It's worth stating that no-one in the Hitachi/ASA team believes that Graeme or Conrad will win the world championship; that's not a realistic goal and the team also have other priorities, i.e. winning in Britain and delivering a double British championship for KTM UK. Before you get upset, thinking

Conrad Mewse - 2018

▲ *Conrad & Vas*
Photo credit Ian Cairns

◄ *Photo credit Ian Cairns*

that everyone on the gate should be going for the win I would say that 'yes, I agree', and 'yes, they are'. But there can only be one winner, and looking at the MXGP class for example, KTM have spent millions of euros to support Cairoli and Herlings who start as clear favourites in most pundits' eyes. They also have Coldenhoff on a factory bike. Given that there are twenty race winners in the class, mostly on factory bikes, it's a bit unrealistic to think that Graeme Irwin will come in as an MXGP rookie and win. That's in no way intended to be disrespectful to him; he's a very talented rider and reigning British champion but apart from Herlings and maybe Tim Gajser, no rookie expects to come into this class and win and remember that those two came through MX2 and were MX2 world champions. If opportunity strikes and luck is on his side, of course Irwin would go for the win but it's vital to set more realistic targets otherwise every week would be totally demoralising. Scoring points (points are awarded down to twentieth) would be a great achievement in the early races, and if that happens the personal targets can be raised, maybe top fifteen or top ten. Whilst that may seem fairly modest goals, bear in mind the additional bike time and travelling involved in racing GP's, particularly the fly-aways, which is a new experience for Irwin and adds another demand to adjust to.

For Conrad the demands are no less. Last year he had such a bad time at the early fly-aways that his team manager Jacky Martens sent him home early so that he could get some rest and decide if he still wanted to race. The strain of living in Belgium, feeling lonely and homesick then travelling to the four fly-aways at the start of the season had caught up with the young Mewse (just seventeen at the time) and it was affecting his riding and his health. It's easy to forget that just because a young lad can ride a motocross bike fast (or kick a football well) he still might not be ready to live independently and in another county. While the teams may pay them well and provide the bikes and equipment for racing, they often can't replace a happy home life or the pastoral support necessary to nurture some young talent. It seems glamorous, spending your days practicing and going to the gym but it can quickly become mundane, boring and lonely. It's not much fun going back to an empty flat every day. Simple things like missing your pet dog, your siblings and even your parents (not all teenagers hate their parents!), or just the familiarity of friends speaking the same language can make a big difference, and there are a few riders in the British paddock that haven't been able to adjust to life abroad. Jake Nicholls told me that he absolutely hated living in Lommel as there was nothing to do. He would spend all his time in the gym just for something to do and ended up seriously over training. One year on, Conrad is more mature, but crucially back living in England where he feels more comfortable and supported. There is probably more expectation that Mewse will do well although that does not manifest in any pressure from the team.

The race weekend went okay for Conrad, qualifying in tenth place on Saturday, he was sixth in race one but after starting poorly in race two could only get to nineteenth. Still, that left him thirteenth overall and with seventeen championship points in the bag. In the battle of the Brits, (who six months earlier were all prospective targets for the Hitachi/ASA team) Ben Watson came out on top, fourth overall and just a point away from his first podium. The move to Kemea Yamaha seemed to suit him and with a winter of structure training behind him he seemed more mature, stronger and more aggressive than before. The third Brit, Adam Sterry, was returning to racing after missing almost a year with a knee injury. While practicing in Holland he had hit a metal post, splitting his ring finger open on his left hand. A first turn crash in race one ripped the wound open again although he battled up to thirteenth in some pain, his glove soaked in blood. After getting the wound re-stitched, (nine stitches!) he could only manage twenty-first in race two; little things make a big difference when everyone else is at one hundred percent.

Graeme's weekend was as good as could be expected. Qualifying twenty-first, he earned points in both races with sixteenth and twentieth finishes, a great result in his first MXGP. In truth, all eyes were on the Cairoli/ Herlings battle at the front, as Herlings reeled in the nine-times champion in the first race but ran out of time. In race two Cairoli pulled out an eight second lead before Herlings again put on a charge to catch the champ apparently off-guard. After an epic battle for a couple of laps between the two KTM riders, Herlings made a pass on the last lap to take the overall. TV commentators Paul Malin and Adam Wheeler waxed lyrical about the "changing of the guard" and it being the biggest win of Herlings' career as he put in the fastest lap of the race on the last lap.

The Hitachi/ASA team were happy too. No injuries, points in all four races and plenty to discuss on the long flight home. There would be little time once they got back as the first Maxxis British championship round in Lyng, Norfolk was scheduled for the next weekend.

Unfortunately, there are thieving scum bags everywhere. The Dixon Racing Team had rented a house for the team to stay in and while Tommy Searle was in bed on Saturday evening thieves broke in and stole his bag containing his goggles and more importantly his wallet and passport. It could have been worse but it's a headache to arrange travel documents to get home that he and the team could have done. He seemed quite philosophical after the race when he was being interviewed, joking about having to stay in Argentina and competing in their national championship. As luck would have it, the first British Championship round at Lyng was cancelled. Heavy rain had left the track and parking area saturated and with more rain forecast, series manager Stuart Drummond had no choice but to postpone the event until October. The 'free weekend' meant more time to get over the jet-lag from Argentina and allowed the team to focus on the next MXGP in Valkenswaard the following weekend.

> **Conrad Mewse.**
> When you're young its normal to have sporting heroes that you look up to or admire. They often seem much older, much more accomplished and worldlier. As I've gotten older I realise that most of these sporting stars are considerably younger

than me and whilst they have a special talent that has put them in the public spotlight, they're still growing and developing just like any other young man or woman. Conrad illustrates my point perfectly; he has incredible talent on a motorcycle but he's still only eighteen years old and has been growing up with the weight of a factory contract on his shoulders when most kids his age are playing football with their mates or chasing girls.

Like most schoolboy moto crossers, Conrad's dad Steve got him into racing.

"We started off in schoolboys, just doing club races in my area and we had some success, we started winning races and it just went from there. We never had any setbacks, and everything was going great, all through 85's and then we moved to racing in Europe. Even in the first year we nearly won the 85cc championship. I was still in school full time, so it was difficult for me to practice in the week and to get to the races. I would usually take Friday off school and we would head to the Dutch championships, or the European races. Actually, me and my dad would fly, and my nan and Granddad would drive with the bikes and all the food, so we had a good team around me, it was very small, but it worked."

This family team probably isn't that unusual but to me it shows how deep those ties are and why he would later struggle.

"Everything was going great and we moved up to the 125's in 2014. I had a practice crash in Dunkerque during my winter training and that was a big set-back for me. I'd just signed a deal with Factory KTM, but I was out for about six weeks and we just struggled. Everyone knows how intense that class is and missing a lot of the off season, we weren't prepared."

For 2015 KTM created a junior team, headed up by ten times world champion Stefan Everts. Everts has a reputation for being....... how shall we put it?.......it's got to be his way or no way, which is fine if you agree but can create some difficulties if you don't agree with him.

Teamed with Jorge Prado and Josiah Natzke, Conrad would experience a difficult year.

"It was a good experience for me, but it was tough. I moved to Belgium on my own and lived in the workshop with my mechanic."

Conrad was still fifteen years old at that time which seems incredibly young for such a move, and a big step to take. Not only moving away from your parents and family but also your friends

"It is. I was nowhere near prepared for it. A fifteen or sixteen-year-old is usually at home with their mum doing everything for them and that's where I was at the time; my mum was doing all my cooking and cleaning, just like a normal kid. Before I left we would finish school and go up the field for a game of football, and obviously that all had to stop. This is the point in my career where it went from being a hobby to a job. In a way it took my life away a little bit. Everything was motocross, motocross, motocross. I moved to Belgium because that's where I needed to be. But it was better; we had some good results and we were heading in the right direction. To be honest, we didn't win many races and I still wasn't where I wanted to be."

I asked about his experience with Stefan Everts, was he as bad as some people had said?

"It's difficult. Like you said, Stefan is 'his way or no way' but he's a ten times world champion so he knows what he's talking about, he knows what works and what doesn't work but the thing I found difficult was that not everyone is the same, and what works for some didn't work for me. I'm quite different to some people; I like to be around a family orientated team and everyone get on, just more of a friendly vibe which makes me a happy rider and makes me perform at my best. But Stefan's a great guy, he did a lot for me and made me

realise a lot of things. He taught me about work ethic and realising that when it's your job it's no joke; you can't put ninety-nine percent into it, it's all or nothing"

There's always talk about pressure and with someone like Everts instilling the message of hard work does that put any pressure on a rider? What about the knowledge that the whole team is there to support you, does that create any pressure to perform?

"I don't get pressure from other people, the pressure I have comes from myself. I want to win so bad, so I put that pressure on myself, but I do know how much work goes on by the team and I want to give them the best results possible. There's a lot of mind games in this sport and sometimes it's difficult to overcome them but I feel like I'm in a good place now and I have overcome them. I've been through quite a lot already and ridden for a few factory teams and I'm still only eighteen; I'm happy where I am now, and we've learnt a lot over the last few years of my career that has made me a better person."

For 2016 Conrad moved to the Jacky Martens' owned Rockstar Husqvarna team, the official MX2 factory Husqvarna team. Martens was the first man to win a modern era 500cc world championship in 1993 on a Husqvarna and has an impressive set-up based in Lommel. (The Hitachi/ASA team rent a workshop on the same site as Martens base.) Conrad was signed to race in the EMX250 championship and convincingly won both races at the opening round in Valkenswaard.

"By the start of 2016 when I was signed by Husqvarna and Jacky I was starting to get used to everything, living in Belgium and it being my job. Everything was coming together nicely, and the team was great. I started training with Joel Roelants and that made me realise a few things, he taught me how I should train and just picking bits of everything that work for me and putting them into a plan. We had a very good winter; I did a lot of riding and a lot of training. Coming

into the first round in Valkenswaard I didn't have a clue who I was racing, I didn't know who was supposed to be the top guy, I was just coming here to have fun and do my best. It was good because I was working hard, doing my own thing and we came to Valkenswaard open minded. It was a fantastic weekend and I went 1-1 on the day. It was a big buzz; where I'd been for the last few years and to finally get back on top on this stage of racing. It was great for me and of course, all of the team and family who had worked so hard."

After such an impressive race many pit pundits felt that 2016 would be Conrad's year to dominate to EMX250 championship and build some confidence and momentum, but team boss Martens had other ideas.

"After the race we got straight back into training, and I remember the moment when I was out cycling, doing my last bit of the ride when I got a call from Jacky saying to come around and that they wanted a meeting to talk about a few things. For the rest of the ride and all the way to his house I was kinda panicking a little bit; I didn't know if it was gonna be a good thing or a bad thing. I'd just come off the back of winning the first European, but I had no clue of what it was about or if I had done something wrong. When I got there, he congratulated me on the win and a fantastic ride and said how did I feel about moving into the MX2 class. Obviously, Thomas Covington was injured at the time so maybe that had something to do with it. My dream has been to be MX2 world champion since I was a little kid so when I got that opportunity I just took it with both hands and didn't think twice or look back. Sometimes now when I do look back and think 'was it the right decision, should I have stayed in EMX250?', but either way even if I had won the EMX 250 I would still have been in the same situation when I moved to MX2 so I'm glad I did it sooner rather than later".

"MXGP and MX2 are the top. The depth is incredible. Anyone in the top fifteen could win a race. when I won the EMX race in Valkenswaard I put 4 or 5 unbelievable laps in then backed the pace off and just came home with the win. In the MX2 class I did that but when I backed off they're still there, and they start making passes and I'm going back and back. I wasn't used to riding at that tempo for that amount of time and it wasn't my physical shape, it was mental. That was the main struggle for me when I moved into MX2."

Mewse found his feet towards the end of the season but wasn't a threat for race wins as Herlings dominated the class, but his rookie year had been OK and with Herlings moving into the 450 class for 2017 the class would be wide open, not necessarily for Conrad to win but certainly consistent top ten. However, the season couldn't have started worse (barring an injury). The first 4 races were fly-aways, which meant long-haul flights, hotels, hire cars and temporary pit shelters. Conrad had a terrible time, scoring no points in Qatar, just 6 points in the mud-fest of Indonesia and no points in Argentina. He was at rock bottom and Jacky Martens knew that something had to change, not just for his racing career but for his welfare so he took the decision to send Conrad home, missing the Mexico MXGP.

"We changed a few things after '16 because it didn't end very well but I didn't have a great winter, we still made the same mistakes, so I wasn't physically or mentally prepared. Looking back now compared to what I've done this winter (2017 –'18) it was a complete lack of training, but also mentally I just wasn't 'there'. I think a lot of it was down to confidence and where I'd finished the year before, I hadn't done a fly-away before and it all just got to me. It was difficult."

The talk at the time was that Conrad was homesick. He wasn't enjoying living away from home in Belgium and was missing his family.

"Well when the results weren't there, and things weren't going well, it did hit home that I was getting a bit homesick. I just wanted to go home and spend some time with my family in a normal environment with the people around me that know what I like. It sounds pathetic but it all adds up and it does get to you. The first two fly-aways were a disaster; I was riding so tight and nothing was running smoothly. Indonesia was a washout and I just felt so far away from home; I wasn't used to it and I got quite sick. After Argentina we sat down with the team and knew that something had to change. It was difficult because I wanted to do well for so many people not just me. I was travelling with the team and my dad would meet us there but it all came crumbling down. I went back home and missed Mexico, but I continued with training and riding; it was just the fact that I was back home, riding my local tracks, seeing everyone and feeling comfortable. I was so glad to get back to the race in Italy (Trentino), it was steady, and I had a tenth and sixteenth. The next week was OK then I had my first good result of the year in Latvia with a ninth and a third. I'd started getting comfortable and riding well again then I came up short on a double jump at my local track and broke the bottom of my ankle, so I missed Teutschenthal; I couldn't get my boot on or even walk. I came back after that, but it wasn't a great year. I got told in the middle of the year that Husqvarna were down-sizing to two riders in MXGP and MX2; the two Thomas's were performing great, they'd just signed TKO (Thomas Kier Olsen) and Thomas Covington was going really well so it was a no-brainer to let me go. We made some changes about half way through the year, I started training with Tommy Searle's trainer Kirk Gibbons. He was helping me a lot and things started to turn around but there's only so much you can do in the season and not be tire for the races. We gave it the best we could and the last few races were a step in the right

direction; Assen was good. I was third in the first race and closing on Jonass and Prado when I crashed with about 5 minutes to go then I led the second race for fifteen minutes. It was partly physical and partly mental; I knew my winter training hadn't been good enough and I knew I couldn't last the whole race, even at that stage of the season. It's the worst feeling ever, knowing that you've done the hard bit getting in front but you're not sure you can last the race".

"

Chapter 7

ROUND 2, MXGP OF EUROPE, VALKENSWAARD; UNDER PREPARED AND COLD. MEET THE MECHANICS.

Round 2 of the MXGP series was The MXGP of Europe in Valkenswaard, Holland. Driving to the track on Friday had a familiar feel to it and the waterlogged fields and continuous drizzle all indicated towards a difficult weekend for all concerned. Some in the paddock question the wisdom of scheduling an early round of the world championships in Holland (it was March 17th/18th) when the weather is almost certain to be cold and wet while southern Europe has much milder conditions, but Valkenswaard is one of the traditional early races and the sandy soil is able to deal with a lot of rain and still give a rideable surface. Temperatures dropped on Friday night to minus 4 Celsius and a dusting of snow greeted the paddock on Saturday morning. The track wasn't frozen, but it had a marshmallow like texture. At the European MXGPs there are always support races for the EMX 125, 250 or 300 classes. I'll briefly explain how the system works.

The EMX125 class is for schoolboys (and girls) ages 13 – 17 riding 125cc 2-stroke engine bikes. Its seen as the development class for young riders with the 125 viewed as a great way to learn bike craft such as corner speed, momentum and gear selection. It is very competitive! In Valkenswaard there were ninety-two entries trying to qualify for forty spots on the gate.

Some of the young riders are factory supported but it's also a great way to show-case your talent if you (or your dad) have aspirations for a career in motocross. 2 timed qualifying sessions each seed eighteen riders into the championship race with a further 4 coming from a 'last chance qualifier' or 'LCQ' making a forty-rider gate. Riders have to qualify at each round regardless of their championship position, no-one is seeded directly in.

EMX250 is the 'feeder' class for young talent progressing into MX2. Riders must be 14 years old and ride 250 cc bikes. A rule change for 2017 opened the class to 2-stroke 250cc bikes where it was previously a 4-stroke only class. Again, some of the riders are supported by big teams or even factory supported, and the series is supposed to help develop the future stars by getting them used to the same tracks, conditions and crowds as their peers. Riders qualify for each round in the same way as described for the 125 riders above, 2 qualifying sessions and an LCQ. It has proven to be a very successful formula for developing and progressing riders with Conrad Mewse being a good example of someone who was talent spotted at a young age and moved from 85's to EMX125's, EMX250's and on to MX2 with factory support. Hitachi/ASA KTM don't have any riders in the EMX championships this year as they're focused on MX2 and MXGP.

The EMX300 class is for 2-stroke only bikes. Riders must be 15 years old. In reality this class doesn't form part of the progression path to MX2 or MXGP but is for the 2-stroke fans, both riders and spectators. There is usually only one group with the fastest forty in timed practice qualifying for the championship races at each round.

All three EMX classes provide one vital thing; revenue! It costs about three hundred euros to enter. For that the rider will get and entry to try and qualify plus 3 additional passes and a camper permit. At Valkenswaard there were one hundred and fifty riders entered in the 125 and 300 class, generating forty-five thousand euros for Youthstream. There's no prize money and you don't get a refund if you don't qualify. That sounds like a good business model to me! Each class gets free practice which runs into a timed qualifying session (as described above) to decide the qualifiers and gate position. Each class gets two races, one on Saturday and one on Sunday. All that provides enough track time to give the spectators something to watch in between the main attraction. The downside for the EMX riders is that they are used as the cannon fodder to clean the track. Out first, they get to soak up any mud, puddles or in this case snow and establish some lines around the track. Last year the first 125 practice was out at seven o'clock in the morning so this year the 300's had it relatively easy when they went out first at nine o'clock but its then a long time to wait until their first race at three twenty-five. In fairness to Youthstream, it would cost more than three hundred euros to bring 4 adults and a camper if you were paying to get in so in effect the race entry fee is free, but the subtle difference is that the race entry goes to Youthstream whereas the spectator entry and public camping fees go to the organiser of the event so you could argue that Youthstream is benefiting from the additional revenue at the expense of the organiser. Ultimately, if you want to race then you have to enter, simple as that.

Back under the Hitachi/ASA awning, the team were still chasing their tail, but so were a few other teams around the paddock. The awning was a bit old and tired with a few leaks and repairs so a new one had been ordered back in October, along with new flooring, printed back-drops and partitions for the hospitality area. For whatever reasons there had been a delay and it wouldn't be ready for another couple of weeks. The old awning was still in use, as was the tired ground sheet. With no back-drops or partitions the awning looked big and empty. With no heaters and a biting wind it felt like a big barn, the mechanics would have a chilly weekend especially as all their metal tools were like ice. Team issue uniforms had also just arrived so there were boxes of shirts, trousers and jackets to give out.

There was an even more pressing issue; Steve Fry the new truck driver had failed his driving test due to an overly robust, newly qualified examiner, then had the re-test cancelled due to a puncture. It baffles me why this had been left so late but apparently there's a long waiting list to get booked on a LGV driving course. The driver from 2016 had been called back into action (he's a mate of Roger) to bring the truck to the track. Steve's absence meant that some of the hospitality that he normally takes care of was missing. With Roger and the whole team due to attend this event it wasn't the best start.

Usually the awning acts as a meeting place for the team and any invited guests. With the weather being so cold and everyone struggling to keep warm it felt a bit empty. The hospitality table was lacking its usual selection (although Ali did rustle up some soup and sandwiches on Sunday) and to me it felt like one of those days at work that you just want to get through.

I feel sorry for the mechanics on days like this. There's plenty to do at any race, basic bike prep includes checking and double checking every nut and bolt, replacing filters, engine oil and swapping wheels. Suspension adjustments are carried out by the WP technicians for the Hitachi riders but if forks or shocks need swapping it's the mechanic that changes them over. Any crash damage needs to be repaired and the bikes get power washed after every time on track so three times on Saturday and three more on Sunday. Then every nut and bolts checked again. Everything feels easier when you're winning, or for the mechanic, when your rider is winning. It's the same amount of work regardless of position but the 'feel good' factor of a win is immense. Even the 'feel good' factor of a good ride shouldn't be underestimated. As I said earlier, no-one is expecting Graeme Irwin to win the world championship but everyone in the team will know when he's riding to his full potential and that's all you can ask of anyone. But even if your rider is having a great day, its such hard work being a mechanic on weekends like this. All your tools are ice cold, your fingers are probably freezing but you can't wear gloves for some of the dexterous work. The power wash area is freezing, and you're bound to get over sprayed by the mechanic next door. Some of the power washers froze overnight too. The awning is freezing and to top it off you'll get issues with the bike that you never get normally. I saw mechanics with heat guns trying to de-frost and dry out brake callipers. You'll probably end up changing a clutch or two as even the gentlest of riders will be on the clutch in the power sapping corners. There's additional prep for mud races; hand guards and coarse foam to pack cavities and stop mud accumulating.

To add to the Hitachi/ASA mechanics woes, the new boiler in the race truck had frozen on Friday night when the temperature plummeted. There was nothing they could do to defrost the frozen pump so that meant no hot water for the shower or sink. On Saturday the electrics blew. They weren't sure what caused it. At the MXGPs, the organisers are required to provide mains hook-up for the teams, usually done via a series of strategically placed generators. The rank that the Hitachi/ASA truck was in all blew but the truck would not re-set so no electricity. You would think it couldn't get worse, but it does.

Someone had used an old petrol can to put detergent in without marking the can. The truck driver filled up the generator that the team carry but wondered why there were bubbles coming back out of the filler opening. It was too cold and horrible to sort out then; put 'draining the genie' on the to-do list for Monday. So, no hot water, no mains hook up, no portable generator and no compressor for the air-line. The air hoses had been 'forgotten' but that was academic as without a power supply the compressor couldn't be used anyway. Whilst it may seem like a comedy of errors, other teams were suffering similar issues with their trucks as pipes froze, 'snags' were discovered, and power washers froze.

The biting wind didn't let up all weekend making it feel like minus ten degrees. All the teams kept the blinds down on their awnings and the crowd was sparse; the public camping area was only about a quarter full. It must have been a financial disaster for the organising club who recoup their expenses from ticket sales and camping having already paid Youthstream their sanctioning fee. The whole event lacked any buzz as everyone struggled just to keep warm, which was a shame as there was some great racing on track. In the MX2 races, Factory KTM teammates Pauls Jonass and Jorge Prado dominated both races but Conrad Mewse had a very mixed weekend. He crashed in the qualifying race on Saturday, injuring his right hand and twisting his bike so that he had to retire, this meant last gate pick in the main races on Sunday. It seemed like a disaster for the team as a broken hand could wreck his season, but it was just soft tissue damage and after a hot bath, massage and stretching in the hotel he was able to race.

The horrible track conditions miraculously improved overnight, leaving it dry and firm for Sunday. With a fairly even start gate a lower pick wasn't as much of a disadvantage as it can be at some tracks. Conrad raced to fifth and fourth positions for fourth overall, one of his best rides in MX2 and easily the best British rider. He was physically tired after two great rides around the brutal Valkenswaard circuit but knew that the efforts put forth during the winter months were now paying dividends, his confidence and motivation both rightly boosted.

> ## The mechanics; Bryan Connolly (BC), Vaclav Lavicka (Vas) and Paul Whitehead (Minty).
>
> *BC and Vas work for Graeme Irwin and Conrad Mewse respectively. BC comes from Fife in Scotland and is typical of many in the paddock in that he raced as a schoolboy, did an apprenticeship in a road bike dealership before becoming a motocross mechanic. He worked for Bryan Mackenzie from 2004 until 2016, then Adam Sterry at CLS Kawasaki in 2017. When CLS shut its doors Sterry moved to F&H, hoping to take BC with him but the deal wasn't right and after a phone call to Roger he was hired.*
>
> *Vas has a similar story, growing up in 'a motocross family', his father raced but Vas only claims to ever be a hobby rider. He worked for Ricci racing and STR, turning spanners for Jake Nichols before joining Jacky Martens' Rockstar Energy Husqvarna team in 2015 and working for Conrad Mewse then Thomas Covington.*
>
> *Both have long-term girlfriends and BC has a daughter plus another due in April. It's not the ideal life for a family man but they*

recognise that it's not easy for their partners. Vas said "I see my girlfriend maybe every two weeks. It's a hard lifestyle, people only see the race weekends but that's the easy part. The travelling and long days in the workshop make it hard".

They've both worked for factory teams so is it different working for a smaller team like Hitachi/ASA KTM?

They both agreed that 'factory' is just a word, they have a bigger crew and more budget but it's just the same. With modern four-stroke engines, teams all have an engine builder and suspension specialist, the mechanic just swaps whole units. Vas said the Hitachi/ASA team was more relaxed, without the pressure from the factory team, and if anything, it's easier because at Jacky Martens' team he had to go practicing with Covington as well.

BC said it was easier than working with Bryan Mackenzie because he was more emotionally involved there. "Bryan was more like a brother, I even put my own money in for parts like ignitions and valves, things to make the bike go better. I even bought a dyno, still have it. But because of that you get so pissed off if it doesn't go well, you expect 120% every time."

Vas also has a connection with his rider. "Conrad lived with me when he first came over to Belgium when he was fifteen. We became friends and when he left Husqvarna he asked me to come with him here".

Although BC hasn't been with Irwin that long, they have developed a bond. When Irwin went to America in November to train, BC went with him. Both mechanics agree, you need to have a connection with your rider, it's not just a job; it can't be just a job.

They work well together and the atmosphere in the team has been so much better this year, but there's an unwritten rule; mechanics don't work on each other's bikes. They're happy to help disassemble, for example taking suspension off for servicing but each takes responsibility for putting the bike back together, so they know every nut and bolt is tightened correctly. Peace of mind for the mechanic and rider.

Minty

Paul Whitehead, aka Minty is in his second year with the team. Last year he was Josiah Natzke's mechanic but this year he doesn't have a rider, so he is the general assistant, his extra pair of hands used to help with the awning, set up the power-wash bay, fetch and carry tires and anything else that need doing.

"I started off working with Jason Renee in the AMCA, then moved on to Wulf sport TM with Stuart Edmunds. I spoke to L.P.E. at Hawkstone and there was an opening there. Steve James has been great, we grew up close to each other and used to do a lot of the same things without knowing each other. I was at L.P.E. for about eight years working with riders like Gert Krestinov and Tanal Leok. We did outdoors then I did the arenacross with riders like Fabien Izoid, Julien Bill, Jason Clement and more. I had some great times with Steve, through thick and thin."

It's a nomadic lifestyle, and Minty lives most of the time in the team truck at the workshop in Lommel.

"It's not the sort of job that comes up in the job centre. I got into it by being here, talking to team managers and looking for the chance to do it. You've got to have a passion for it, I always have, and I wouldn't be here now if I didn't. It's not like working in a factory where you just do it for the money."

In the MXGP class Graeme had a more torrid time, which was disappointing after a positive debut in Argentina. Factory KTM is seemingly all powerful in the current era and dominated the weekend. Jeffrey Herlings showed why he is the 'sand king', passing the reigning world champion Antonio Cairoli in both races in a masterful display. Graeme's weekend was less spectacular. He tangled with another rider on the first lap of the qualifying race after a good start and crashed, dropping right down the field. A second crash sent him over the handlebars, his KTM cartwheeling into his back. The tough Irishman remounted and got back to twenty-fourth but would feel the effects of the impact on Sunday. Struggling to find his rhythm in the first race he could only manage nineteenth for two championship points. In the second race, he washed the front end, twisting the bike and subsequently his front mudguard fell off; he ended the race in twenty-first place. It may not seem impressive, but to score points against the calibre of rider in MXGP takes some skill. Irwin finished twenty second overall and of the riders in front of him, four had won world championships and seventeen had won grand prix; that's a pretty deep talent pool

For riders in Graeme's position, i.e. trying to move up to the elite, international level of racing from the national level the difficulty will come as the season rolls on and he must maintain his self-belief and confidence when he's getting 'beaten up' every week. The theory (and hope) is that he will make incremental improvements in MXGP as he gets used to the extra speed and more demanding tracks which should also pay dividends when he's racing against a less deeply stacked field in the British championships.

Chapter 8

ROUND 3, MXGP OF LA COMUNITAT VALENCIANA, REDSAND – WORKING OUT OF A SPRINTER, CULHAM & LEE TOLAN

The problem with leaving things until the last minute is that you run out of time. While the trailer unit was in its winter storage, the internal refurbishments were carried out and it had its annual ministry of transport test. The cost of the refurb was minimal but the hoses on the tail lift were old and obsolete and when it went for its M.O.T. the rear suspension airbags were perished; one side needed immediate replacement whilst the other side would pass the test but would surely fail at some point, so it would make sense to spend the money on preventative maintenance and change both sets and get the hydraulic hoses on the tail lift changed. Roger didn't want to spend the money so only the one side was changed to pass the M.O.T. I don't know why Shaun and his mate didn't just lie to Roger and say they both needed changing, along with the hoses but they didn't so at some point you know the airbags and hoses will fail causing massive inconvenience to the driver and team and probably great expense to Roger. The old phrase 'penny wise and pound foolish' springs to mind.

The new boiler had been fitted on the day the truck was leaving its winter storage to go back to the workshop in Belgium. With no water in the truck the plumber had not been able to commission the boiler. He had tested all the gas connections and made sure it would fire but had not been able to carry out a full function test. It turned out that the old boiler was faulty but so was the gas regulator valve, so the new boiler would fire but wouldn't stay alight because of the faulty regulator which a function test would have uncovered so small wonder that it froze. Add another job to the 'to do' list.

The new awning for the race truck was finally ready but there was no time to get it fitted now that the season was underway. Steve had now got his licence so at least the team now had a driver, but it was too late to get the truck the 1000 miles from the workshop in Lommel down to Spain. The team decided that the best solution was to work out of vans for the race at Redsand and get Steve to take to truck to Stuttgart in Germany to have the new awning fitted, that way it would be ready for the next MXGP in two weeks' time.

On the eve of the GP Youthstream announced the addition of another MXGP. The Swedish MXGP scheduled for August had been cancelled when the host club decided they could not afford the sanctioning fee demanded by Youthstream after losing their sponsorship from the local government. Many secretly gave a sigh of relief as it meant a bonus weekend off, less travel expense and less time away. There were still 19 rounds so it's a busy schedule. The announcement of a further MXGP in Bulgaria would bring the championship back up to 20 rounds with EMX250 and EMX300 also getting an additional round. For the teams competing in the Maxxis British championship the new GP clashed with a British round at Hawkstone. Would the ACU rearrange their championship? Its not that easy as usually national federations wait for the MXGP calendar to be published then fill in the available dates, thus avoiding any clashes. By Saturday the answer was clear as social media posts reported the date for Hawkstone being moved forward two weeks to the date vacated by the Swedish GP.

It also creates some issues for the teams who will have to stretch their already tight budgets to include another round. Youthstream would probably say that they are merely trying to showcase the MXGPs over the full 20 rounds in as many markets as possible thus maximising the exposure of their partners and sponsors, a business decision.

Canvassing opinion around the paddock, it seemed to range from indifference to mild annoyance that no-one was even consulted; everyone got an e-mail with a press release announcing the new date. For teams in the MXGP and MX2 classes it didn't really make much difference as they would head on up to Turkey for the following GP rather than having Turkey as a 'stand-alone' event. And there is one further reality which is that for every team that may complain or withdraw from the sport, there is another team full of ambition and ready to step in. Revo Husqvarna are a British team racing in the EMX250 championship and I interviewed the riders and team owner for a website feature on Sunday. The team have a clear three-year plan to move into MXGP with their strategy and business plan mapped out. As I said in the beginning of this book, the racing may be a sport but running a team is a business......and Youthstream know that better than anyone.

Media duties are a part of all the rider's obligations. MXGP TV produces the television shows that include studio shows and the live TV coverage of the races. Paul Malin is the studio host and race commentator with Lisa Leyland co-presenting and doing the live interviews with riders before and after the races. Malin is a former GP racer and winner of the MXON with Great Britain in 1994, so he's been around the sport for years. The shows are produced at the track so Malin and Lisa Leyland are at every event, walking the track, mixing with the riders and teams. This presence on site and 'hands-on' approach has paid dividends as they are both very knowledgeable and work well together on screen. The TV coverage of the races is also sold to other networks with commentary, and they employ their own commentators who describe the action. For example, Eurosport have veteran commentator Jack Burnicle and analyst Rob Andrews. The downside to this method is that the pair work from a booth in London and basically talk about what's on screen rather than any of the back-ground information that being at the event offers.

At Redsand, Conrad Mewse was a guest at the Saturday studio show, filmed live while the EMX250 LCQ was going on in the background. Mewse talked about his winter training, moving back to England and his new team, and sounded very professional. Some teams give their riders media training to ensure they are a polished as possible, and while this approach has its benefits it's nice to see a rider who is natural and intuitive. I'm a big fan of Max Anstie for that very reason; it comes across that he is professional, works hard and has a great team set-up but also that he's having fun and enjoying being a racer. He's an enthusiastic and funny guy, and his podium celebrations are pure joy. I remember watching Jeremy van Horbeek on the podium at Valkenswaard in 2017, he had finished third and narrowly missed second place. He looked so miserable on the podium you would think his dog had just died! For goodness sake, a podium is an amazing achievement, at least enjoy the moment!

The track layout at Redsand was exactly as it was in January when the team were there testing and training so no real surprises. The soil is a red, powdery dirt that looks sandy when it's harrowed and disked but has a hard-packed base. Although all the team had spent plenty of time there through the winter it was not known how the track would develop with the extra EMX250 and 300 riders besides the GP action.

The temporary set-up under two 'easy-up' shelters with a van at either end worked very well for Hitachi/ASA. Each rider had a van as their changing area and there was plenty of room for the mechanics to work. There was also a good atmosphere in the team, better than at any point last year. The mechanics work well together, each doing their own thing but happy to help the other and with Minty doing the peripheral jobs it was working well. Both riders seem happy and positive which also makes a big difference. Conrad has a positive personality and is very easy to work with. He knows what he has to do, has his inner circle that includes his dad and riding coach Justin Morris, and just gets on with the job. As race time approaches he sits quietly with his music on, getting focussed and ready. Graeme seems equally relaxed off the bike, chatting and enjoying being at the GPs. MotoGP rider Jack Miller from the Pramac Ducati team dropped in on Sunday to see Graeme and catch up. The pair know each other well and were chatting about riding through the winter. Miller is apparently quite

▼ *Vas gives encouragement*

◄ *Conrad battling the factory KTMs of Prado & Jonass*

◄ *Ian interviewed live on MXGP-TV. Out of his comfort zone!*

Photo Andy Gee

good on a motocross bike and uses them for training. They also discussed weight as Miller was keeping his weight as low as possible, something that is much more important in MotoGP than on MXGP. It's not unusual to see riders and drivers from other motor sports at MXGP, (after all we're all petrol heads whatever our preferred branch of sport) and it's nice to see the mutual respect for the different disciplines; they all understand the work, commitment and sacrifice needed to reach the top in any sport.

The qualifying races on Saturday proved that a good start would be essential. The track was very fast and flowing with plenty of lines and options but nothing technical that separated the riders; they were all going flat out and doing the same things. Because it was so fast the track didn't become as rough as usual, so the races became something of a highspeed procession. Conrad would finish fifteenth and Irwin eighteenth.

A much bigger crowd on Sunday, certainly a lot more than had braved the Baltic temperature the previous week in Valkenswaard, filled the grandstands on Sunday morning with Spanish rider Jorge Prado of the Redbull KTM team the fans' favourite. Prado has a full factory bike and is Mewse is to regain the factory support its riders like Prado that he needs to beat or at least show that he can match on slightly inferior equipment. And that is exactly what he did in race one. A great start saw him narrowly miss the hole-shot but slot into second place. He would soon become the filling in a factory KTM sandwich as Pauls Jonass led, with Conrad second and Prado third. By lap five Jonass had pulled a small gap of four seconds on Conrad but Conrad in turn had pulled away from Prado; the Hitachi/ ASA team were ecstatic as Conrad looked comfortable. As the race hit twenty-five minutes Prado had eroded the advantage and was on Conrad's back wheel and past him into second spot. Conrad retaliated immediately regaining second place, exactly the fighting spirit that the team want to see. The intensity of running at maximum speed had taken its toll on Conrad and a small mistake at the end of the wave section proved costly. He hit a small bump slightly wrong, the impact ricocheting his bike off course and losing momentum, it was enough for Prado and Thomas Olsen to dart past.

If anything demonstrates the parity and intensity of grand prix racing that was it; after thirty minutes of racing a small mistake (and not even a crash) would cost two places. It's not just the physical strength and endurance required but the mental focus, and ability to adapt to changing track conditions whilst attacking the rider in front and simultaneously defending attacks from the rear. The first three riders, Jonass, Prado and Olsen were all on full factory engines against the semi-factory engine of Conrad, so it was a fantastic achievement. Whether it was the extra 500rpm and 2hp from the factory engines that made the difference it's hard to say, although that advantage wouldn't have hurt but more likely it was that the first three are more experienced at running at the front and therefore more comfortable with the pressure. It's all part of the riders' development, incremental improvements until you 'belong' at the front, but performances like that don't go unnoticed by other team managers.

While Conrad was battling in second place, MXGP TV presenter came to the pit box to get a live interview with Hitachi/ASA team manager Ian Browne. Ian isn't the most outgoing personality, certainly not a man to seek the limelight but reluctantly agreed to be interviewed. As the cameraman lined up Ian with Lisa Leyland at the edge of the shot, she received to signal from the director to go. Ian was live.........for the shortest interview in TV history as he responded with a one-word answers. Certainly not as polished as his riders, but it made me chuckle as the coverage went back to the race action and Lisa Leyland wondered off down pit lane. It's strange how many people are happy to talk all day but when you put them in front of a camera they feel very embarrassed and uncomfortable and don't know what to say. Just try filming your family at home and see what reaction you get.

The second race didn't go quite as well, fourth around the first few corners, he would lose places to Darien Sanayei, Hunter Lawrence and Jed Beaton after a small mistake on lap one, settling into a good pace in seventh. A late charge by factory Honda rider Calvin Vlaanderen and Ben Watson on the factory Yamaha pushed Conrad back to ninth at the flag, perhaps the energy expended in the first race also being a factor. Sixth overall in the GP and up to fifth in the championship, it had been a great weekend as he continues to harry the factory riders with his raw speed and meet his own expectations of being in the top seven.

Graeme had a more mixed day. In the first race he was in a comfortable twelfth place, with good lap times that meant he wasn't losing ground. A small mistake on lap seven cost two places but he also lost his rhythm and another place on the next lap. Still in fifteenth place, he was at the back of a group of four within a second of each other. Unfortunately, a last lap pass by Jasikonis meant he finished in sixteenth place. In race two the rider next to him on the gate moved early, hitting the gate. The distraction was enough to cost Irwin a bad launch and he was almost last around the first corner but sliced through and was up to twenty-second on lap five when a mistake undid his efforts and dropped him to twenty-ninth. He would battle back to twenty-fourth, but it just wasn't a track that lent itself to lots of overtaking. In an interview after the race, Wilvo Yamaha's Jeremy Seewer talked about how difficult it was to overtake in the MXGP class. He was runner up in last year's MX2 championship and said that even with a bad start he could still move up to the top five but in MXGP you are working just as hard to make progress inside the top twenty as in the top ten. That should be a comfort for Graeme, but he still left disappointed with a no points from race two.

Realistically, it had been a good weekend for the team as Conrad was exceeding expectations but probably delivering what the team secretly hoped for, that is mixing with the factory riders, and Irwin was meeting expectations in the stacked MXGP. We talked about pre-season testing in an earlier chapter, carried out at this very track. Irwin was riding the bike differently in the races than he had in the pre-season tests. During testing he was able to ride in a higher gear and use lower engine RPM, but under race conditions he was revving the engine more and using more clutch. The team made a mapping change to suit the more aggressive and racy riding style. This illustrates how hard it is to simulate race conditions at the practice track but also the value of testing so that information is available to make changes when they're needed, and the fact that the process is continuous.

It was a story of mixed fortunes for the other British riders. On the first lap of Sunday warm-up, Anstie hit a kicker as he took off across the big Monster Energy table top jump at the back of the course and crashed heavily. I didn't see the crash, but reports were that he lay on the track for some time. His team put out a statement that he was badly bruised and would therefore not be racing but there was suspicion that he had been knocked out and suffered a concussion. Anstie is a tough competitor and very fit so if it was possible to race I'm sure he would have. He was walking about watching the racing later, so you must think he wasn't that badly hurt physically. If, however he was concussed I really respect the team and Anstie for not racing. There's mounting evidence of long term health issues arising from blows to the head and sportsmen not taking sufficient time to recover from concussions, mostly in contact sports like rugby, American football and boxing but motocross is not immune. This is purely speculation on my part, but I think there is still a fear by teams that if they admit to a rider being concussed it will mean that the rider is forced to sit out for longer so a rather generic press release about being battered and bruised is an easy cover story. I hope I'm wrong because we have a duty of care to protect these young riders, even to protect them from themselves as their competitive urge and desire to win championships can cloud their judgement. It was a good decision not to race, confirmed when Max revealed the truth to me two months later.

The 'good news' story of the weekend was in the EMX250 championship where Revo Husqvarna rider Mel Pocock took a very popular and emotional win in the first race. Pocock won the championship in 2012 but lost his right thumb in a crash at the start of 2016 that nearly cost him his hand. It's been a long road back, with lots of surgeries and rehabilitation so the win was both joy and redemption. It was a massively popular win as those that knew him knew how difficult his last two years have been, and his social media pages were awash with 'likes' and good wishes on Saturday evening. His teammate Martin Barr would win race 2, giving their team a huge boost as they build towards competing in MXGP next year.

The Hitachi/ASA team headed back to Britain immediately after the race. The benefit of the temporary pit set-up was a very quick tear-down and on the road. Graeme's mechanic BC had extra reason to get home as quickly as possible, his wife was due to give birth soon and there was a doctor's appointment he wanted to attend with her. That's the drawback of a job like his, you're away from home a lot and it's not always possible to down tools and leave.

The weather forecast was atrocious all week but with the first British championship set to run next weekend on Easter Sunday at Culham, it was probably worth getting a muddy practice session in, although finding a place to ride wouldn't be easy. Practicing is part of the job and teams will provide practice bikes for that purpose, saving the race bike for racing. It may sound obvious but the maintenance intervals on a full race engine would mean it needed rebuilding every week if it was used for practicing. If riders want to race outside their contracted events, in this case Graeme and Conrad are only contracted for MXGPs and British championships, the riders have to seek permission from the team, not only to race but to use a bike. Both Irwin and Mewse had been asked to race on Good Friday in the Huck Cup, at Marshfield. All through the '80's and '90's there were non-championship races, usually on bank holidays where riders could earn start money (the stars would be paid to attend) and race for prize money, much like the Hawkstone international. The Hants Grand National was the traditional Good Friday race, held at Hamer Warren in Ringwood or Matchems Park, the event and tracks now sadly gone. The Huck Cup is an attempt to revive the tradition of a big race that will attract the top riders, and to commemorate the life of Mark Hucklebridge, a former grand prix racer from Marshfield who succumbed to cancer in 2017 at just thirty-seven years of age. The meeting had been held on Good Friday for years and had been known as 'The old friends race' in memory of Mike Brown, a local racer who was tragically killed in 1988 in an industrial accident. The meeting had become one of the biggest event on the local calendar and the addition of the Huck Cup pro race would hopefully cement its place in motocross fixture lists for years to come. Mike Brown's brother Alan and his son Tom run the local Kawasaki dealership, Motoxtreme and had worked hard over the years to support the event and this year to ensure a top line-up in the Huck Cup. Graeme Irwin and Conrad Mewse were the biggest names but lining up against him would be former GP racers Josh Coppins, Stephen Sword and Tom Church plus a host of British championship riders. There is some risk involved when you enter a race like this with mixed displacement bikes and possibly a target on your back, but the advantage is that its actual racing rather than just laps on a deserted practice track ahead of the British championship race just up the road on Easter Sunday, and of course the chance to win a few quid.

The rain lashed track was a muddy mess but Graeme and Conrad took a first and second a piece, enjoyed the day but most importantly got some good mud racing practice and left uninjured. Even with rain falling all day and spectators being towed in and towed out there was still a decent crowd and both Hitachi/ASA riders were in demand all day for autographs and pictures. For a lot of fans who don't go to the MXGPs or British championships this may be there only chance to see them race or meet them, and I was impressed with how friendly and available both riders were throughout the day.

Culham.

From a very soggy Marshfield the team moved about fifty miles east to the Culham circuit in Oxfordshire for the first round of the Maxxis British championship. It was supposed to be a four-day festival of motocross incorporating amateur races on the days before and after but those all got cancelled due to the weather. With the first round at Lyng already postponed it would be unthinkable for the second round at Culham, (which had now become the first round) to be called off but with a stroke of luck the rain stopped and the loamy silt that forms the track was in great condition on the Easter Sunday.

The Maxxis would see the British championship side of the Hitachi/ASA KTM team for the first time. The deal was that ASA scaffolding owner and team sponsor Lee Tolan would provide the race truck for UK events with

Irwin and Mewse under his awning with an additional rider in MX2, Michael Ellis sponsored by Tolan, who would himself be racing in the two-stroke championship.

The race truck looked very smart with four riders under the awning but there was no hospitality on offer. It was my first chance to sit down with Tolan and find out what he had planned.

Lee Tolan.

"I've always been a keen rider and always wanted to be part of a team. I did a lot of work with Roy Emberson before because he lived near me. I was always helping him out here and there but never enough to be recognised but with the idea of being involved. My business went from me going out on my own in a lorry and just trying to get by, to now having thirty men and ten lorries. Business is booming. Asa is my son's name and the company is named after him, I love him to bits and so I named the company after him. Things started small, but they've just gone really well and ended up where they are today. I've known Graeme for a long time, just saying hello. About three years ago he came to my track, I own Mill Lane MX, he came to the track when he was riding for Dave (Thorpe) and we just developed a relationship. We started talking about him riding for me and we just get on really well, we're like brothers.

The British championship is my team, this is under my banner, but we would have confused everything because Roger has the deal with KTM, but Graeme has a deal to ride for me. We've amalgamated so that Roger does the GPs and I'm doing the British championship, that's why it's my truck, my awning and all the expenses are from me. I'm not just a personal sponsor for Graeme, he rides for me and I pay his wages, and everything is down to me. We all know where we are within the team, so if people want to see me a Graeme Irwin's sponsor that's down to them. The actual nitty-gritty of it is that the British championship team is mine, Conrad rides for Roger, Graeme and Michael Ellis ride for me. Where it gets tricky is that the bikes come from Roger. "

I had met Lee at Ottobiano last year when he and Irwin were scouting for potential MXGP deals and he had mentioned wanting to see the British championships have a better profile.

"I'll never be in control of the rules or the way this is run but all I can do is bring a good set-up and hopefully that will help raise the game of others. The paddock is dwindling to easy-ups and vans, it's not exciting anymore. I know it's an expensive sport, but I just feel that our sport is dwindling down. I want a more professional appearance, so we get more spectators, it doesn't look any more than a club meeting when you come here sometimes. I race all the time, and the MX Nationals are run better in some respects. I'm not criticising the ACU or saying it's anyone's fault, but if I can put my spin on it maybe it will make other people want to do it.

We have a two-year deal with Graeme and Roger and we'll just see where it goes. I've been the beneficiary of having Conrad come on board, that was nothing to do with me but it's great that we've been able to amalgamate, and all be one team. I couldn't ask for it to be any better than it is at the moment. We had a few teething problems when we started but everything is good now."

I couldn't let that last comment go without a further question. What were the teething problems?

"Graeme was signed to me, but for him to achieve his Grand Prix goals I agreed to sign up with Roger, but I didn't want to. Graeme was my signing and it was my deal, we were gonna do it on Honda and we've ended up doing it on KTM because it was better for Graeme. I've tried to put my own personal goals aside I wanted it to be about Graeme and I didn't want to be selfish and make him do British championships for me. I did want this journey to start off like that, I wanted it to be for Graeme because I knew he has the fight in him to do his best, you don't have to ask him to do anything. If he does badly you don't have to tell him off because he's already gutted about it and I didn't want to put him in a position where he couldn't achieve his goals.

Then everything was Roger, Roger, Roger and I'm thinking 'hang on, I'm putting half a million pounds into this' and wasn't getting any recognition. I was getting the hump about it, it started off about me and Graeme and it felt like I was getting rode out of it. It wasn't anyone's fault, but it was getting to me. It was grinding me at first but we're all happy now; I've accepted that no matter what people think, we know what the deal is. Graeme puts everyone right, but I have put my issues to the side and this is about Graeme."

It was good to hear Tolan's opinion, but I couldn't help feeling that he was missing the point that it's a marketing opportunity and whilst having a big shiny race truck might look good you have to be accessible and you must look after the people who are looking after you. There were some team sponsors in attendance, but they couldn't even sit down or get a cup of tea. If I was putting tens of thousands of pounds into the team I would expect to be welcomed into the awning with open arms and made to feel important and special. Instead, everyone was kept outside, Lee didn't want anyone in the awning and especially not inside the truck, giving orders for the place to be continually swept and kept spotless. Perhaps he's just too used to barking at scaffolders, but this is motocross not a building site, and these are sponsors paying a lot of money into the team not labourers who can be replaced easily.

There is also a bigger problem with the British championship (in my opinion) and that is star power. I don't want to offend any of the participants when I say that there are no big names to draw the crowds, and by big names I mean current MXGP riders. The Dutch Masters ran at the same time with thirteen Grand Prix riders entered. They race in the Dutch Master for a number of reasons; they live nearby in Holland or Belgium; their teams are based there and want them to race in the teams' national championship but also because everyone else is there, so the competition and practice is better. Back in the 'good old days' (up to the late '90's) riders were required to race in their national championship to get on the grading list which was the only way to get an international licence. With that requirement now gone, riders can choose not to race in Britain and with many of them choosing to race abroad the British championship lacks the lustre it once had. The Hitachi/ASA duo and Evgeny Bobryshev are the only GP riders committed to the British championship, Tommy Searle was supposed to race but is injured and that is it. No Max Anstie, Shaun Simpson, Ben Watson or Adam Sterry. I understand why they race abroad and also why their sponsors don't want the expense of getting everything across the channel eight times a year when they can race a couple of mile up the road from their workshops, but without some top names battling for honours it diminishes the prestige. It's a shame because the organiser managed to pull off a decent event in Culham, despite the weather gods being against them all week. The track was well prepared, and the paddock was fine although it seems so amateurish that the bikes are power washed randomly around the paddock rather than in a designated area like they are at the GP's.

On the track the team had a dream start. The MX2 class was first on track and Conrad set the fastest lap, two-and-a-half seconds quicker than anyone. In the races his superiority was even more emphatic, with his best lap times over three seconds quicker than the second placed rider, winning both times by almost thirty seconds.

Graeme had the weight of the number one plate to carry, the defending champion always has a target on their back, but it didn't show as he set the fastest time in his class although only by a tenth of a second. With a deeper field than in MX2, Graeme would have his work cut out but got to the front in the first race and took a convincing win. A mid pack start in race two left him with work to do and he lost too much time getting past Ivo Monticelli and could only get to third place. It was enough for the overall, and the red plate. He was visibly annoyed after the race, I'm not sure if it was with himself or Monticelli, but that's racing.

Roger Magee and Lee Tolan were happy, their partnership delivering the results that both had hoped for, two overall victories!

Chapter 9

ROUND 4, MXGP OF TRENTINO, PIETRAMURATA; THE NEW AWNING & GRAEME IRWIN.

Tucked in the shadow of the Dolomite Mountains in Northern Italy, Trentino is possibly the most picturesque venue on the calendar whilst simultaneously being the biggest pain in the ass to drive to. Access is either via the Brenner Pass, the alpine route from Germany, through Austria and across the Alps or from the west through France and another route across the alps, both involving a lot of long, winding and narrow roads. Vineyards line the valley roads, the grapes used for Chardonnay and Pinot Grigio and when you arrive at the track huge grey cliffs provide the backdrop to the first hard-pack race of the MXGP year. The paddock is small and spread over several terraces with barely enough space to accommodate all the teams, WMX and EMX riders, so motorhomes are held at the welcome centre about three miles away and brought down a few at a time. It took me five hours to get in on the Friday, not through anyone's fault, it just takes that long to park everyone.

Hitachi/ASA were on the third tier of the terraced paddock, a nice spot but it meant quite a hike to the start line and power wash bays. MXGP is built on hierarchies and the paddock parking illustrates that perfectly. The big hitters like Redbull KTM and the other factory teams get the prime spots with the 'lesser' teams further away, until you get to the EMX riders who are often parked in adjacent areas or scattered around the paddock. Youthstream plan all of this in fine detail with the paddock marked out with painted grids, the big race trucks required to arrive on Thursday to be positioned in their allocated spot, with the campers and motorhomes not allowed in until Friday. Trentino is always one of the busiest events as many of the sponsors and partners of MXGP are Italian, all wanting front row parking at their home GP. The limited space meant that even getting into the car park was impossible as they were full up early, with the public camping areas well over a mile away also full.

The new awning was debuted, much lighter than the old one with 'Milwaukee' written large across the roof sheet, perhaps in preparation for a bigger sponsorship involvement from them next year, although the new floor mats and back drops hadn't arrived, so it still looked like something was missing. Steve had got the truck in without incident although he claimed that he hated every minute of the drive, frustrated by the 56-mph restriction as opposed to the 90-mph he usually travels at in his van. It was certainly a baptism of fire getting the forty-tonne rig down the narrow alpine roads.

With time to spare on Friday, I sat down with Graeme Irwin.

> ## Graeme Irwin.
> *"My dad was a professional road racer, my eldest brother is five years older and he had a bike, and I just started riding when I was about three. My dad was still racing, and we would do local races, a grass track, whatever. I'd been going to these races since I was in nappies, I was born into racing, it was our life. My dad stopped racing when I was about four and we just started racing Irish stuff, Donegal championship and fun stuff. I started racing when I was four. I probably shouldn't say this, but I had a fake birth*

certificate and I was racing under some other kid's name. at the first round of the Ulster championships at Desert-martin a woman knew I was under age and they pulled me off the line. They changed the age limit then to six, and I had to wait another year or so. I can still remember it now, just wanting to ride, I'd do laps around the pits."

With a dad and two brothers all road racing, was there a time when Graeme could have gone into road racing too?

"I was the fastest motocross rider of us all. That's not saying I was better than them it's just maybe my love for motocross was just a bit more than theirs. We're all so competitive as a family, if we all sit around the table its nuts, everybody wants to be the fittest, everybody wants to be the fastest, 'I train harder, no I train harder, we do this better, he's better in that area but I'm better in this area', you can just imagine, yet we all have so much respect for each other. None of us are racing against each other."

If they had all raced motocross professionally would that have made them even more competitive?

"I think so, but when we were riding together, from quite a young age I had the edge. Glenn is two years older, but I always had an edge over him, so maybe he could see that making it professionally in motocross is really tough. I believe that motocross is the toughest sport of all to do professionally and get to the top level; the skill, the fitness, there's so much that goes into it. My oldest brother Ross never went into short circuits, he stopped and loves surfing. Glenn is next and rides for factory Ducati in BSB (British super bikes), he's won a race and proved that he's a very talented guy."

I've seen riders from other disciplines come to MXGPs as guests of their sponsors before and the one thing that impresses me is the mutual respect between the racers from different sport. Is that because the sacrifice and discipline required to succeed at the elite level is the same?

"Oh, for sure. I'm good friends with Jack Miller and Cal Crutchlow, they love motocross and Jack started on a motocross bike and is really good. He has a lot of respect for what I'm doing, and I know his game and it's not easy. My wee brother Andrew rides in world super sport. I would say it's the first year he's really taken everything seriously, not that he wasn't serious before but there's a difference between taking it serious and doing something about it. He's putting the work in during the week with his training and his preparation is second to none. I think he's got a bright future."

Graeme had ridden for Roger a few years early, racing a 350 but ended up injured. At that time was racing in the grand prix a step too far?

"I rode for Phil McCullagh in Moto one and he taught me that you need to have a heart to be any good at motocross, you have to have a passion for it. I never gave him enough credit. He taught me that you never back down, never give up and never quit. I rode for him for two years before I went to Roger in 2009, racing in the British championships. The next year with Roger was supposed to be my first year in MX2 in the world championship but I dislocated my shoulder the week before the first round of the British championship. I won the first race, it was the first time I'd even been in the top five. Second race wasn't so good, I was inexperienced. The next week my shoulder came out again and that was the week before the first GP. I got the operation to fix it, we decided it was better to take the time to heal up properly then go out strong later in the year and start preparing for the next year. I was off for four months, then back on the bike for two weeks and my other shoulder popped out. I got that shoulder fixed but the season was over, we scrapped that year. So, then I went from riding the British championships to riding the GP's on a brand new 350 in 2011. I didn't know how to test or anything. I didn't know what I was doing really, I was just getting on the bike and twistin'

it, trying to go as fast as I can. I had the speed I just didn't have the 'head' to go with it. I was always thinking with the right hand. I just wanted to go fast but never took a step back and think about how to go fast. I was just 'I have to go faster...faster...faster', and sometimes I was going fast but then it was 'eject'. So that season was horrendous, there were only about twenty-one riders in MXGP that year and everybody had a podium in a race, if not won except me. I broke my neck in France and that was my season done, and that was it with Roger. I wasn't getting paid then, but he was giving me the opportunity, which fair play to him, I wasn't bringing any money in and when I look back he was giving me the opportunity of a lifetime. I took a step back. I got an offer from Roy Emberson, it was the first time I ever got paid. Fair play to Roy, after the bad years I had he still paid me. The way I looked at it was the more money I had the more money I could put back in. That was probably the main problem I had when I was with Roger, I didn't pay for a coach or just someone to come with me to help out and take the pressure off. Sometimes you need someone to just say 'relax Graeme' or think about lines. It was just me and the mechanics, that's the way it was. I moved away from home, I was living with the mechanics. The budget I had to live off was ridiculous, I was trying to practice and do everything, and you just can't do it. So, I think as much as the opportunity was there with Roger I just didn't have the private funding to do it properly."

Graeme then had three years with Neil Prince on Suzuki, 2013 on a 250 the '14 and '15 on a 450, then two years with Dave Thorpe on Buildbase Honda. The Honda set-up always impressed me, they looked the most professional in the British paddock with a full-sized awning and bikes that look special. Graeme had an outstanding year in 2017, winning the British championship. He had previously told me that even if Jake Nichols and Tommy Searle had been fit he felt he would still have won, so what had changed for him?

"We always had the ingredients to go fast we just needed them to click together. I just found out what works for me and did it. People tell you to try this and try that, but I knew what works for me and what I wanted to do. Nobody knows you like you know yourself. Before I would have been riding little goat tracks but when I was with Dave I started going to Belgium and places in Northern Ireland, riding tracks that were rough as ass-holes, so I could be fitter, faster and stronger. Dave or Neil never told me how to ride the bike. I think this is the biggest thing; they are not going to go for riders that need telling what to do. Dave knows how a rider's mind works, he knows what to say at the right time to get you going or what to say to piss you off. Neil Prince too, they know what we need and if they didn't think we could do the job they wouldn't sign you. I think they both believed in me. Some people need to be told 'you're the man, you're gonna win', but for me that doesn't work, the only person that can make me win is me. Don't get me wrong, this team uses Justin Morris at the races for lines, and his race craft and experience, but it's an easy way out to say, 'oh the team didn't tell me'. I think when I was younger and had the opportunity with Roger maybe I did need that guidance, but I had that from Stephen Sword when he was my teammate. He let me ride and train with him, so I saw what he did. There were days when I was thinking we should be doing more, just going hell for leather, but now when I look back at it I totally understand what he was doing. He was there for the season, not training for one race. As a kid I was going to the gym thinking you should be bust, bust, bust. If you're not crawling out you haven't done enough."

(Note, both Roger and Shaun Osmond have told me on separate occasions that Stephen Sword is the most professional and motivated rider they've ever met.)

For 2018 Graeme had a couple of options but really wanted to get back to the MXGPs. He had committed to ride for Lee Tolan in the British championship but had also spoken to Roger about a deal for grand prix. The only way it would work would be for the teams to combine, with the same bikes and graphics supplied by Roger. The team would use Lee Tolan's race truck in Britain which meant the team could leave the articulated truck in Belgium.

"There were a few ups and downs, like who's the boss here and who's the boss there, why's my name not mentioned. It's like two chiefs walking into the room and wanting to see who's the bigger chief, but it's all worked out in the end. They're both really professional and they know what they have to provide for the riders to do a good job."

I asked Graeme about his experience with the team and testing earlier in the year.

"Whatever I want to try, they will do for me. If I said I want to try a lower sub-frame the guys will make one, it's not like they say oh we're a privateer team so we can't get it. If I want something they'll get it. We've tested foot-pegs, suspension, engines, ignitions and that's all on-going, it never stops. I feel a lot on the bike, I'm very sensitive to how the bike is. Sometimes having a fast bike isn't always the fastest bike on the lap chart. I'm a guy that doesn't like to change gear all the time, I like something long (broad power band) and I'm really fussy. If it isn't right I'm a real pain in the ass for everyone."

I asked about the example earlier in the book about Ken Roczen having the head supports tapered to allow more frame flex. Would Graeme be able to feel that?

"When I was with Suzuki I went to Japan and did a race there for factory Suzuki. The guys there told me 'you must test them and make

the triangle into an L shape, then the back of the bike is so much better'. And honestly, that made a massive difference. Until you test it back-to-back, but you must test it on the same track on the same day, you'll feel it. It's the stupidest things; I'm really fussy with the throttle, it must be light and if there's any grit in there I'll hate it. I run my back brake pretty high. The thing is that the KTM is really good from stock, they have a hydraulic clutch but on a jap bike with a cable it must be lubricated every time because that's your feel, the throttle too. I just like the controls to be nice and fresh, nothing even a bit gritty. BC is great, I've been fortunate with all the mechanics I've had but when you first meet them, and they say 'what, you want a new throttle cable between the first and second race?' and I say, 'yeah it's a bit off' they look at you like 'what the fuck?' "

The season had started well with points scored in six of the first eight races and an overall win at the first round of the British, but what results would Graeme consider a success year?

"In the MXGP's, if I end up in the top fifteen at the end of the year I'll be happy, that'll be a good year for my first year. I really feel like I'm not riding like myself here, it's so frustrating, everything just hasn't clicked. It will, I'm sure one hundred percent, but I've had to learn a new series, a new race format, new team and bike".

At an MXGP the riders are on track three times on Saturday, free practice, timed practice and qualifying race then another three times on Sunday with morning warm-up and two races. Has the amount of riding at the weekend been a factor?

"A massive factor. These tracks are so much faster than I'm used to. There's eighty good GP riders on the tracks, the lines form differently, how the race goes is different. I just need to relax. Me and Roger spoke and said just get the first three rounds out the way without anything stupid then we can start ticking things off. Now I know I just need to line up and worry about myself I'm not thinking 'right, what are these guys gonna do.' I just need to go and ride the bike how I know I can ride a bike, and not change it because I'm here. The depth of talent is exactly what I was expecting, I'm realistic, I don't live in the clouds. It's about stepping up and building up, we know we can be better but its about building up and going in the right direction."

We talk a little about how grand prix racing has changed. I've followed the grand prix since the late '70 and in my opinion this is the most competitive era, with all the best talent concentrated in the main MXGP class rather than diluted across three classes as it used to be, 125, 250 and 500.

"It's the intensity now too. I've watched the old videos and the intensity then was nothing compared to what it is now. Don't get me wrong some guys were intense but they were long motos and they used to pace themselves."

And finally, what about the British championship, is defending the title a priority?

"That's the plan, we want to win that. I'm happy with the first round, to walk away with the red plate. Last year people saying, 'oh yeah but there weren't many people in it', all the key-board warriors saying it'll be different this year. I don't look at that stuff, but I know what people say, I might be the same if I was outside looking in and didn't know any better. It doesn't bother me, people only remember who wins the championship. Unless it's the world championship you can always say 'aw, you only won it because so and so wasn't there' but you can only race whoever's on the gate. It's cool having the number one plate, not in a cocky way just because it was such a good year."

There's always a number of media events across the weekend, the usual press conferences with the riders on the podium and sometimes a featured 'partner' or sponsor. On the Friday evening there was a drinks party in the Skybox restaurant with a presentation from the organisers of the MXGP of Turkey on the 2nd of September. A few speeches welcomed everyone and a short video showing all the tourist attractions nearby before trays of assorted nibbles and Turkish Delight were brought around. The event is obviously a big deal for the local economy with involvement from the regional government, which is probably one of the best indicators of how big the MXGP brand has become as countries vie to hold an event. Youthstream president Giuseppe Luongo asserted that the preparations were well under way with improvements to the track and facilities, confidently predicting that the Turkish organisers would be strong candidates to win the best organisation award. The short event was very civilised as team managers discussed the best route to get to the event from Bulgaria the week before then back to their bases in northern Europe, although I must admit to feeling slightly under dressed in my shorts and T-shirt.

Earlier in the book we mentioned the debacle with Benoit Paturel and the BOS team where they split before the season started with much finger pointing on social media. BOS soon found a replacement in the form of Evgeny Bobryshev and Paturel was seen on a private Honda, riding in the French championships. He returned to the MXGP paddock this weekend after signing a deal with Marchetti KTM. The strange part is that when he fell out with BOS it was allegedly because he didn't want to ride a KTM but he's back on a KTM team. We will probably never know exactly what happened, but it was good to see the talented Frenchman back on the gate and just goes to show that there's always a second chance.

Graeme and Conrad didn't have any media duties to fulfil and it was quite relaxed in the camp. The track conditions proved deceptive as the loose, stony soil got pushed aside, the hard base with square edges bumps came through and the ruts solidified. In the qualifying races Conrad was fast in three sectors of the track but seemed to be too cautious in the final bowl turn before jumping back onto the pit straight. Third for a couple of laps before first Thomas Covington and then Ben Watson passed him in the same place, the final bowl. He finished in fifth spot, with Watson fourth. Interestingly their best lap times were just one thousandth of a second apart. In the MXGP-TV studio show, guest Lewis Philips from the website MX Vice compared the three British riders and felt that Watson was best placed to succeed this year with Mewse being a couple of years younger, and Sterry rebuilding after being injured last year.

Graeme's Saturday saw steady improvement, with the super sensitive rider feeling a problem with the front brake in free practice but going quicker in timed practice before a qualifying race that was both good and bad. Bad because he tangled with another rider on the second corner and went down but good because of what followed. Restarting in last place he put on a charge back up to twenty-second with some aggressive overtaking and real determination in his riding as he passed Max Anstie and chased Max Nagl across the line. The qualifying race is always a bit of a strange race; you don't want to expend too much energy as there are no points at stake just a gate pick, which at this track wasn't too important but it's always good to see your rider looking a bit racy and fighting for positions so the team were happy with his efforts. I had a long chat with Shaun Simpson that evening and he told me that he had changed his strategy on Saturdays, trying to expend less energy in qualifying races that don't pay any championship points and are merely there to give the crowd something to watch rather than a boring timed session.

By the time the main races started on Sunday the WMX and EMX riders had soaked up all the water and the track was hard, rutted and dusty in places. The organisers always grade the start and any jump faces that are dangerous but most of the track was rough and gnarly, or a 'proper motocross track' as some of the opponents of man-made tracks would say. The huge crowd in Trentino occupied every inch of hillside, the big triangle of grass by turns three and four covered in the yellow and red of Tim Gajser's fan club with Italian flags all around and a big group of '222' Cairoli fans by the finish line jump.

Conrad had his worse race of the season, gating poorly in mid-pack and staying there to end in twentieth spot. The team weren't impressed, *"he was riding like a twat, no effort at all. He got a bad start and his head went down, you can't just give up because you don't get a start, or you don't like the track"* said team sponsor Shaun Osmond afterwards. Perhaps it was a harsh assessment but it's hard to reconcile that ride when he was dicing with Prado two weeks previously and Prado was now leading the race by thirty seconds. There was also the small matter of a factory engine. The team had been promised factory engines if he was in the top seven after the first three rounds and good to their word, KTM had delivered the promised engine and he was having his worse ride of the season. To compound the problem still further, his championship rival Ben Watson put on a charge and moved up from twenty-sixth to eleventh, passing more riders than anyone else including a fall that cost him time and three places that he re-took. It was his best ride of the season, with his fastest lap coming on seventeen of nineteen.

Riders and teams often talk about pressure, usually saying that the team don't put any pressure on the rider, it's the rider's competitive nature to put pressure on themselves but there's definitely an expectation that the rider will at least perform to the best of their ability and Mewse's first race came well short of that; no fight, no intensity in his riding and a poor finish.

Between races he sat in the race truck with his practice mechanic Paul Keates and whatever was said a different rider went out in race two, gating around seventh he would battle with championship leader Pauls Jonass and benefit from a clash between Jacobi and Vlaanderen to finish in fourth with his fastest lap coming in lap eleven and improved again on lap fourteen. There's no doubt about his speed or fitness but it's the mental side that seems to need strengthening. A poor start doesn't mean you give up and ride around in twentieth if you want to win a championship or keep hold of factory engines. It's that sort of inconsistency that he and the team were hoping to eliminate. He would remain in fifth place in the championship but Ben Watson leap-frogged him into fourth but looked much stronger in both races.

Graeme doesn't carry the same weight of expectation at grand prix as Conrad, which is no disrespect to him just a reality in a class packed with factory backed super-stars. A decent start in the first race was undone a few turns later when he was hit off balance and quickly lost a dozen places as he was shuffled back to the mid-twenties, the intensity of the first few laps being very costly if you're not on full pace from the start. He would struggle to make any progress on the dry, hard-packed track. The power delivery of the race engine was too fierce and wasn't 'hooking up', instead it was 'beating up' Graeme. Between races his mechanic BC and Minty swapped engines, putting a standard 450 engine in place of the race engine. To his credit he battled to the flag in both races and claimed two points in race two, perhaps proving that you can sometimes go faster on a slower bike. Many of the top riders prefer a smooth and tractable power delivery; it's fine having lots of power but if it's wearing you out then you're probably not using it anyway. I noticed that Shaun Simpson's factory Yamaha sounded very flat in qualifying and he said he was using more traction control to help get grip, so it wasn't just Irwin that needed a modified power band.

Graeme's press release afterwards was the most downbeat so far, especially the first paragraph.

'Well two points is better than no points! Another tough weekend and I suppose that's as positive I can be. Scraping low amounts of points is not where I expect to be after four rounds in, but I believe in myself and the people and team around me believe me I know what I need to do.

I'm comfortable with the amount of riding now at a GP weekend and by Sunday I know the track - so that's no excuse. But the pace at the start of the races is so hot - it's not like a British championship race where you kind of let the race settle and then get up to speed. Here you have to come straight out of the blocks and smash it; with speed and rhythm.

Despite these hard rounds, my riding is improving and my lap times in the second half of the race match that of the top 10. I just need to make the starts count and pull the pin from the off'

It turned out to be a difficult weekend for the British contingent. When Bas Vassen and Thomas Olsen clashed over one of the blind downhill jumps the marshals were slow to react and Adam Sterry landed on Vassen's bike as it lay in the middle of the track, sending Sterry flying down the hill. He was lucky to escape with cuts and bruises, but as two more riders hit the downed bikes before the marshal reacted, the marshal needs his ass kicking! Four riders out of the race, fortunately no serious injuries but it could have been much worse. Max Anstie withdrew from the races on doctor's orders after qualifying. Quite clearly not himself, he apparently felt ill after the qualifying race. When the F.I.M. doctors examined him, they refused to allow him to race, the symptoms of the concussion he suffered in Redsand two weeks previously were still present, even though it was never publicly declared that he suffered a concussion. He was also told he could not race in Portugal the following week, even though he competed in the Dutch Championship between Redsand and Trentino. It disappoints me that he raced in Holland then tried again in Italy when he had clearly sustained a serious head injury in Redsand, his team trainers and manager should know better than to allow it, let alone put pressure on him to race. No race is worth risking permanent brain injury for. And finally, Shaun Simpson crashed on the last lap of race two trying to pass Jose Butron for the last point. He landed heavily on his right shoulder, at first thinking it was broken or dislocated as he was in so much pain. An x-ray in the mobile medical centre revealed nothing broken and after a few hours the pain had subsided. It would be a long drive back to his home in Lommel and a visit to his personal doctor on Tuesday for further investigation and treatment. A CT scan revealed no serious damage and he would be back in action at Agueda after resting the shoulder all week.

By nine o'clock the awning was down, and everything packed away in the race truck. The bikes had been washed but no work done on them. Ian and Shaun had already left to drive for their hotel ready for an early start, Ian going back to Lommel and Shaun back to England to be home by Monday evening. There's a restaurant at the track in Trentino so the mechanics, Minty, Steve and myself went for a well-earned beer and some food. Minty is the fussiest eater I've ever met and only wanted a bowl of chips as we tucked into some delicious pizza. Antonio Cairoli was at the next table with his crew, enjoying a relaxed meal. Most of the riders get away from the track as fast as possible, trying to get home so they can go about their normal routine on Monday. Cairoli uses a luxury motor home at the track and only lives a few hours away, so I guess it's easier to have another night at the track then drive home in the morning although he had done a podcast interview on MX Vice in which he said it's hard to remain motivated after fifteen years at the top and he sometimes misses training. There was much speculation on line about that comment in the following week, but from the evidence so far, he was still the only man who could run with Herlings.

Steve and Minty would take the race truck straight to Portugal, a one thousand three-hundred- and-fifty-mile journey across southern Europe. Steve was quite nervous about it. He would struggle to cover the four hundred and fifty miles a day necessary to get there by Thursday morning, restricted by the number of hours he could drive and the 56mph speed limit on large lorries. Realistically, every team in the paddock would have the same problem, including Youthstream who ship about twenty articulated lorries full of equipment between each MXGP. The Youthstream riggers start dismantling the scaffolding pit lane and sky boxes as soon as the presentations are complete and by Monday lunchtime there not much left to suggest an MXGP took place, the signs, banners and structures all en route to the next event. It would be a busy set-up on Thursday and Friday in Agueda!

Graeme Irwin - 2018

◀ *Lee Tolan (L) & Graeme at the Dirt Bike show*

Chapter 10

ROUND 5, PORTUGAL, AGUEDA; TROUBLE IN PARADISE, STEVE FRY – RACE TRUCK DRIVER & CANADA HEIGHTS.

By seven o'clock on Monday morning the paddock in Trentino was virtually deserted, most of the race trucks had already left to get a head-start on the road. All truck drivers are restricted on the hours they can drive so it makes no difference what time you start but they all use the service stations and rest areas for their overnight stops and by five in the afternoon most of them are starting to fill up. There's nothing worse for a trucker than being out of hours and struggling to find a place to stop, especially if its dark, so many will start their day early to ensure they get parked up by five or six o'clock.

Everyone uses sat-nav these days, so everyone was on the same route, not quite a convoy but more of a conveyer belt. On Tuesday evening I caught up with Steve and Minty in a service station on the D1, La Pyreneenne motorway which runs along the bottom of France in the shadow of the Pyrenes mountains. I wouldn't say Steve was emotional, but he was certainly wound up.

"I can't do. I'm jacking it in. I hate it. Hate it! HATE IT!"

As we sat in my camper having a beer he told me that he'd made a mistake. He thought this would be his dream job, but he hated the driving, being stuck at 56 mph, he hated having to stop and he was so worked up at the thought of driving to Portugal that he didn't even watch the racing in Trentino.

" Steve Fry – race truck driver.

I should tell you about Steve before we discuss his current situation as it will help with the context. Steve is a plumber and gas engineer. One of the nicest guys you will ever meet, he lives for motocross and works long hours during the week so that he can travel on a Friday and be at the races as much as possible. Like many self-employed trades-men, he's a grafter and in many ways a work-a-holic; if he's not working he's not earning. Unfortunately, the work was taking a toll on his health and even though everyone was telling him to slow down he just carried on. When Roger decided not to keep the previous truck driver on, Ian and Shaun spoke to Steve about the job. Steve already did a lot for the team and would now be getting paid for it. He would have the winter to pass his LGV test and finish up any plumbing jobs, it seemed like a win-win, the perfect man for the job, a safe pair of hands who could do all the little jobs on the truck and at the workshop in between driving duties.

Steve had been mates with Ian and Shaun since the early two-thousands, meeting them at RWJ Honda and moving around with them as teams and bikes changed before they all landed with Roger. Steve's role in the team is probably best described as chief-cook-and-bottle-washer, doing bits of anything and everything that help the team, from working on the truck to providing the hospitality. Although not considered a sponsor, he pays for a Sky subscription so that they team have satellite TV in the truck and has bought tables, a fridge and repaired the truck gratis over the years, as well as preparing the hospitality and keeping everything clean and tidy. He likes to help out and feel like he's contributing, another piece of the jig-saw that keeps the team working. Anyway, he was now on the pay-roll, Roger had paid for his driving course and test, and Steve hit the road to Trentino and Agueda. "

Back in my camper, he was starting to calm down, but he was adamant that he wouldn't continue. *"I've f##ked up, I thought this would be the dream job but its doing my head in. I can't stand sitting there for nine hours. Its gonna cost me thousands, I'll pay Roger back for the test but that's it."*

As we discussed his feelings I suggested that he hadn't really given it a chance, it was his first road trip and he just needed to adjust to a different lifestyle, but his mind was made up.

"And I didn't enjoy Culham, when I arrived it was like 'what the f##k are you doing here'. That's not how it should be, it was the at same at Hawkstone. People usually come in for a chat, it's a good job it wasn't raining. We ended up sat in the Revo awning. There was one plate with a few sandwiches (in the Hitachi awning) and the mechanics had them; its f##king shit!"

It wasn't just me that thought the British championship regime was wrong then. I've known Steve for a few years and never seen him this stressed, but he was talking about selling his camper and not even going to motocross anymore which was a real shock as he hasn't missed a British championship for about twenty years.

And there was more on his mind.

"I don't mind working, you know that, I love getting on with stuff. But that trailer has been there all f##king winter and they end up fitting the boiler the day its leaving. The bloke never even commissioned it, but I know why, they probably said 'leave it mate, Steve will sort that out'. I had to get my mate to open up his warehouse on Good Friday to get me a regulator before I left then I spent a day cutting holes in the ruck trying to change the bloody regulator which they had built in and it still isn't right, it needs a new flue. Its sucking the gas back into the burner and keeps cutting out. The old boiler was OK but the new one's are more sensitive. I put a fan there and it sort of worked but it's not right, it pisses me off! The f##king satellite dish was broken last year, and nothing's been done about that, I was on the roof of the truck with a portable dish trying to get a signal so we could have the TV on."

We had some dinner in the service station and he started to calm down, but I knew he was not only upset but disillusioned, and that would be much harder to get over.

There was a story on-line that the MXGP could be cancelled as the track and paddock was under water. These stories sometimes come up, it's a good headline to grab your attention. The reality is that Youthstream wouldn't cancel an MXGP at such short notice if it was possible to run. Yes, they might cancel the support races or alter the weekend program but with so much money at stake as well as television slots to fill there would need to be something almost biblical to stop the event. The main issue is parking the articulated race trucks. Forty tonne trucks don't like soft ground and at over half a million pounds each, factory teams don't want their rigs dragged in and out by tractors. As much as the 'purists' like to criticise modern venues with paved hard standings such as Assen with the cheap shot 'who cares about the parking, it should be about the track' that's not the reality of a modern MXGP. Youthstream came in with a plan to elevate the sport and that includes a paddock that is not a mud bath, so that sponsors, guests and spectators can walk around and enjoy a professionally presented experience dressed in street clothes. The paddock in Agueda is not paved but is covered with a layer of crushed building rubble. Last year it was dry, even dusty but this year the rain would make it soft.

The trucks started to arrive on Wednesday night, Steve getting shepparded in before it was dark. After manoeuvring through the gate, it was a one-shot deal to aim for the allocated area as straight as possible at stop. At this event near enough is good enough, the wet ground not allowing any shuffling about or levelling up. Despite his stress about not making it on time he had done just fine but that still wasn't persuading him to stay. He called Roger and gave him the news. He would take the truck back to the workshop in Lommel and that was it as far as truck driving duties went. He also told Roger how he felt about the situation at the British, and Roger assured him that it would change, he had spoken to Lee already. Colour me sceptical on that one.

Thursday started with rain. And continued with rain...all day. Steve and Minty started putting the awning poles up but it was too windy to put the roof sheet in without more pairs of hands. The rest of the team were flying in, so it would have to wait until reinforcements arrived rather than risk tearing the new roof sheet or dragging it through the mud. As the rain continued to fall speculation about cancellation increased so I e-mail Youthstream to see if there was an official statement coming. 'Cancellation is fake news, this is motocross, we don't mind some mud' was the answer in a nutshell.

The organisers had done as much as they could, bringing in hundreds of tonnes of dry stone to firm up the paddock. They got all the big race trucks in, but the area allocated for the campers was a squidgy mess. The road outside has two lanes in each direction, that only lead to an industrial area. One side was closed and became the paddock area for all the campers and smaller trucks of the EMX250 and WMX riders, as well as media types like me. It was a stroke of luck for all of us, parked on level, dry tarmac; what a result!

Walking around the paddock on Friday morning it was a muddy mess. The trucks had churned up the soft ground and there was so much surface water that it was percolating through the ground-sheet in place. There was some relief from the rain though and as the track crew worked on the track all day with large plant it looked to be in great condition, albeit a bit soft in places so we could expect plenty of ruts to form.

While Steve and Minty had travelled across Europe Ian, BC and Vas had been back at the workshop. It was a typical week but illustrates the point I made earlier in the book; it's not a nine-to-five job. What does a typical week look like for the mechanics and team co-ordinator?

It was an early start on Monday in Trentino. Ian had already left the hotel with Shaun while BC and Vas would leave the track by 7:00, driving the Sprinter back to the workshop in Lommel, their plan was to take turns driving the six hundred miles and get there by the evening. They all got back by about 18:30 Monday evening, Vas going to his apartment, Ian and BC to a hotel, and Shaun heading back to Bristol.

On Tuesday they were all at the workshop by 7:45, BC and Vas would then have two days to prepare two brand new bikes and crate them up for the Russian MXGP which is the next fly-away race, two weeks after Agueda. The standard bikes would be stripped, checked, lubricated and reassembled with a factory engine going into Mewse bike. Ian would drive to John Volleberg's workshop to pick up a new engine for Irwin to try, then to WP for suspension before returning to the workshop by 14:00 to order parts and prepare his visa application. They would leave the workshop at about 19:00.

By 7:30 on Wednesday morning they were back at the workshop to carry on working on the bikes, different suspension, wheels, exhausts, ECU's, handlebars, grips and graphics are fitted. Ian had to work on Irwin's practice bike until 10:30 when Irwin arrived at the workshop. Ian, BC and Graeme then went to the Lommel track next door to test the new Volleberg engine fitted in the 'Russia race bike'. Graeme was happy with the new engine, slightly softer power delivery than the previous version yet still fast. They had tried to soften the power previously by remapping the ECU but that hadn't worked, the mechanical changes had given him the feel he wanted. Back to the workshop, the bike was washed off and refreshed then the bikes were packed into the travel crate with enough spares to cover any eventuality ready for collection. They left the workshop at 20:30, for a six-hour journey to Stansted airport in Britain to meet up with Shaun, arriving at 1:15 UK time as they had gained an hour coming from European time, grabbing a few hours' sleep in the hotel.

The reason they were flying from Stansted to Portugal was to make it easier on the Monday after the MXGP. They all had appointments at the Russian embassy in London to get their travel visas.

Thursday morning came quickly and after a couple of hours sleep they went to the airport at 7:30 for a 9:20 flight to Portugal, (which was delayed for 2 hours due to fog), so they didn't arrive at the track until about 15:00, where they would help put up the awning in pouring rain. BC and Vas sleep in the race truck at GP's so Ian and Shaun would leave then at about 19:00 and head to a hotel, while BC, Vas, Minty and Steve had a well-earned beer at the track.

Friday is the easiest day of the week. BC and Vas would prep the race bikes that had been used in Italy for the weekend. With the race expected to be a mudder they weren't fitting many new parts; the bikes had been fully prepared before Trentino, so it was mostly checking that everything was OK. Irwin wanted to try some different handlebars, and parts like brake pads get changed as a matter of course. BC had said to me before that people only see you (the MXGP mechanics) on a Sunday and think it's easy. Driving across Europe, building two bikes then more driving and flying back across Europe to rebuild two more bikes under an awning, and all in five days is the unglamorous reality. Ian and Shaun arrived at the track about midday as Steve left to get the shopping for the weekend. Ian looked like he could hardly stay awake, the visa application form still causing him some stress, so he and Shaun left for the comfort of the hotel and some free wifi by about 17:00.

Saturday and Sunday would be spent at the track from about 8:00 until 19:00, later if there was a problem with the bikes on Saturday, and until the awning was down and put away on Sunday before the whole process starts again. Ian said that some weeks there may be more time spent driving or flying, or maybe more hours at the workshop especially after a muddy meeting when it can take all week to clean everything up.

There was also a bit of tension brewing in the camp between Vas and Minty. When you're living in close quarters little things soon blow up. Minty can be a bit negative and combined with his fussy eating and constantly being on his phone it had started to wind Vas up. When the sink in the race truck blocked and it turned out to be because of Minty's contact lenses words were exchanged. Ian got involved to try to defuse the situation, but I think this could end in tears. Hendo had butted heads with Minty last year, the pair never got on but perhaps Hendo felt the same frustrations as Vas. You have to make allowances when you work so closely but when someone starts to annoy you it suddenly becomes much harder as you noticed every negative trait that only serves to reinforce your opinion. BC had other things on his mind, his wife Emma was due to give birth to their second daughter on Tuesday so he would be flying back to Edinburgh on Monday afternoon as soon as he had sorted out his Russian visa application so that he could be with her for a few days, flying back to Canada Heights for 8:00 on Saturday ready for the second round of the British championship. Most expectant dads would be taking time off work but it's not that sort of job. You definitely need an understanding wife if you're in the MXGP paddock. I did say at the beginning that teams are like families.

Youthstream must either be better connected than we thought with a direct line to the weather gods or just very lucky as despite the rain all week and predictions of a mud-fest Saturday dawned with blue skies and broken cloud. The work carried out at the track had paid off, it was in prime condition as the EMX250's rolled out for practice at 9:00.

As I watched the EMX250 LCQ with Shaun he said *"Graeme won't do any good this weekend, he's already lining up the excuses. I've heard it a million times over the years, they just slip it in on the Friday or Saturday, 'oh, I've got a bit of flu' and you know they're gonna have a shit weekend."* A bit of a harsh prediction when Irwin had been testing and had apparently had a good week.

"We've had it loads of times, xx was the worst". (Note, I won't name the rider even though Shaun was explicit) *"He had the A to Z and Z back to A of excuses, fucking pathetic! If he had a row with his girlfriend, didn't feel well, his dog was ill, any excuse. Then they fuck about with this and that, one click here as if that makes any difference. When a rider's winning everything is brilliant but when they're not this is wrong, that's wrong, suddenly the bike's shit, the suspension's crap, the team, the engine. A month ago, it was all brilliant! And they picked the engine, they picked the suspension and it was all fantastic; we haven't changed a thing and now its shit and you start getting the excuses.*

Do you think Herlings carries on like that? He would win on a standard bike. When they start making excuses on Friday you know they aren't ready. I can tell by their mannerisms, a little cough and a comment, 'I'm not feeling too good'. You wait and see."

I like his honesty albeit a little 'black and white' but I suppose that's the product of age and experience.

There was no relief on track as both riders had their worst weekend of the season. Neither Hitachi/ASA rider shone on Saturday, Conrad eighteenth and Graeme twentieth in their qualifying races. Between timed practice and the quali race BC had swapped engines, putting the race engine back in, this time with a different ECU, creating the same package that Graeme had tested on Wednesday in the 'Russia' bike. On Sunday morning Graeme looked ill. *"I've been as sick as a dog"* he told me after warm-up. In the first race he would retire on lap nine, unable to hang on any longer. It was doubtful that he would go out for the second race but to his credit he did. After some rest and fluid, he lined up. Despite getting a reasonable start he lost places in the early laps before he got going, dropping four seconds off his lap time on lap four. He admits that he's struggling to get up to full speed from the first lap and feeling like crap probably didn't help but he needs to fix it. In his mind he's a top fifteen guy but by losing so much time in the first three laps he's more like a twentieth to twenty-fifth place rider. Twenty-third in race two and no points for the weekend.

As we walked back I asked BC how he felt. *"F##ked right off!"* was the unequivocal answer. *"What bothers me more is him losing ten places on the first lap"*.

On Conrad's side of the awning it wasn't any better. After his outstanding rides in Redsand and Culham he had been below par in Trentino and there was something amiss here. His dad and granddad were with him, and everyone was trying to get him in the zone. Shaun had a theory, "I bet it's something stupid, he's met a girl or something. At the start of the year he was military with his training, his diet, going to bed, everything was spot on and now he's moping about with his head down. How can you ride like he did in Redsand and this week he's riding around at the back?"

A first lap crash in race one put him in twenty-eighth, but as he came past pit lane on lap three he was pointing at the bike. Making no progress, he pulled in on lap ten saying the bike was losing power and was unridable.

The crash had ripped the air filter off it's housing and the bike had been sucking unfiltered air. The lack of an air filter would change the fuel/air mixture, sending the ECU into confusion which was the most likely cause of the power loss. Vas would have to do an engine swap between races in case there was any mechanical damage caused by sucking dirt.

Race two didn't go much better, dicing with riders he lapped a couple of weeks ago he would finish in twenty-first. No points scored, he dropped to seventh in the championship. After the race he sat in the awning with his shirt pulled over his head. The truth about his malaise didn't take long to come out and Shaun was right; girl problems. It's easy to dismiss such things when you're older but for a teenaged kid (and that's what he still is) it's a massive thing. Having said that he's being well paid to leave that stuff at home and ride the bike fast but not everyone can compartmentalise their life and if there's a problem in one area it can mess up the whole thing.

Everyone will have a bad weekend at some point in the championship. In Agueda Clement Desalle and Gautier Paulin both had bike failures (on factory bikes) that put them out of the race and Thomas Covington injured his knee, ending his weekend. The old cliché is that you win titles on your bad days, when you limit any losses to a minimum, so a bad weekend is just a fact of life. Irwin said it was the worst weekend he'd ever had, Conrad was in a bad place and there was a black cloud over the team as they packed up; everyone was hurting.

Ian summed it up, *"it's demoralising. Everyone's working hard, and you get repaid with that sh#t!"*

Canada Heights.

The beauty of our sport is that no matter what happens you get another chance next week so despite the disappointment in Portugal, the second round of the British championship at Canada Heights, near Swanley in Kent offered a chance for redemption. It was a busy week; Ian and BC got their visas before BC flew home to Scotland. He would become a dad for the second time on Tuesday when beautiful baby Sophie arrived. Graeme got over his flu bug and had a good week training and Conrad also sorted himself out. I spoke to him at Canada Heights and he was back to his usual self. *"We know what the problem was, and you won't have another GP like that"* he assured me. Conrad had his nineteenth birthday on Saturday, but whereas most nineteen-year-old lads would be out drinking with their mates he was fully focused on making amends.

Roger had a different angle on it after such a promising start to the season then both riders under-performing. *"Both riders have held their hands up. I had a lengthy e-mail conversation with Conrad and today he's apologised for it and assured me it won't happen again. He knows he's messed up; OK, the first race wasn't his fault totally because he got hit off on the first lap and the impact dislodged the airbox and affected the bike, but race 2 was just unacceptable. He knows that, he's just turned nineteen yesterday, he's still learning but it has to be a short, sharp lesson so that he doesn't let himself down above everybody else."*

With factory engines being supplied because of his early performances, does the Portugal race affect the team's support from KTM?
"No, everybody in this sport is experienced enough to know that anyone can have a bad day for whatever reason, it happened to some of the factory teams last week with DNF's. we've just got to learn from our mistakes and take it on the chin. Graeme too, he said he didn't feel too bad on Friday but by Saturday he was ill, the concentration wasn't there but he's recovered this week and almost put it on pole this morning 0.07 behind Bobby."

The British championship set-up using Lee's race truck was still creating a 'them-and-us' feel to the team. I was told that both Roger and Graeme had spoken to him after Culham, but nothing had changed. Steve Fry had driven the grand prix truck back to the workshop in Lommel, cleaned everything up and come home. He was at Canada Heights with his camper, providing hospitality for the team and guests at Roger's request. They had had a meeting and despite it being an obvious set-back for the team Roger had responded in a very mature way in my opinion. I asked him about the hospitality arrangements and the driver situation.

"For a good part of the week before Culham we didn't think it was gonna run so we probably didn't cover all the bases. We needed to sort out somewhere for sponsors to sit and I didn't realise there wasn't enough room under the awning for the sponsors and the bikes. For the next rounds we'll have something with easy-ups, at Desertmartin it'll be different with so many guys from home being there. We'll look at a mini marquee. We won't bring the truck from Belgium, it would cost about £2,500 for fuel and ferries. Regarding Steve, no matter whether it's the team or normal business, you don't want to put anybody under that much pressure to do a job that you don't get the best out of them. Steve's been very loyal and faithful over the last seven or eight years and I want to keep that and keep an important member of the team together. I've listened to what he had to say, he was looking forward to doing it but found it just wasn't for him so we've a couple of options to look at this week. Fortunately, we've got a couple of weeks where we don't need to take the truck, so we'll see what the best option is, even if its temporary for a couple of weeks and then something else for the rest of the season."

Steve's camper was set-up behind the race truck, the small awning seating about twelve people, including all the team staff bar the mechanics, and as the coffee and snacks flowed there was a nice atmosphere as friends popped by, largely ignoring the race truck. Whatever Roger had said to Lee, it appeared to me that he was managing around him rather than dealing with the situation as no-one was aloud in his awning. Without Steve I don't know what he would have done.

On track it was almost business as usual. Conrad was again fastest in timed practice by two seconds but made hard work for himself with mid-pack starts. Never-the-less he won both races, coming through methodically and without any panic. Graeme was seven hundredths of a second behind Bobryshev in timed practice, but the real drama came in the second corner of race one. He ended up on the ground and dead last, his KTM refusing to restart for thirty seconds. The old cliché is that you win championships on your bad days, so this race could be pivotal later in the year. He charged back up to eleventh spot. In race two he would finish in third place, and fifth overall. He would lose the red plate to Jake Nicholls and fall fifteen points behind. While the MX2 championship looks to be Conrad's to lose, the MX1 title is much less certain.

Chapter 11

ROUND 6, RUSSIA, ORLYONOK; A POLITICAL 'HOT–POTATO', SHAUN OSMOND – SPONSOR AND ASSOCIATE & BLAXHALL

When Youthstream added Russia to the calendar in 2017 it wasn't met with overwhelming enthusiasm, particularly by the EMX riders. The EMX classes are supposed to be European championships so a difficult and expensive trip to Russia wasn't what anyone wanted with most people under the impression that Russia wasn't part of Europe. Brad Anderson had won the first round of the EMX300 championship in Germany but hadn't planned on going to Russia. With a championship in his sights he managed to get his bike transported to Estonia then taken into Russia by his mate Tanal Leok. The effort was worth it because he would ultimately win the title and without going to Russia he wouldn't have done that. Regardless of any grumbles the event went ahead, and Hitachi mechanic Steve Henderson told me it was the best event of the year.

Fast forward to 2018 and Russia was the host of round six of the MXGP with the EMX250s and EMX300s in support. It's not just the distance to get there, almost two-thousand-three-hundred miles from Calais if you're driving to the Black Sea town of Orlyonok. Crossing a handful of former Soviet Union countries where delays at the border for no apparent reason other than to make life difficult are commonplace. There's also the added complication of visa requirements and the political and diplomatic unrest that was at it's highest since the cold war. Following the poisoning of the defected former Russian spy Sergei Skripal and his daughter who were living in Salisbury, Britain was in a diplomatic stand-off with Russia and had expelled a number of Russian diplomats, followed by a similar number of British officials being expelled by Russia. The war in Syria where Russia backed the Assad regime had brought them into conflict with America, Trump and Putin engaged in a political 'man off'. The foreign office travel guide advised British visitors to 'be aware of anti-British sentiment' and avoid large crowds or protests when in Russia. On the weekend of the MXGP in Agueda just two weeks before the MXGP in Russia, coalition forces from America, Britain and France launched missile strikes on Syria in response to a chemical weapons attack by the Assad regime on a rebel held town of Douma that killed at least seventy people including children. The chemical attack on civilians provoked international condemnation further ramping up the diplomatic tension between Russia and the west.

A visa is required to travel to Russia. Brits must apply in person at the Russian visa application office in London, even Brits like Shaun Simpson who lives in Belgium have to go to the visa office, complete a forty-seven-question form that requires detail of your parents and children including their date of birth and place of birth for both, all the countries you have travelled to in the last ten years including dates of entry and exit, financial details and any military history. The most difficult part of all of that is trying to recall the travel information for a GP team member, nigh-on impossible as they travel so much. The visa costs about £340 pounds including using an agent to help the process and your passport is kept for four days so you have to plan the application for when you won't need your passport. The week before a British championship was ideal. It's not just the Brits, all European nationals have to get a visa from the embassy in their country.

Once the visa is granted, via a stamp in your passport, you have a tourist visa. Russia refuses to issue a sporting visa to allow athletes (riders) to compete in another tit-for-tat diplomatic quarrel over doping and the

Russian Olympic athletes being banned. So, technically the riders could be arrested for racing at the GP. It seems unbelievable to me that with all these issues there is still an MXGP in Russia but apparently, it's an important and growing market. The trip would cost the team about £9000 to send the travel crate containing the bikes and spares, plus the two riders, two mechanics, Ian and Shaun. Roger had sorted out the travel arrangements with S.E.L. but co-ordinating everything else was delegated to Ian.

" Shaun Osmond – sponsor and associate

Shaun has been around the MXGP paddock since the 80's, as part of various teams, as a team owner and now as a sponsor and associate of Hitachi/ASA KTM.

"I started out helping Stuart Coyle, we were doing British championships and GP's on an Irish licence because it was so packed and strong with UK riders. We did that for a few years then with other riders like Jon Barfoot, then Daniel Smyth was the start of the Albion Honda days. We were on hybrid Honda 500's which was expensive because we were buying the aluminium framed 250 and making them into 500's with help from Colin Dymond engineering in Barnstable. We also did 125's then switched to KTM with Stephen Sword around 2000. I first met Roger many years ago and my involvement started with bringing riders to the team, James Cotterill came as a second rider then Jordon Booker, and from then on I just helped out and eventually started giving then vans to use, that's probably been for ten years."

You go to nearly all the grand prix and British championships, so how would you describe your role in the team now?

"I supply the team with vehicles and Roger pays my expenses for the GP's, I travel with Ian, so it doesn't cost Roger much. I chat with Roger and Howard a lot, about riders and anything else but Roger

is the main man and ultimately makes the decisions. He's not always there so he listens to the feedback from me, Howard and Ian but it's good to have feedback from different people. Roger has been very shrewd over the years."

You've worked with a lot of other teams and run your own team so how has this team developed since you've been involved?

"They've progressed slowly over the years, but I think Roger one of the cleverer managers in the paddock because he manages the team within their expectations and budget. We can all run a team and have a big awning, a big set up and expensive riders but you have to be cost effective and work with what you've got. Roger has been sensible over the years, not getting carried away like many others have and don't last the distance. Roger's been there a long time, and he's always going forward slowly, never two steps forward and one back. Other teams explode onto the scene then they're gone but he's been clever with his strategy and helped by individual people contributing in different areas."

The team have two very talented British riders this year with a lot of expectation on Conrad but maybe less expectations for Graeme in his first year in MXGP. Could the team handle them differently?

"If I was running the team it would be different but that's my way of dealing with things. Some people are more laid back and only time will tell if that's good for Conrad. There was an issue earlier and it was trial and error trying to resolve it. Roger wants results and if Conrad can win the British championship and finish in the top ten in the world I would say the team have done a good job. Graeme and Conrad were both very professional in their build up to the season, and Graeme impressed me a lot in the early season but when he got to the GP's I think it was a culture shock. Completely different track to what he was used to in Britain and Ireland, different depth of riders and I think it takes anyone a year to find their feet in that class. I think he's finding it more difficult than he anticipated, the depth of talent is the deepest it's ever been. You can't come in and expect to be in a certain position, you've got to fight wherever you are in that field and the guys at the back are fighting just as hard as the guys at the front. It's also learning the tracks, the travelling and being away from home and it takes time to adjust to a different way of life. It's a big learning curve and not just on the bike."

Arriving in Russia, the intention was to get taxis to the track, but the team found a mini-bus and along with the Revo Husqvarna team, piled on board. The 130 km journey should have been about an hour and a half but in horrendous traffic it took four hours. With twelve guys, no air-con on the bus and temperatures touching thirty degrees it wasn't the most pleasant trip.

The organisers pushed the boat out with opening ceremonies and because everyone arrived on the Friday they all had plenty of time to enjoy the hospitality.

The race 'weekend' in Russia was on Monday and Tuesday, to coincide with the spring Bank Holiday and Labour day, a very big holiday in Russia. The combination of expensive travel costs, visa requirements and political uncertainty had potentially all contributed to a lower than usual number of entries, particularly in the EMX250 and 300 classes. How low were they? Just thirty-eight in the 250's and that included nine Russian wild-cards who all failed to score, and only fifteen in the EMX300 class with three Russian entries. The GL12 team owner Bob Buchanan summed up what many believe in the team press release after the event. *"Russia to all intents and purposes is a 'flyaway' event, for small teams and private individuals it's a logistical nightmare and an horrendous expense and because of this it has no business being on the EMX calendar which was reflected in the entry.2*

The track at Orlyonok is hard packed and stony Paul Malin described it in his commentary as having an 'old school feel, rough and rocky'. Last year it was a mud fest but with thirty-degree temperatures it was hard, blue-groove in places and slick in other parts where the water sat on the surface. Only twenty-three riders were on the gate in the MX2 class, but it was business as usual with the factory KTM's at the front, although unfortunately not Conrad who scored a fifteenth and nineteenth, dropping another spot in the championship. His ability to separate his personal life from racing and his emotional resilience again being called into question.

In MXGP Clement Desalle broke the KTM stranglehold taking victory with a 1-2. The track obviously agrees with the Belgium rider who won last year in the mud and hadn't won since then. Graeme got two great starts, around tenth both times but lost places as his old nemesis, first lap intensity, got the better of him. He would finish nineteenth in race one and pull out of race two with blistered hands. Struggling to find a rhythm and riding tight, he was gripping too hard and chewing his hands up, so as he was outside the points and decided to save his hands for Blaxhall. He said in the week *"it was a bummer, I got two good starts but struggled to get up to pace. In the second race I wasn't riding relaxed. I wanted to save my hands for Blaxhall, I need 3 days for the blisters to heal so I'm not riding this week."*

The team flew home on Wednesday, arriving at 1:30 on Thursday morning. Graeme checked into the nearest hotel before heading for home after lunch time. He was very positive about the trip despite the results. *"It was a cool trip, and to be able to say you've raced in Russia. It was a lot simpler than I expected, even getting the visa was easier than getting my American visa. There was no hassle, they give your passport a good check but that was it. The place was a lot like Europe, like the small villages in Spain with little supermarkets. We found a good place to eat so went there every night. The hotel was OK, but the breakfast was a bit depressing. The track was awesome, very fast but nice to ride."*

So, despite all the concerns beforehand there was nothing untoward and everyone seemed to enjoy the trip, notwithstanding to expense for the EMX boys. For Roger though it was an expensive trip for little reward. *"Based on the results it was a waste of time. Conrad has something niggling him that we haven't got to the bottom of yet. We've had another long chat and he assure me he's OK. The situation with Ben (Watson) makes it worse, I've asked him (Conrad) if he wants Ben to be the only Brit on the podium this year, he can do it. I think Graeme has never ridden on a track like that before."*

When Conrad was interviewed by MX Vice after Blaxhall he just put it down to Portugal and Russia being his worst tracks and 'off' weekends, not any underlying issues.

There was some good news for Graeme on his return as the Irish MX Commission had announced the team for this year's MXON with Graeme in the MXGP class. *"It's nice that they have confidence in me to represent my country, and it's good for the team to get sponsorship and bikes sorted so we're not chasing it at the last minute"* a delighted Irwin told me.

Social media was in full swing and Roger posted a congratulatory message to Ben, a nice touch I thought. A press release from KTM UK was conspicuous by its absence, much to Roger's annoyance; how can you keep sponsors happy if you can't even get a press release out in a timely manner? There was however plenty of news from MotoGP where Johann Zarco had signed for Factory Redbull KTM to replace Brit Bradley Smith and Tech 3 would also be switching to KTM for 2019. Let's hope KTM aren't blowing all their money on road racing at the expense of motocross.

Blaxhall.

It was a short week for the team travelling back from Russia. The sandy, Suffolk circuit is popular with the riders and spectators, and with unusually good bank holiday weather forecast it was set to be a good race. It would be an eventful weekend for the team, and for all the wrong reasons.

Team owner Roger goes to all the British races and as many MXGPs as possible with flights that fit around his kidney dialysis. A computer glitch meant his hotel for Saturday night was cancelled as Holiday Inn had overbooked, and as Roger had booked through Booking.com he got bumped. Not the end of the world, but on a busy bank holiday weekend they ended up in the last room available in a Best Western a bit further away. His travel woes continued when the EasyJet flight back to Belfast was cancelled meaning an extra night in a hotel by the airport. The rest of the team had also left it too late to get their usual hotels so were spread around the area wherever a room was available.

On the track there was drama. In the first MX2 race, Mel Pocock and Conrad were penalised five places for jumping the table top under waved yellow flags, dropping Conrad from third to eighth. His rear brake cylinder had broken on the first lap making his ride to third more difficult. After the race the team weren't even told officially, and when Roger wrote out a protest to dispute the decision he was told that no protest would be accepted as it was a statement of fact. The race director claimed to have seen the incident although Conrad was insistent that it was a held yellow flag, not waved. When officials choose to act arbitrarily and without even informing the teams or riders officially it devalues the sport. Apparently, another team manager with a reputation as a sore loser had also been involved much to Roger's dismay, pouring the fuel of bad sportsmanship on to the fire of poor officiating. Conrad would come out swinging in race two, he hit the slow dropping gate and had to pull his bike backwards to release it, so dead last. He would charge to the front, winning convincingly and retaining the championship red plate.

Graeme had a much tougher day with consequences going beyond the race weekend. His blistered hands had recovered although he was still feeling the effects of the long trip to Russia. A crash in the qualifying session saw him sustain serious burns on his back and left arm when he was pinned under his bike, the hot exhaust melting his shirt and body armour into his flesh. Fortunately, the ACU doctor was present and dressed the wounds before each race and after the second race before Irwin went to hospital. In a remarkable show of determination and fortitude, he rode through the pain to take 4 – 7 race results for fourth overall. Holding off Bobryshev for much of the first race took a lot of energy and combined with the pain from the burns he did well to take seventh in race two. He would spend the next couple of days in hospital while the medical team decided if skin grafts would be necessary. The tough Northern Irishman was determined to ride in Latvia, but Roger was more reserved, *"We'll wait for the proper medical opinion before we decide. At the moment I think he may have to miss Latvia and Teutschenthal. I can't send him and risk something worse happening or getting an infection if the doctors advise against it"* he told me on the Monday. Sometimes you have to save the riders from themselves.

A WINNING COMBINATION

Hitachi Construction Machinery UK
Proud Sponsors of the Hitachi KTM
UK Motocross Team

hitachicm.co.uk

HITACHI

Chapter 12

ROUND 7, LATVIA, KEGUMS; HOWARD AND ALI – TEAM PLAYERS, AND THE SOURCE OF CONRAD'S MALAISE.

Sad news broke during the week as one of motocross's legends, Eric Geboers, drowned in a boating accident on a lake in Holland. The diminutive Geboers was the first man to win world championships in 125, 250 and 500cc classes and his death at just fifty-five years old under such circumstances was tragic, as his stature in the sport was reflected in the tributes on every motorcycling website. The MXGP paddock would remember the great man with a minute's silence before the start of the first race, and each rider displayed a "Mr 875" sticker on their front number plate in honour of his unique world championship haul.

The aftermath of Graeme's qualifying crash was greater than anyone had suspected on Sunday. He had suffered four third degree burns to back and right arm and whilst the adrenalin of race day had helped him to get through the day these injuries were serious. He would spend the week in hospital undergoing laser and chemical treatment, and narrowly avoiding the need for skin grafts. He was in a lot of pain, a good sign as it indicated that the nerves weren't dead, although it doesn't feel good when you're lying in a hospital bed. Infection is the main concern as it can lead to further complications and even be life threatening. Nevertheless, he was determined to race in Latvia until Roger stepped in on Tuesday to inform him that he would not be racing in Latvia or Germany. Graeme was initially concerned, not only his competitive instincts urging him to race but also concerned about the loss of income as there is an injury clause in his contract. Roger assured him that he would be paid, the injury clause would not be invoked. (We'll explore the detail of contracts later in the book).

Speaking to Roger on the Wednesday after Blaxhall he said *"I told Graeme yesterday that he's not riding in Latvia or in Teutschenthal. The main thing is to get healed and healthy for Matterley, St Jean and Ottobiano. He's got two GP weekends off then the only free weekend so that will hopefully be enough time to recover and get fit but if he's not ready for Matterley he won't be riding there. I didn't realise how bad the burns were until I saw the pictures afterwards. The first race took a lot out of him, battling with Bobby, and in the second race his body wouldn't let him give any more. He wants to race but his health is the most important thing right now."*

The ACU doctor, Iain Dobie, who treated Graeme has some history with Irwin and the team. He was spectating at St Jean d Angely in 2011 when Graeme crashed and broke his neck. He would assist the local medics and travelled to the hospital with Roger and Graeme, speaking in French and English to ensure the best treatment and diagnosis for Graeme who was also concussed. Dr Dobie is and orthopaedic surgeon at Belfast hospital and also rides himself. Roger said *"Iain has become a close personal friend since then. He knows what riders need and he became the ACU doctor after Mel Pocock's crash in 2016. He's the honorary Hitachi team doctors, paid in ham sandwiches. When he was there in St. Jean, he was very reassuring and has a very calming way with things. He dresses Graeme's burns in Blaxhall, so he could ride and a lot of doctors wouldn't have known what to do."*

Every cloud has a silver lining and with Graeme out it meant his mechanic Bryan got a couple of weeks paternity leave to spend with his wife and new baby. A nice gesture by Roger and fortuitous timing for Bryan.

There was also the issue of a truck driver still to be resolved. Roger had interviewed a potential driver and there was also another name in the frame. The team would again use the sprinters for Latvia, made a little easier since now it was just Conrad. Most of the GP teams use articulated lorries but the Jeyzek team from Spain use a converted coach, a decision that would prove costly when they were pulled over at a German police checkpoint. The 'coach' was tested in Spain as a camper, passing their equivalent of an M.O.T., but the Germans inspected it as a coach, requiring a higher standard. It failed…. miserably. The coach was impounded, requiring 15,000 euros worth of repairs, on top of a few hundred euros in fines before it could be driven. The team hired a couple of vans and crammed the bikes, tools and as many spares as possible into them, leaving a couple of staff with the coach. Rather than pay the inflated repair bill, they hired a low loader to transport the coach to the Czech Republic where it was repaired for much less, then driven to the next GP in Germany. The team also had to find hotels food as they usually live in the coach. Team owner Carlos Marchou is a big, jolly fellow and even this drama couldn't stop him smiling.

I travelled to Latvia with two of the team's long-term supporters/ associates, Howard Smith and Alison Rowland.

" Howard and Ali – team players.

I asked Howard to describe his role. *"It's a voluntary role, I don't get paid only a pass and car parking pass. I support Roger as much as possible with expertise and knowledge, sourcing material and cash, negotiating and introducing deals."* Howard was a one-time Team Green racer until injuries curtailed his riding but with many years of contacts both inside the paddock and beyond he brings that contact list to the team. A long-time friend of Roger, he says their *"mutual respect and friendship goes beyond motocross"*, as they speak on the phone weekly and play golf together when they can. Those talks can be about any pressing team issues, riders or just about the weekend. Howard also analyses lap times; who's fast, consistent, fast late in the race and compares the EMX250 times to MX2. *"We're always looking for the next 'big thing', we look at schoolboys and MX Nationals, Roger does the same in Northern Ireland."*

Ali is Howard's partner. Together they go to all the British championships and six to eight GP's. As they both work for Bott who are one of the team sponsors she is the liaison but also does much of the hospitality for the team. *"The team has changed and grown in stature over the years and there have been some growing pains, but I love it. Even if Howard didn't want to come I would still come."* As one of the financial controllers at Bott she understands how important budgets are. *"With more budget we could do a better job, but you have to be realistic. Every time Youthstream add another fly-away race it's another £10,000, so that ten grand you just got from a new sponsor over the winter is used up straight away."* Howard chips in, *"Youthstream does a great job with TV and promotion but that comes at a cost to the teams. We pay £10,000 a year per rider to enter and there's no prize money so you have to pay bigger salaries and bonuses."*

With Graeme absent all the attention focused on Conrad. He had a full entourage in attendance; manager Jamie Dobb, riding coach Justin Morris, practice mechanic and man-friend Paul Keates as well as some family and friends. After a strong ride at Blaxhall following two less than stellar GP's everyone hoped he was back on form and when he finished fourth in Saturday's qualifying race it was all smiles. Come Sunday he almost grabbed the hole-shot in race one, pushed out by Prado but a decent ride netted eighth. More importantly, in the second half of the race he was on the pegs and charging. After the race it was all smiles as his family and entourage carried out the race autopsy before he took a nap.

But in race two it was a different Conrad. Another great start in second place but by the end of lap one he was in sixteenth, looking lacklustre and seemingly not trying. He said later that his hole-shot device hadn't released, holding his forks down for a few corners but that didn't explain the next sixteen laps. Ian wasn't impressed in the pit box, nothing obviously wrong with the bike. He would drop to eighteenth and regain a couple of places to finish sixteenth. Before I returned to the Hitachi pit after the race he had gone but I was told there had been some drama as his family comforted him as he was distraught.

By sheer luck we were all on the same flight home on Monday. I'm always wary of asking riders for interviews over the weekend as they must focus on their riding, but I had agreed with Conrad to have a chat at the next GP in Germany on Friday as part of this book project. We ended up sat next to each other so decided to use the two-and-a-half-hour flight to do the interview. He seemed in good spirits as we started talked, my plan was just to re-cap the season, so I could fill in some blanks in the book. We started at Redsand where he battled Prado and just missed the podium. *"At the start of the season I was in a really good place, just enjoying everything, enjoying training and looking forward to the races. Suddenly the fun has gone, I'm not really enjoying the build up to the races. It's difficult because it's my job but I've got to enjoy it. Last week has been a bit military and it's not working for me, some riders can live mx, but I need to take time off and relax, just see my family. When I'm happy I ride great, there's no doubting my speed, my strength or my talent."*

I wasn't expecting such an honest answer, I didn't know him that well at that time. I asked about Portugal and told him I had heard it was girlfriend trouble that had affected him. *"I'd been seeing someone, but I'd kept it quiet. I was in a happy place, then people started finding out and made a problem out of it. It wasn't a problem in my head or what went wrong. I've always been controlled by teams and people around me and it never works. When I have fun in the week I ride better. At Redsand I was doing my own thing and it worked. I had a mishap in Portugal and its back to other people being involved, too many people giving too much advise."* The upshot was that he had been told to end the relationship with the girl by his entourage, something I thought was incredible. *"I've asked to have that independence, but they don't seem to trust what I do".* By now he was becoming slightly emotional, it was obviously something that really bothered him. "At the British championships my family are there, joking around and it takes my mind off it, it doesn't feel like work but the GP's feel so serious at the moment because I haven't had the best results, so I've got a lot of pressure. The British championships are good but after about the top five the depth isn't there, but in the GP's it's a battle to get in the top fifteen. People need to understand I don't want to be in fifteenth, I give 100% every time but I've been inconsistent. There isn't any support when you get those results, it's the same in all the teams but that's when you need it. The team need to work on that, it's not there at the moment."

The 'team' is quite a generic term so I asked him to be more specific. *"Jamie is good, he doesn't tell me what I already know, he does help turn it around but he's too controlling, I just want him to manage my contracts and do what I'm paying him to do. Paul and Justin are there to make me perform at my best, I've known them both a long time, and I get on well with Vas, I lived with him for a long time and we had a laugh. I just don't need to be controlled in the week, I like it when I do my own work in the week. If I'm gonna fail I've got to be allowed to fail, sometimes I feel like putting the bike in the van and never riding again".*

As we went through the list he didn't really have a big issue with any individual, just the feeling that everyone felt they knew what was best for him. I asked if he had spoken to Roger about this or told his dad how he was feeling. It was apparent that he felt unable to speak to either, Roger was his boss and his dad was convinced that Jamie held the keys to unlocking his potential even though Conrad saw him more as the jailer. He knew that everyone had his best interests at heart but in his eyes, they didn't go about it in the best way, and actually it was his own entourage that were creating much of his stress.

When we arrived back in England he was off to see a sports psychologist on his way home. He also had some strained knee ligaments, damaged the week before Russia so the plan was to take a week off and visit his mum and sister. Hopefully the week would give him some head space, and maybe the strength to tell the right people how he felt.

I spent the week mulling over what he had said. I had asked for his permission to raise it with Roger and his dad, which he granted, but I wanted him to make his own decisions and not for me to become another voice telling him what to do. In the end I decided to speak to him in Germany and see if it was just a conversation for this book or was he really reaching out for help.

Chapter 13

ROUND 8, MXGP GERMANY, TEUTSCHENTHAL & STEVE MEWSE – THE DAD'S PERSPECTIVE.

There was some good news for the team on Friday. A new truck driver had been hired and would start in time for the next round at Matterley and Graeme had messaged Ian to say that the doctors were pleased with his recovery and he would be able to start riding next week, which should give him a good week to prepare for his home GP. I met with Vas, Ian and Shaun and the talk turned to Conrad and some conversations during the week. I had just finished typing up interviews with Jamie Dobb and Justin Morris which are included later in the book, and what struck me was that everyone seemed to know what the problem was but not recognise that they were each part of the problem; too many advisers. Shaun was as 'black and white' as ever, 'he just needs to f##king man up' while Ian was more measured and realised it wasn't that simple. While Conrad wanted more control of his own life he wasn't able to wrestle back that control. He's a very young nineteen and has been coddled and looked after all his life. Having more control would also mean doing more for himself, even simple things like goggle prep. A conversation in the week between Ian and Steve Mewse, Conrad's dad, had resulted in his practice mechanic Paul Keates being left at home so Conrad would have one less voice in his ear and the team starting to control who has access to Conrad at race weekends. I was glad that Ian had come to the same conclusion as me without me getting involved, and hopefully it was a step in the right direction for Conrad. It also transpired that Keates had become more controlling over where Conrad practiced and trained and was allegedly having some relationship issues, played out on Facebook which were also impacting Conrad. These things happen gradually so it would be interesting to see if his absence made any difference.

After interviewing Conrad earlier in the book, I was quite surprised that he had been sent to Belgium on his own at such a young age, so I was curious to get his dad's perspective. As a parent I'm quite protective of my kids but when an opportunity comes along that's too good to miss I understand the dilemma. Here is Steve's perspective.

Steve Mewse – the dad's perspective.

"I bought Conrad a little PW50 Yam when he was 3, we spent some time on that. He did his first race when he was 6 and it just progressed from there. We did club stuff then BMA, in 2009 on a 65 he won the BYMX, BSMA and Redbull pro-nationals as it was then.

We did a couple of years on the 85 and he won one of them the BYMX or Pro-national, I can't remember which one it was.

In 2012 we decided to do the Dutch championship, because a guy in Holland was doing his engines. First one he rode was at Mill and he finished 3rd there, 2nd round he was 2nd then he won the 3rd round and he started to win that, so we decided to go to the Europeans. The Europeans had already started, and we missed the first couple but still managed to get it. He had a puncture at Matterley Basin otherwise he would probably have won that.

In 2013 he won the 85cc world championship. After that he got noticed by KTM

When he was 15 he moved to Belgium and he told me that was when it went from a hobby to a career, what was your thoughts as a parent at that time.

If I had my time again I wouldn't have done it but when you win something like that and Stefan Everts comes along, you think that they're gonna take you to the next level, which I think they tried but he was too young, and his mentality was too young. What Stefan was saying was right but trying to instil that into a 14-year-old child with no parents there was very difficult. I think that's why Prado has done so well, because his dad stayed with him throughout.

He was living with a young mechanic for a year, Ade Phelpstead who works for James Dunn, but it didn't work out they were booth to young. Then he had Hendo Steve Henderson which didn't work out because he was far too old and miserable"

Did you have any concerns about his welfare or was it just a case of trying to support his dream?

"It's difficult really because he dislocated his shoulder in the January before the season started so when he initially went over I didn't know if it was the injury that was the problem, or solely going to the team. Obviously now that I've been around the sport and experienced the big teams and not so big teams and gain some experience myself, if I had to do it again I would change a few things".

I interviewed Eddie Wade and his parents, and they said they'd had a long conversation with you which had helped them decide what to do, I guess you never had the opportunity to speak to anyone for guidance?

"I think apart from Prado he was one of the first riders to be picked up by the factories at such a young age. Harry Everts spotted Prado in the 65's and Conrad in the 85's and that's when the factory started buying riders up, like Eddie but because it didn't work with Conrad they though they'd better do something else which is when they started the factory juniors that Stefan ran. That's when you had

Prado, Conrad and Josiah Natzke. I think they might have thought they'd made a mistake initially, that's why now they keep their riders like Rene Hofer out of the limelight".

What would you do different now or what advice to a parent of a hot prospect now?

"I said this to the Wades, just because they've won the world title on an 85 you think that's it but it's not. Look at Brian Hsu, he's done nothing, Conrad hasn't done a huge amount, Maxine Renout hasn't done much, I know he's been injured but when you look at the path if I had my time again I'd come to a team like this, Hitachi, where you're surrounded with British people, I'd keep him at home, I'd monitor things a lot more. But we had no idea about the physical side of things, I didn't know how far people go into it, the Europeans are more knowledgeable about how they progress with their child. Conrad never went to the gym, he just used to ride a couple of times a week. All of a sudden, you're out cycling 3 or 4 times a week. I think if they're gonna be good they will be good wherever they are. I don't think being in Belgium or Holland with a factory team at that age is good. If you look at Ben Watson now, he's done it right. He's got to 19 or 20 and then he's going when he's matured a bit and understands. To ask a 14-year-old kid to wash his clothes, cook his tea, go to bed on time, put his phone down......it just doesn't work".

At the start of 2017 Jacky Martens sent him home, was that the low point in terms of missing the family.

"No, if you look he went with Jamie Dobb before the world championship in 2015 for a month and he nearly won that. When he was home, riding with Jamie and Justin he started going well. Its similar this year. I don't think it's where you are I think it's the people you're surrounded by. It doesn't need to be family it just needs to be s someone that can look after the kids and treat them as a kid. A bit of

safeguarding and mentoring. At the end of the day, to the big teams it's just a job and they want to pull someone through that's gonna make sales later on. They should maybe manage it a bit differently."

Do you think it's just a 'sausage factory' and if the kids fall by the wayside so be it?

"No, KTM have been pretty good to Conrad, they put him on a 5 year deal and although he's gone from the factory to Roger at Hitachi they've still kept him and made the effort so I wouldn't say they push them to the side, that would be unfair because they have put a lot of time and effort and money into him, but at the end of the day it's a business and they want results. They've stood by him for 5 years, so we can't complain."

Has all the ups and downs affected your relationship? I see you every week, and his granddad too. Has the experience of him going professional and you both learning together made you stronger?

"I think if this year goes to plan the last 4 years will have been worth it, although they've been difficult and at times it hasn't been great, that's made him a stronger person. If he doesn't get too many wobbles. To be honest he's been away a lot in the last 4 years, so I haven't seen a great deal of him, I've got a business and commitments. For example, this year they went to Spain for a month, when he was with Jacky they went to Sardinia, and he lived in Holland, so he hasn't been home much. If the GP goes well he comes home for a couple of days then he's back up to Derby and stays with Jamie, Paul or his auntie and does his training then flies out with Paul on a Friday. He's a bit of a travelling gypsy really."

Conrad arrived later in the afternoon with his dad and Justin Morris and told me he had had a good week at home, still done some riding and felt a lot happier as he set off on a track walk with Justin. Sleeping in the camper instead of a hotel, he was getting back to the simpler set-up that he liked. Saturday started well with fifth fastest in free practice and eleventh in timed practice. The times aren't that important other than to give an indication of which Conrad had arrived and he did look good. The qualifying race was a disaster as he crashed in the second corner, dropping to the back. I watched the race with Ian and could sense his frustration as Conrad circulated, only make three passes. About eighteen minutes in, he seemed to come alive and start attacking the track but with the riders in front strung out it was too little, too late in a twenty-minute race. Ian looked at me with a face that said, 'what the hell am I supposed to say about that?'

It's funny how we measure success. Race one started with a crash on the start straight, Conrad locked bars with the rider next to him and went down. He had to pit immediately to straighten his levers and would end up on twenty-third place but despite not scoring a point Ian was happy. *"The result was a disaster but at least he was trying, I thought it was a good ride. He's had worse results when nothing has happened".*

Race two was another disaster, twenty-second place and no points. Starting at the back he was battling with a gaggle of riders that he should never be involved with, it looks more like a last chance qualifier as they trip each other up allowing the front group to ride away. After the race he said his shock had blown, a statement which would come back to bite him. The team all wanted to get home as fast as possible, so the rear shock was removed and given to WP who would test in at the factory, while everything else was packed away as quickly as possible, without a de-brief. I spoke to him at his camper, just to get a comment for my magazine race report. He looked dejected, and with his shirt off I could see he was battered and bruised from the first race crash and the brutal roost, but the hurt was more mental than physical. He just said he was pissed off but there was nothing he could do.

It's important to put some context in here. The GP was one of the worst I've been too; the track was very fast and although there were plenty of lines only one was fast so where you started was where you finished. Cairoli is usually a master at overtaking, but he was stuck behind Desalle both times, trying every line on the track to find a way past without success. In the first MXGP race there were only two over takes during the whole race in the top ten, Gajser passed Paulin and Bobryshev passed Seewer so perhaps Conrad has some defence. But his lap times were off the pace and he was lapped in race one, and narrowly missed getting lapped in race two.

Shaun had delivered a new van to Germany for the team to use but had no need to go back to the base in Lommel so came back to England with me. It was a thirteen-hour drive with an overnight stop, so we had plenty of time to kill. *"When Conrad walked up to the awning for the first race I knew we were f##ked; he had no spring, his chin was down, you could just see it in his body language. I looked at Browner and he knew it too."* Shaun does tend to see things in rather black and white terms, but he is quit an astute judge of character and body language. We discussed a variety of potential solutions to get Conrad back to his early season form but without anything obviously broken it's hard to know what to fix. Shaun was also sceptical about the 'blown shock'. *"I didn't see any oil. WP will put the shock on a dyno and measure everything, they won't be happy if he's saying it's blown and it's not. The track was just rough, and he was riding shit, I bet there's nothing wrong with that shock".*

Conrad had now dropped to thirteenth in the championship, from fifth place just after Redsand. It was likely that KTM would withdraw the factory engines as they were conditional on being seventh or better. There was also the issue of the fly-away races to Indonesia. Roger would have to decide if he was going to send Conrad and/or Graeme on the long and expensive trip to the double header. It would cost about £20,000 to send the two riders, mechanics, bikes and Ian for the two-week trip. With limited budget and no realistic championship challenge, it might make more sense to stay home a train. The next GP at Matterley would be key.

Chapter 14

ROUND 9, MXGP GREAT BRITAIN, MATTERLEY BASIN, ROGER'S FRUSTRATIONS, MAX ANSTIE'S REDSAND CONCUSSION & THE AFTERMATH.

There was a week off between Teutschenthal and Matterley, meaning no MXGP or British championship but that doesn't mean a week off for the riders. With all the bikes prepared the mechanics did get some time at home, BC still with his new baby in Scotland while Vas spent a week working on his house in the Czech Republic. Graeme was back on the bike for the first time since Blaxhall. It seemed like a long time but was in fact only seventeen days, remarkably quick considering the severity of the burns. On the continent there were championship races in Belgium, France, Germany and Italy with GP riders in all of them. Graeme just needed time back on the bike while Conrad needed to re-group mentally, so they weren't racing.

The team had hired a new truck driver. Jakke Van Bael is an experienced motorsport trucker having worked most recently for Kemea Yamaha and Yamaha Europe. He lives near Lommel meaning he can go home when he's not working which makes the living conditions much easier. He came with a recommendation from his long-time friend, Jacky Martens and is a big motocross fan, telling me

"I have many friends in GP paddock. I been coming forty years, my friend is Andre Vromans (Factory Suzuki and Honda 500 rider in the early '80's), *he lives in the same village. I like this life."* Roger and Ian were both happy with the new appointment, he seemed to fit right in and understood the job was more than just driving from A to B. His first job as to bring the truck to England and get the boiler commissioned en route to Matterley by the plumber who had fitted it in March. With a new flue fitted it was finally working and that only took three months!

Elsewhere in the paddock there was bad news as the 8Biano Husqvarna team folded suddenly, siting financial reasons. Their riders, Iker Larranaga and Brent van Doninck were left looking for a home for the rest of the season, as were the mechanics and team staff. Van Doninck was interviewed by MX Vice (https://mxvice.com/77599/chatter-box-brent-van-doninck, published on 22/5/18) and said he hadn't been paid or given the equipment he was promised. It goes to illustrate how close to the edge some teams are financially, and as I've already said, it's easy to make promises and over commit but that doesn't ever end well. Within a couple of days it was announced that Larranaga and Van Doninck would join the DIGA-Procross team (after Husqvarna had stepped in), to complete the season.

Whilst the sudden demise of 8Biano was unfortunate, there were some much more concerning rumours circulating that HRC Honda was planning to withdraw at the end of the season. HRC Honda is still the most glamourous team in the paddock much like Ferrari in Formula 1, with most of the top riders aspiring to ride for them at some point in their career. The bikes look like works of art and with a long, rich history of winning and a no-expense-spared approach to racing they were to team to be on for many years. Recently they haven't had things their own way, the big push by KTM has transferred some of that winning magic and even big money riders like Tim Gajser and Ken Roczen (in America) haven't delivered the championship success that HRC demand, although Gajser is the 2015 MX2 world champion and 2016 MXGP world champion. The HRC teams have been hit hard by injuries on both sides of the Atlantic this year. In America

Ken Roczen and Cole Seeley were both injured in supercross, then fill-in rider Cristian Craig tore his ACL at the second outdoor national and was out. Similar misfortune befell the MXGP team as newly signed Brian Bogers injured his foot before the season even started and missed the first half of the year while Tim Gajser broke his jaw before the first MXGP and was below par, any championship hope effectively slipping away before it begun. Todd Waters was brought from Australia as a fill-in rider and promptly broke his collar bone in his very first qualifying race in Latvia. Despite a new sponsor in the form of HSF Logistics, a Dutch transport company, HRC was spending millions and not seeing the return on their investment, so the Japanese bosses recalled their most senior man in Europe and put him in charge of building mopeds at the Honda factory in Japan. The mid-season move was viewed by many in the paddock as Honda planning their exit strategy as well as a 'punishment' for the individual concerned because he had failed to deliver the expected results. It was impossible to get official confirmation from anyone at HRC which only added to the rumour mill but the loss of another factory team following Suzuki last year, would be bad news for the sport.

The British MXGP is one of the most important events of the year for Hitachi/ASA KTM. It will be the only GP many of the sponsors attend and along with the British Championship round at Desertmartin, it's the chance to shine, hopefully on track as well as off it. The hospitality area was about three times its usual size as the team hosted some important guests with a selection of drinks and a buffet, as well as 'meet and greet' sessions with Graeme and Conrad.

Roger can explain. *"The majority of our sponsors are from the UK, so we want everything to be 110% right for them. Its our biggest guest list of the year, we're entertaining up to 60 guests from all the main sponsors and some of the junior ones. Its just a matter of showing them what we can do at every event if they have the guests to come to it. With this set up hopefully we can entice more people to be part of the team. We get a maximum of 15 passes from Youthstream for any event so Hitachi will eat up those plus additional passes here, so we go out and buy the rest or do a deal with the organisers for car-park passes as well because it's important that sponsors that are putting a lot of money in don't have to wait in lines to get in, it gives them a bad impression, so those are things that might seem small to some people but they're a big deal to others. We try to give everyone a good experience.*

KTM UK have loaned us the inflatable tent that they use in BSB, we did ask for one earlier but they're 12,000 euros, we also have the two easy-ups and the new Stegmaier awning that we bought this year, so we can probably seat about 40 to 50 people. We provide food and drinks, water will be popular this weekend and as much tea and coffee as they want. We also have Milwaukee here this weekend with their own trade stand, with guests coming tomorrow including the marketing director so its important he knows what the set-up is, and we meet face-to-face.

The results on track are important because the team then gets a higher profile on TV, but its also to do with how the sponsor connects with the crowds at events, so they can get feedback and those people go home and buy their products."

There were plenty of frustrations with the organisation of the event. In the living area there is supposed to be electric hook-ups provided but there were too few and no electric anyway. There's always issues with passes, but I spoke to a few people who had paid for V.I.P. camping only to be told there was no record despite an e-mail chain.

Roger had his own issues with the organisers. *"We try to do everything properly with e-mails confirming everything. We brought Milwaukee to the table as a trade stand and agreed a price with Dixon (the organiser). We sent them a list of personnel, vehicle registrations coming on site, the number of passes needed and when they turned up at the gate as we told them to, no-one knew anything about it. we'd agreed a place for the trade stand by us, but they put them on the other side in the trade area. That's just an example of the bad organisation of the British GP. It's always the same but everyone glosses over it. Another example, I said to Steve Dixon weeks ago that I needed hotel rooms, he said it was arranged. I've been asking him for the reservation code, never got it and when I got to the hotel last night the guy said, "that twat Steve Dixon, I've been having problems with him for three years". We can all be critical of each other, but I don't think he has the organisational capability to run an event like this properly, yes, it's a big undertaking but it needs a structure in place to make sure certain people deal with certain things. This morning I needed some car park passes and they're not there, just simple things but it causes a lot of headache. I needed a pass to get my 85-year -old dad down here so he doesn't have to walk miles from the car park, its not sorted. I want to try and support the organisers but not when you're getting treated like sh#t, it puts unnecessary pressure on everyone. It's very frustrating."*

Beside some smoozing in hospitality Roger also had his riders on his mind. I asked him to talk about the recent weeks, both Graeme's injury and Conrad's slump in form.

Graeme first. *"What Graeme did at Blaxhall was phenomenal, to ride two races with those burns. We took the decision to carry on riding out of his hands, his health is more important, so he accepted that. Fortunately, the chemical treatment that the burns specialists used has worked well so he's been riding for the last ten days. After free practice this morning he said he doesn't have any issues with it, just a matter of keeping the dressings in place and keeping any dirt out."*

And Conrad. *"We've agreed with Conrad and his dad to go back to basics and try to get to the bottom of whatever has been affecting his over the last few weeks. What they do as a small family unit seems to be working, the feedback I'm getting is that on the practice track his speed is back up to podium level speed, but we're waiting to see if he can transfer that to the race track with other riders around him. I spoke to him after free practice and said there's no pressure just because it's his home grand prix, just enjoy it. I think once he gets the first podium we're away. He wants more control of his life so that's what we've given him, we've got the family unit back and pulled back some of the other team members who weren't*

Livin' the Dream

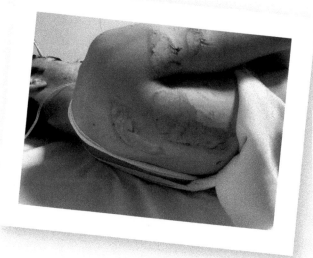

◀ *Graeme's burns from Blaxhall*
Photo credit Graeme Irwin Instagram

After the chemical treatment ▶
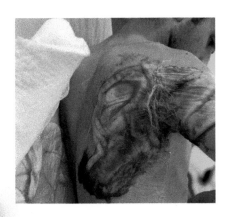

◀ *The Blues Brothers.*
Graeme & BC

British MXGP ▶

doing anything intentionally to his detriment but weren't pushing him. He seems to be the sort of kid who needs the right guidance and his father knows him better than anyone. His dad knows how to plant the seed, then next thing you know his lap times have dropped. Looking at the big picture he's nineteen years old but in his full development he's not nineteen, same as we had with Ben last year and we've seen what he can do this year once he matured and got away from his family. It's the flip side of it, maybe Ben's dad wasn't pushing him enough, it's not a criticism just an evaluation, we just have to find the key to open the lock."

At the MXGP Youthstream get the home country's riders at the Saturday press conference, alongside the qualifying race winners. Tommy Searle, Max Anstie and Ben Watson were the chosen ones. It's a valuable bit of exposure and P.R. for the team and riders involved, but because the Hitachi/ASA duo were languishing in the championship table they weren't there.

Matterley Basin is very much the home race for Max Anstie, who grew up just a few miles away in Winchester. Anstie now rides for the Factory Rockstar Husqvarna team but I've included his story to illustrate just how quickly a season can turn and the dangers faced by the riders. Anstie had a big crash at round 3 in Spain, suffering a concussion that continues to affect him.

> ## Max Anstie; Redsand concussion and the aftermath.
> There's growing evidence about the long-term effects of concussion injuries and particularly secondary concussions which happen when a person is knocked out after a previous injury. Contact sports such as American football have become more aware of the dangers and require players to take a mandatory break after a concussion rather than the old 'walk it off' approach; no race or football game is worth risking permanent brain

damage for. The F.I.M. has also been working to improve rider safety with increased standards for helmets among other things but there is still work to do.

Max Anstie is one of my favourite riders in the paddock. You always get one hundred percent from Max but what I really like are his podium celebrations; he is a picture of pure joy and really embraces the moment. When he crashed in Sunday warm-up at Redsand he was knocked unconscious and forced to miss the races. Unfortunately, the effects were more serious than he realised at the time and the consequences would bother him until the middle of the season. Thankfully fully recovered, I sat down with Max at the German MXGP, two months after the crash, to ask about the injury and his recovery process. As you would expect he was honest and open. His story offers an insight into how the riders and teams deal with head injuries, with some lessons for all of us to learn. This is his account;

"I started the off season well, everything felt like it was going well. The team were working hard, and we had stepped up with everything, the structure, the training, planning, blood tests; everything felt good. We went to Argentina for the first GP and that didn't go exactly to plan, a bad start in the first race and I came through from the back and in the second race I crashed at the start. I don't know if it was a bit of nerves, but first round so no biggy, we can push on. Everyone in the team expects podiums, we've gotta be on the box and no one's happy if you're not. That comes from everyone, the team, the sponsors, the brand; but we work hard to do that, that's the goal. We were pushing really hard in the week, went to Valkenswaard and I was in a position to be on the podium and I crashed on the last lap. I was battling Coldenhoff and I ended up sixth overall.

We wanted to step up again and I'd been training really hard with

Gautier, pushing each other in the week. I went to Velthoven in the week before Redsand and it was a little bit frozen, they were still getting that weird weather and it was really cold in Belgium. I'm not used to riding in the cold, but it wasn't frozen enough to be a problem, just a couple of bits in the shade. I'd just started my moto and I crashed my brains out; that was a big one on the Wednesday before Redsand. I landed on my head and I remember being on the floor thinking 'man that hurts'. I was only there with my practice mechanic, everyone else had already gone to Spain so I phoned them up. I didn't think it was that bad and I probably played it down at the time, I was 'yeah I'll be fine'. My head hurt but it's no big deal, crashes happen, and you've just got to deal with it.

Saturday in Redsand was OK, we were working on set-up and I think I was seventh in qualifying. Then in Sunday warm-up I hit a kicker. I can remember up to it, I was going fast but not mega. I hit the kicker and was endo'ing, but I wasn't worried or panic revving, I remember thinking in the air its fine, but I landed a bit short in all the soft stuff and it just caught my front wheel and I must've gone over the bars and landed at the bottom up-side-down but I don't remember that because I was knocked out.

I remember waking up and Antti (Antti Pyrhönen, team manager) was there, and thinking I better look OK because if I look bad there's no chance he'll let me race. I was saying 'yeah, yeah, I'm alright'. I didn't even go to the medical centre, the main F.I.M. doctor hadn't got to me by this time, just the local Spanish medical crew had stretchered me off the track. I got up thinking I'll be alright and walked back to the truck. I didn't realise how long I'd been knocked out, but I saw the track clock and it said five minutes to go but the session is fifteen minutes and I crashed on the first lap.

There was no chance of me riding there in Redsand. It was weird because I'd only knocked myself out once before and then I wasn't unconscious just repeating myself and being weird, but I had three weeks off after that. This time I was obviously knocked out, but the rest of my body didn't feel too bad. Other riders were saying 'you were there for two laps', but I didn't feel bad, just a bit of a headache. The team knew I was knocked out, so they knew I wouldn't be able to ride. I was asking if there's anything they could give me to make me OK, but they said I needed to rest.

I didn't realise how much it could affect you. I didn't ever go to the medical centre. It was bad timing because from there I had to fly back to London to get my Russian visa, so I was sat there for four days because it takes so long. I was just loosening myself up thinking I'll be fine, I'm just a bit stiff. I came back from there and went straight to the Dutch championship the next Sunday.

I just felt really weird. I knew there was something wrong, I could go fast for five or ten minutes then I just wanted to go to sleep. I could do it but only at fifty-percent, I couldn't be intense. I didn't know if it was the effects of the crash. I went back to the team and they were saying OK, we've got to push on and dig ourselves out of this. I was saying yeah, I wasn't being honest with them, but I wasn't being honest with myself. They were asking lots of questions, have you been sleeping OK? And I was like, 'well yeah, sort of'. There were a lot of little things that were a bit off, but I was brushing them off.

We went training in the week and I felt really bad. I could only do fifteen minutes then I dropped off, I was in zombie mode. I just thought, 'OK, we'll keep going'. We went to Italy (Trentino) and I struggled a lot, I couldn't push on Saturday. I came in and said, 'look, there's obviously something wrong and we need to get this looked at'. I went out on Sunday with a plan to build up, but I only did three laps and felt really sick, I thought 'this isn't good'.

So, after that I saw the doctors. They did all these scans and could see there was bruising on my brain. I did some tests and they said I was off, my co-ordination, checked my eyes and did all those things. The doctor advised me to have a week off completely doing nothing, then build it up with physical training and then start riding after that. What had been the issue was that I'd already hit my head before Redsand. If' I'd just hit it once I would probably have been alright, but I'd made it worse and prolonged the recovery by not recognising that and resting straight away. But it's a tough one, especially when my body felt alright and it was just my head that hurt when I rode.

Then the recovery plan started but by then I'd already had two weeks of milling around and not really doing a lot, trying to ride but not doing a good job and making it worse. I had a full week off, then started back on the program. I went riding a few days before Russia, but I knew it was probably a little bit early. I did one twenty-minute moto and felt good but the second one I felt like I was on the limit and the third one, the team stopped me and said no, you look tired. When you've run out of time it's tough, I want to race, and the team obviously want me out there, we need to be out there for the sponsors, for the brand. There's pressure from everyone asking questions. It's actually easier if you break something, if I had broken my arm it's easier to say you have to give it this amount of time to heal whereas with this I looked Ok and I could ride just not really sharp. Anyway, we went to Russia and I felt good on Monday, but I was tired on Tuesday (It was run on a bank holiday rather than a weekend). It was so intense and fast, I felt more tired than I would have liked, but I felt like I was on the recovery train.

We had a good couple of weeks training then did the Dutch championship and I felt good; then we went to Latvia. I was really pleased that in Latvia I did two solid days and every moto felt good. I felt physically tired in the motos on Sunday, my legs were tired but that was because it was hot, but my head didn't feel tired and I didn't feel out of it. Latvia was really good, and I was pleased with that, the next step was just bike time, and race time, just sharpening up those areas. You've got to be so 'on it' with this class. The doctor said to me that for me riding is like walking, you can do it and from the outside it looks o.k. but to be at the very top level, to compete for race wins and podiums, anywhere near that sharp end, there's ten or twelve guys that can all be in the top five and they're all at one hundred percent, so if you miss a bit of time, and I missed a good month, then it's hard to get back into it.

The doctor told me to rest but I didn't see him until two weeks after the crash. Maybe it's an experience you've got to go through, but you've got to listen to your body. It's tough, I trusted the people around me to make the right decisions and we thought we were. A little bit more knowledge might help but you can't tell someone who hasn't had a head injury. They might read this and then forget about it, it's not important at the time. Next time if I knock myself out it will be 'right, put the brakes on and treat it seriously, see the doctors and be on the safe side'. At least with an arm or shoulder you know you can just deal with the pain, that's it but with a head injury it's a weird one. There's the potential to end up bad, and the doctors did tell me that. It's important to take the time that is needed.

One thing I've learnt recently is that you've got to take control of yourself. People were telling me but it's hard, I want to go and perform, it's not that I don't tell the team, but you put on that you o.k. because you want to be good then you go back to your camper and think 'oh my god, I'm struggling'. You've got to listen to yourself and admit there's an issue. I kept going and going, I thought I would be fine but actually made it worse and prolonged it. If I would have knocked myself out then said, 'o.k., it was a big one, I need to have two weeks off then start again', I would probably have been a lot better off, but because my body felt OK and I didn't want to lose time or miss days of training because I feel like I'm gonna get slower. You've got to listen and take everything into consideration. Whether its yourself or you have close people around you, you need to listen and make the right decision".

I spoke to Max regularly through the season and he assured me that there were no residual effects. His results were back on track with some podiums and he felt that he had fully recovered.

Beautiful summer weather provided the perfect backdrop, but the crowd still looked sparse to me. The price of tickets, pit passes and camping just too much for a lot of people. On track the action was intense with factory KTM making all the headlines in both classes, especially the Herlings/Cairoli battle that ended with Cairoli on the floor. He was fuming and refused to attend the press conference afterwards (the official excuse was that he had an early flight booked) but there is little doubt that Herlings is on another level at the moment, as he rode around the outside of Cairoli in race two, stood on the pegs in a rutted off-camber turn.

The Hitachi/ASA duo had less newsworthy weekends. Despite his practice track speed Conrad was again lacklustre. Seemingly giving up as he crossed the start gate, standing up in the first turn and starting at the back in both races. Fourteenth and twenty-second place finishes, only seven points scored wasn't enough to make anyone happy. I asked one of the team what was wrong, *"same sh#t, doesn't know what he wants"* was the reply. To compound his woes, the 'blown shock' from Teutschenthal had been thoroughly tested by WP, stripped and examined; it was working perfectly.

Graeme had a better weekend even if his results didn't reflect that. Sixteenth in timed practice, eighteenth in the qualifying race, the nineteenth and twenty-first in the races might not sound great but he was glad to be back and riding well. I asked BC (his mechanic) if he thought the imposed layoff had done him good. *"Yeah definitely. He's really hungry and he's got a bit lost before trying to figure out what he wanted with the bike. We're back to the original race engine now with a softer hit so the power rolls on better."*

In race one Graeme was thirteenth for over twenty-five minutes, overcoming the lack of first lap intensity that had been his nemesis. I thought it was the best I had seen him ride at a GP, and despite losing six places in the last few laps through tiredness and silly mistakes he looked good. In race two he gained a couple of places but the time away had cost him endurance. Afterwards he was buoyant as we talked about the weeks since Blaxhall.

"Honestly, it was just adrenalin that got me through that day. The first race when the gate dropped I just tried not to think about it, just go-go-go as fast as I can and get the adrenalin going. It worked but half way through my body wasn't as strong, I had four full thickness burns on my back and my body was fighting that, I felt totally drained. In the second race I just thought give it everything, it's a long championship but I couldn't get it going. I was in hospital for five days. The first option was skin grafts, but I told the doctor my situation and he was really cool, East Grinstead hospital is really good, they treated people in the war. I ended up having a chemical treatment, it's a new treatment but it got me back a lot faster. It wasn't just five days in hospital, it was the ten days house bound. I wasn't allowed to get my body temperature up, if I did it was complete agony and the burn would itch and feel like someone was digging it up with their nails. That

lasted fifteen days, I couldn't do anything just lying on the sofa trying to get a cold breeze. At the time I wanted to try and ride the next week in Latvia but realistically I wouldn't have been able to. I'm not a quitter, I'm the complete opposite and I'll do whatever it takes. Roger and Lee both said take time off and get better. I feel like maybe the break has helped in some ways. Not with bike fitness but we also had things to work on with the bike which we've done in the last two weeks since I started riding again, just making it for me, and the team are all behind me, they know that when I'm comfortable is when I'm fast. I've been putting the work in but I just need to get stronger now and hopefully build on this. The start of the year was strong then we had a bit of a downward spiral but today has been a good up, I think the weekend as a whole is probably the best I've ridden. There was some discomfort, but it didn't slow me down, I was thirteenth for most of the race and then fell back because my fitness isn't a hundred percent from having a couple of weeks off."

Chapter 15

ROUND 10, MXGP FRANCE, ST. JEAN D' ANGELY, THUNDERSTORMS, RUTS & CONTRACTS.

The week following Matterley was all about Herlings and Cairoli. Cairoli had led both races at Matterley but Herlings had passed him in the final laps of each race. Riding around the outside of Cairoli in a rutted, off camber turn while standing on the pegs in the first race was one of the all-time-great overtaking moves with comparisons drawn to Everts doing the same thing to James Stewart at the 2006 MXON. When Cairoli retaliated Herlings again passed him, in doing so they touched and Cairoli ended up on the floor. In the second race Herlings again won and Cairoli rode straight past him after the flag, and also skipped the post-race press conference; the heat was definitely getting turned up between the two sides of the Redbull KTM team as every motocross site had video of the clash and plenty of opinion as to who was at fault. Herlings remained humble but resolute; he hadn't intended to knock his teammate down but its racing, and with a 52-point lead in the championship he was in a strong position.

Conrad's performance had everyone scratching their heads. He had been given what he said he needed and it hadn't made a difference. It was probably unrealistic to expect things to turn around in a week but his practice track motos showed he still had the speed but put him amongst other riders and he seemed to give up. Roger had some ideas to put him with a different trainer 'to toughen him up in a controlled way' but I had my doubts. KTM had seen enough, the factory engine was taken back and there was also talk about contractual consequences, so it seemed like a good time to talk about contracts with Roger.

" Contracts.

"In the early days we didn't have contracts at all because we weren't getting the level of support we're getting now, so even with riders in the early days it was a hand shake. E-mails were starting to come in, but as things got more involved we decided we needed to have contracts with riders. We got a specimen contract from another team and adapted it; we're still using that contract today with a few amendments. For the sponsors, its more a case of sitting down with them and finding out wjat they want to get back out of it; do they just want graphics on the bikes, the truck and media or guests at each event, hospitality and at which countries then we structure a package to suit that sponsor and agree a figure. With the main financial sponsors, we have a structure so we get a lot of the finance at the start of the season because we have a lot of expense then. We have to pay Youthstream, we have fly-away GP's, new kit to buy such as suspension and wheels. Other sponsors such as Dunlop tyres and Enjoy graphics give us product to use free of charge. We have two contracts with KTM, one with the factory in Austria and one with KTM UK. The one with Austria is really for the bikes, parts and bonuses for world championship events, then KTM UK top it up with additional budget and bonuses for British championship events. Within that, KTM have the option to take riders from us into the factory team.

The rider contracts start with the term, one or two years. Then its structured with the salary, sometimes with a clause that if they finish in the top ten in the world championship the salary will go up in the second year. On top of that they have expenses per GP and the bonus structure from KTM, which they keep one hundred percent of. Then there are other product sponsors such as Twin Air which offer an incentive to win the world championship which can be pie-in-the-sky for a satellite team but its in there. There are clauses in there about behaviour and what they have to do, especially about social media; they have to be careful about what they post and don't bring any of the sponsors into disrepute with any comments they have. We ask them to tell the truth but in a way that can't be used by others as a stick to beat us with. Its training them so that if/when they get to the next level this is what will be asked for; turn up promptly at promotional event, have their own vehicle and changing area at events, just simple things but these are the rules and just go by them. There is also an injury clause. It depends what caused the injury; if it was a mechanical failure then it wouldn't be invoked, and we didn't invoke it on Graeme after his burns at Blaxhall. It's like a normal job where you get sick pay rate, so it's a reduction but with Graeme's case we knew it was only short term and he would be able to focus on his recovery better."

With two fly-away races coming up I had heard that the riders would not be going due to their position in the championship and a performance clause in their contracts. What does that entail?

"It's in the contracts that if you're not in the top fifteen then you don't go, or you have the option to pay for it yourself. The reason for that is that Youthstream have a cut-off for giving subsidies for transporting the bikes and if you're not in the top fifteen you don't get anything. It hit us a couple of years ago when we had two early fly-away rounds and neither Jake or Ben got on the top fifteen, and we ended up with

a very substantial freight bill that we hadn't budgeted for because we thought they would both be in the top fifteen and it didn't happen. We try to give the riders every opportunity to go pay if they're outside, some have taken it, and some haven't. Graeme is outside the top fifteen, so we've already told him he's not going; with Conrad we'll decide by the 19th June which is the cut-off. If he gets good results by then I think he'll definitely be going but we'll take advice from his family. We don't want to build him up then send him to Indonesia and have a couple of bad races and he's back to square one."

A few weeks ago, Roger had said "I expect you've heard people say I don't always pay them." It was a strange statement, but I had been told that it was the case, not with team staff just riders. Roger obviously wanted to explain his reasons for any non-payments.

"Over the years that have been a number of issues, mostly arising from the rider not reading the contract. For example, if they have an outside sponsor that also sponsors the team then that becomes a team sponsor so any money they get needs to be declared and split with the team, usually 50/50. Another example is where riders have been looked after but when they go to another team they don't return all the goods they've been issued with before the final payment is due. Theft isn't too harsh a word to describe it, anything we give them we document and if it doesn't get returned we can charge them. It doesn't happen every year, in some cases it's been a few hundred pounds in others it's thousands.

Years ago, we had a rider under contract for a year and he wanted to switch teams before his contract with us was up to ride the Belfast supercross. We wrote to him a few times and said your final payment is seven thousand pounds but if you ride in Belfast for another team you'll be in breach of contract and won't be paid; he went and did it, so we didn't pay him. He never queried it, but he didn't speak to me for years.

> *We don't do anything underhand, we copy everyone into e-mails, so everyone involved knows what is happening.*
>
> *It's usually that riders don't understand about the finances involved but more recently it's about the social media stuff that we're looking for. We also have a performance clause that if there's substantial underperformance we can end the contract within a month. It's a bit subjective but we've left it that way. We've never used it, we're not as hard as some riders make us out to be."*

In the team truck at Saint Jean on Friday I asked Ian for his take on Conrad.

"I've never known a rider like it. He's got such a talent and can do it when he wants to but last week he said he's not sure if he really wants to race or if he's got the right mentality for it."

I drew some comparisons with riders like Jean-Michelle Bayle who walked away from the sport,

"Yes, but they did the business when they had to, made their money then went. Conrad needs a reality check, he's making good money and he won't get that doing a normal job. He could've been on factory KTM next year but he's blown that, he's lost the factory engine now."

Shaun joined in. *"Watching him practice last week was mesmerising. I know it's his track but watching him scrubbing, standing up and railing a 180-degree turn, and so fast. He can do stuff on a bike that no-one else can, I thought 'yes, we've cracked it', then he goes to Matterley and just gives up, it's like he's bi-polar or something, just a different kid."*

Ian continued *"we're looking at getting someone fresh involved, who doesn't know him and can come in with a fresh outlook and see if they can work it out."*

I'd been messaging Hendo in the week, and he said he had the same issues in 2015 with Conrad when he was his mechanic on a 125. Hendo said he needs to go and do some club races where there's no pressure and build his confidence back up.

"He does that at the British championships. He goes there knowing he can win and make good prize money and bonuses but its like he comes to a GP and its hard work, he's not earning prize money or bonuses so he's not interested but that's such a short-sighted view because if he's not getting results here he won't be getting a big contract next time."

Shaun also had some ideas. In a two-pronged approach he had a friend in Bristol with a big scaffolding business and had arranged for Conrad to work as a scaffolding labourer for a few weeks when he would be at home instead of going to the fly-away GP's in Indonesia.

"We've got to try something outside the box. If he's saying he doesn't know if he wants to ride then fair enough, I'll help him become a scaffolder cos that's all he's qualified for. He needs a dose of reality, perhaps getting up every morning at 6 o'clock and working his bollocks off all day will help him make his mind up. I've run it past his dad and thinks it's a good idea."

It was certainly a novel idea and perhaps a shot across Conrad's bow that real life could be a lot harder. The second prong was blatant bribery. £100 every time he was in the top five, in any session including free practice as well as races going up to £500 for a podium. The cash would be matched by his dad so the incentive was doubled.

Graeme arrived listening to the Isle of Man TT live on his phone. He'd had a good week with two days riding and the burns on his back had healed sufficiently to no longer need dressings in his street cloths. He looked lean and fit but also prepared, bringing his food for the weekend which he put in the fridge, ready to do his work. At the TT Peter Hickman won the Senior race, smashing the lap record with an average speed of 135 miles per hour, and with the race over the conversation turned to 'silly season' which had become the main topic of gossip and speculation in the paddock. With Herlings so dominant it appeared that everyone else was competing for second place but teams still needed top level riders and with riders like

Van Horbeek, Desalle, Tonus, Jasikonis and Coldenhoff as well as the other three Brits in MXGP, Simpson, Searle and Anstie all out of contract at the end of the year there could be a bit of a shake-up. Both Graeme and Conrad were on a two-year deal which Graeme confirmed was *"Such a relief not to have to deal with all that bullshit".* It's not just the distraction of trying to secure a new deal but then getting to know a new team, learning a new bike and getting comfortable that can weigh on a rider. Graeme continued *"it's easier sometimes when you have a manager negotiating for you especially if you're trying to play off two teams, they've always got the get-out to say, 'well I need to ask my rider', but I'd just rather have a conversation and do the deal myself, that's how it happened with Roger and Lee".*

Saturday was hot and humid but the threatened thunder storms held off until late evening, the track getting more stony and hard-packed as the day progressed. The Conrad enigma continued as he was fifth in timed practice then put on a battling ride to finish fifth in the qualifying race. He was quick out of the gate but lost places on the long drag race to the first corner, Ian remarking that without the factory engine he's bound to lose out. Afterwards it was all smiles at the race truck as the team and his family all welcomed 'the old Conrad' back.

Graeme had a great start but would fade back to twentieth, a combination of fitness and a sketchy track that he didn't want to push too hard. I quietly wondered if there were any residual nerves as this was the track that he broke his neck at in 2011 on the 350 but I doubt it; he's much too focused and professional to carry that sort of baggage.

Thunderstorms lashed the circuit on Saturday night, flooding the Hitachi awning and turning the track into a heavy, sticky mess. The organisers had harrowed much of the track after the last race on Saturday but with hindsight they should have rolled it so that the rain would run off. Instead the start straight looked like a ploughed field and the clay soil was so heavy that less than half the EMX125 riders finished their Sunday morning race.

Additional scraping and grooming meant the MX2 and MXGP riders faced a much more raceable but technical track with long, deep ruts. Conrad got a decent start but was held up in the second and third corner, losing places but unlike the previous week he started charging, picking riders off and working back up to seventh place. Race two was more of the same, losing too many places in the first lap but battling.......... battling hard and to the flag, this time for ninth, and eighth overall. He had bagged 26 points, his best haul for eight GP's and his third highest score of the year. In the awning after the race he looked frustrated; annoyed with himself for losing early places and feeling that he should have been higher. The team and I both thought he had ridden well, showed a lot of heart and determination and the fact that he was disappointed was a good sign. It was too early to say for sure, but perhaps he had managed to put his troubles behind him. At the mid-point of the championship he was 56 points behind seventh place, his stated target for the year but with two injured riders ahead and the rest beatable by an 'on form' Conrad, there was much to play for.

Concern was now being expressed about Graeme though, as he endured another weekend without points. It was his second race back after injury but some of the team members felt that there were two issues. Howard described him as 'lost', trying too many set-up changes and adjustments. Graeme was off the pace by about 5 or 6 seconds a lap, and by that I mean the pace of fifteenth place which was where he had hoped to be at the start of the year. Herlings was 10 to 12 seconds a lap faster, but to be fair to Graeme, Herlings was 3 or four seconds a lap quicker than everyone else except Cairoli. Graeme was frustrated and by his own admission 'thinks too much' but he had tried over a hundred mapping changes, various engines and suspension changes since the season started. He seemed tentative in the ruts and less confident than at Matterley, but the most damning evidence was the stop-watch.

Shaun put it in context. *"The trouble is that you build a relationship with all these companies, suspension guys, engine tuners, mapping guys, and they're giving Graeme the same specs as everyone else but he's not happy. If it's working for the other riders why isn't it working for him?"* That was a rhetorical question. *"I'll tell you why it's not working; he's not going fast enough. And he's not going fast enough because in the week he's going to Pocock's place and riding with Mel Pocock instead of going to Lommel and riding with Herlings and all the rest of them. At the start of the year he was supposed to be moving to Lommel so he could train every day, but he's ended up staying in England, taking the easy* path and now it's showing."

It was an interesting assessment. Jake Nicholls once told me that he had lived in Lommel as an MX2 rider and hated it. There was nothing to do except ride and train, and as a result he said he spent so much time at the gym just to avoid the boredom that he ended up overtraining and ill. When he later rode for Hitachi in MXGP he said he wanted to prove that it he could live in Britain and still be successful as a grand prix rider but had come to the conclusion that it wasn't possible, you need to be amongst the other riders, putting in the hard laps around the sand tracks. Shaun Simpson had told me something similar and took the decision to live in Lommel years ago. You will get a glimpse into his winning training regime in chapter 20.

By strange coincidence, Adam Sterry announced that he was parting company with his long-time trainer Richard-Mike Jones to live in Holland and train with his team's own coach Marc de Reuver, a former GP winner and factory rider. After seeing the transformation in Ben Watson this year, as well as the other GP riders all saying the same thing it seems like the answer lay in the sand of Lommel rather than more fine tuning of the suspension.

Designed to Perform, Built to Last

**UP TO 200KG
LOAD CAPACITY**

**EXTENDED
GUARANTEE**

**COMPREHENSIVE
RANGE**

**RIGOROUS
TESTING**

**INDUSTRY
EXPERIENCE**

**CUSTOM DESIGN
AND BUILD**

bottltd.co.uk   01288 357788

Chapter 16

ROUND 11, MXGP LOMBARDIA, OTTOBIANO, BACK ON TRACK, CONRAD'S TEAM; JUSTIN MORRIS (RIDING COACH) AND PAUL KEATES (PRACTICE BIKE MECHANIC), DESERTMARTIN.

The week between grand prix is all about routine for the riders. Read any interview and they all talk about their 'program' which is all about preparing them for the weekend to come. By getting into a routine the body (and mind) knows what to expect, maintains fitness and builds muscle memory, plus most people like familiarity, eating their own food and sleeping their own bed. For these reasons the riders dash for home on Sunday night from virtually every European MXGP, those living in Belgium would be in their bed by 2 A.M..

The majority of the teams would stay at Saint Jean on Monday, the mechanics getting the bikes rebuilt on Monday before driving due east to Italy, an easy two-day drive in the race truck.

As the trucks rolled out on Tuesday morning, Conrad was on Facebook. He posted: -

"First of all, I'd just like to apologise to everyone for being so quiet over the last month or so, we've had a few personal problems that are now ironed out and we are back heading in the right direction! Massive thanks to my HITACHI ASA KTM UK TEAM and my man @vaclavlavicka for sticking

behind me through this rough patch, I went 7-9 for 8th overall at the French GP which is a good starting point for me heading into the second half of the season."

The comments were all positive, with many admiring his honestly in admitting to personal problems. This one was from Roger: -

"It takes big cajones to admit any issues, but your results at St Jean proved to the paddock that you are once again a force to be reckoned with. Really looking forward to the rest of the season. Nothing is impossible now."

Social media can be tricky and I'll explore that later in chapter 19 but I think Conrad's honesty was actually refreshing and sincere rather than the usual politically correct and non-descript white noise that often gets posted by riders. Hopefully it also marked the turning point.

With the factory engine repossessed by KTM, the team got a new engine from John Volleberg, the Dutch ace engine tuner that does work for most of the non-factory teams. The same spec as Henry Jacobi, it had more torque that should suit his riding style better and help with starts.

As the whole team was trying to support Conrad and get him out of his doldrums, this seems like a good time to introduce two of the people who work closely with Conrad on a day-to-day basis, his riding coach and his practice bike mechanic.

> ## Justin Morris - riding coach.
> Like many others in the paddock Justin Morris has a long history in the sport. He spent thirteen years racing from the late 80's in 125 and 250 grand prix including a stint with HRC Honda where Ian Browne was his mechanic. Now working as a riding coach, he splits his time between riding schools in the UK, working for the Polish federation coaching their youth riders, and working as a personal riding coach with Conrad Mewse and others. I chatted with Justin at the Latvian GP to talk about his work with Conrad.

"I could always go fast and that fundamentally hasn't changed. In those days we earned good money and I was extremely fit, our races were forty-five minutes long and we would ride five times in the week and six times over a weekend. British championship weekends were a lot longer so compared with today we did a lot more. We were all very fit, but I did run the edge and enjoyed my life, I still enjoy my life, we're sat here having a beer now and I was pretty much like that when I was racing. I wasn't getting pissed but I did enjoy myself and probably could have done a few things a bit differently, but would the outcome have been any different? I don't know, I tried it so many different ways to be focused."

Do you think it's about finding what works for you as an individual? Ken Roczen is a strong advocate of having balance, after he's won he'll have a beer and some pizza but be back in the gym on Monday working hard.

"Yeah its exactly that. Sometimes I would take that to the extreme (laughing). The way I lived in my career I possibly didn't achieve as much as I could have done, I've had both sides of the coin. I've had the great races and success, and I've had the bad times and the shit so I'm in a good place to guide riders with what they should and shouldn't do and the reasons behind it. I've had the moment where I should've been better, but you never really know. I wish I'd applied myself with more commitment because it is a short career and you think it's gonna last forever. You wake up one day and you're thirty and you think 'where did that go?' but I've got no regrets really. I'm forty-three now and I'm still involved with the sport that I adore. I couldn't do anything else and luckily I do my job well."

What does your job with Hitachi/ASA KTM involve?

"It's trying to get the riders in the right place mentally and physically. I've taught Conrad since he was eight years old so he's like a son to

me. He's an incredible talent and a very frustrating human being but the talent he has is second to none, so it's trying to get in a good place at the right time and ultimately win races. We work together in the week and at weekends. My job unfortunately is picking holes in it, so you're permanently looking at what we can improve. You're looking for micro-seconds, fine tuning all the time. Whether its lifestyle, riding the bike, the way he goes around a corner, any of it. I've just finished a track walk with Conrad, he knows the track but it's trying to eliminate the mistakes and out an old head on young shoulders."

I wanted to know more about the GP in Portugal where Conrad had been so far below his normal speed. His weakness seems to be his mental resilience when things aren't going well, but as I've already said in this book we do expect an awful lot from these young men.

"The thing with Conrad is that he plays his cards close to his chest so you never really get the true, full reason and I don't know if you ever will. We do demand a lot from these kids, and I use X factor as the comparison. Every week they come here and it's a live audition. Now if you don't perform at the live audition on X factor, what happens? You don't get through. It's that special person who can do it week in week out that makes it and unfortunately, we're in a perfection industry. No one gives a f#ck if you're having a row with your girlfriend or got the shits. We care but the factories don't, it's a very difficult thing to deal with. Conrad doesn't like to talk much about his feelings, so you end up guessing. You can sometimes magnify the problem and make it bigger by talking about it or you can try to move on, 'OK that's done, this weekend is a different track'. All the riders are gonna have bad GP's, it's just that he had two on the bounce. If the rest of the year goes well they'll be forgotten about. Conrad has the potential, he was beating Prado easily on an 85 and 125 but it's like any sport, they go up and down. Prado has his time at the moment, but Conrad

will have his time again, he's still not found his feet really but he's definitely a world champion."

Paul Keates – practice bike mechanic.

"I work with Conrad on his personal settings, getting the bike how he feels comfortable and happy. Vas builds the bike in the workshop and brings it to the track, and because I come to the races I set the bike up. Normally that information would be sent to the race mechanic but because I come I can do it."

I noticed this morning (at the British GP) you were changing the handlebar clamps with Vas, is there any cross over of roles?

"No, in the week when Conrad was practicing he broke the air dampers so I had to put on a set of standard clamps on and he liked them, so Vas put standard clamps on but we had to set the heights and change some spacers."

When you go to the practice track what is your role?

"I do lap times and put them on the pit board. We usually work on times. I do bike set-up, suspension. I watch him ride, see how the bike is handling and make changes. I speak to WP and tell them what I've changed so we can bring that to the races."

Is Conrad good at understanding how the bike is working and communicating that with you and Vas?

"No. his bike is set up by me and he just jumps on and rides it."

How did you become a mechanic?

"I used to ride years ago. I got into the British championship but didn't do very well. I won some expert championships but that was it. I always had nice bikes that worked well and people started asking me to do their bikes and set-up suspension and it just went from there. I did four years with Tommy Searles his practice mechanic, then when he went to Dixon we went to Hawkstone and he had a few

> *problems so I ended up going to every GP. I did a similar job to what I do with Conrad.*
>
> *Jamie Dobb asked me to do the same thing with Conrad so that's how I came here. I've been with Conrad since November."*
>
> The season started well but he's had a few bad GPs in the middle, is that something you work on with him?
>
> "The problem is that we did everything together since November and then I think they thought he was gonna struggle and they let him do his own thing. Now Jamie and all the rest got involved and it's got a bit messed up. He seems to be rebelling, saying he wants to do his own thing but it's too early to tell if it's working or not.
>
> I didn't go to Germany because they say I do too much for him and they wanted him to make his own decisions.
>
> Vas is a good guy to work with, and Minty is sound."

On the Wednesday before Ottobiano the first 'earthquake' hit the MXGP paddock as Jeffrey Herlings broke his collar bone and some ribs whilst practicing in Holland. I say earthquake because it was huge news and could be the deciding factor in the championship. Herlings had already lost two world titles in MX2 through injury; in 2014 he broke his leg at a charity race when he was 155 points ahead of second placed Jordi Tixier with four rounds remaining. Tixier was his teammate but had already been told that he would not be re-signed and promptly went on a tare to win the title by 4 points. In 2015 Herlings was again leading the championship by 139 points at the mid-point when he broke his collar bone. He missed the next round but returned to win the first race at the next round in Sweden before injuring his finger in the second race. With Herlings unable to race again, Tim Gajser clinched the title.

This time Herlings had a 62-point lead over KTM rival Cairoli so much less room to spare, and a much more ruthless and wily adversary. The nine times world champion Cairoli had already shown that he wasn't above a bit of rough riding to unsettle Herlings in his pursuit of championship number ten so with the smell of blood you could expect him to do anything he could to make life uncomfortable for Herlings.

The reaction on social media was almost instant as the 'I knew that would happen' comments piled up, presumably from the same people who had been marvelling at his speed in the weeks prior. The Redbull KTM team issued a statement saying that he would have surgery that evening and was 'a major doubt' for Ottobiano, possibly the understatement of the year, as by the next day Herlings had taken to social media to say he would not be riding.

The track at Ottobiano is deep sand, and last year in 43-degree heat it proved to be the toughest challenge for many as even Herlings, Prado and others collapsed after their races. The epic battle between Cairoli and Herlings saw them rubbing plastic with Cairoli coming out on top and stamping his authority on the championship. In my opinion it was probably his best race and the day that he actually put one hand on the title, as after that race he merely needed to control the points. There would be no repeat battle this year with Herlings out but Hitachi had their own riders to worry about. Graeme arrived on Friday afternoon in a good mood. He had been out in the week with WP for a day of suspension testing and made some major changes so we sat down for a catch up.

'When I left you last week you seemed really pi#sed off.'

"Saint Jean just didn't go as planned, I haven't had much luck at that track and I wasn't having a lot of fun, it just wasn't my weekend. I just didn't feel comfortable to be honest."

'Was any of that to do with nervousness from the accident you had there in 2011?'

"Probably going into the weekend, I had a little bit of that, thinking I just want to get out of here in one piece and not do anything stupid like happened last time but after the first session that was all gone. Once you put your helmet on and get out on track all that leaves you, I just didn't

feel comfortable. It was the same as Portugal, really rutty and I didn't feel comfortable there although I was really sick so it was a little bit different."

'I was watching you past the pit lane and you seemed really uncomfortable in the long ruts on that straight.'

"That was probably my worst part of the track. I feel like I'm normally pretty good in the technical stuff but I just didn't feel comfortable, that's why I wanted to go testing this week. We haven't really done much testing, we did a day in Redsand at the start of the year which I think we made a mistake. We stayed at the same place for a month and we did the test quite close to the end there so we knew exactly how the bike was working around there. Sometimes when you ride a track so much if you're having a problem you ride round it and it starts to feel comfortable and its not until you go to other places that you realise. I feel like we were on the back foot a bit with that and when we did one more test before Valkenswaard but t rained really hard all day, so it was a bit of a waste. Since then we've been trying to change stuff on race day. Its not that I'm always uncomfortable just certain conditions like Portugal and last weekend, but I just haven't felt that I can push."

'What was the testing you did this week?'

"We had a day with Frankie, the team's suspension guy from WP. We used the whole day from 9 o'clock until 5:30. We were at the track by Eindhoven, then the next day at Bergam. It's close to WP so we could nip there if we needed to. We made some big changes, everything you could change was changed to make me feel more comfortable. I believe I'm a lot better rider than I showed last weekend."

'During the conversation I had with Howard in the pit lane last week he thinks you're 'lost', chasing performance with settings. Is he right?'

"That's bull shit, just plain bull shit. If I'm changing something I'm changing it for a reason, I'm looking for something."

'Does that go back to what you said earlier that you found a setting at Redsand but it's not working elsewhere?'

"We didn't really change anything at Redsand, the bike felt good, we

changed the rear spring and that was it. We've never made a change and it's not been better. You're always gonna get people within the team on your bad days be quick to turn around and say 'it's this or it's that' but on your good days you remind people that you're not done yet. I know I can be better than what I am at the moment; I think I was actually riding faster last year, it just takes time to get comfortable on a new bike. The biggest thing I would say is build the bike for Graeme Irwin, not for 'so and so on a KTM is using this'. The bike has to be built for me. I can always ride it but at what speed? When it all clicks and comes together it does show."

'Is there any part of your program that you want to change as we reach the mid-point of the season? You were originally planning on living in Belgium but you've ended up living in Kent.'

"I'm really glad that happened, it's working out a lot better than I thought it would. The main thing is that my family can be in England, my daughter can go to nursery and everyone speaks English and my wife is happy. Obviously in Belgium there's a language barrier. For me I can get up at 7, be on the train by 8, I'm in France at 9:30 when you add the hour time difference, and I'm at the workshop for 12:30 and the track opens at 1:00. It's no stress if I want to go to Belgium for a couple of days, just stay in a hotel overnight and be back home by 8 o'clock in the evening. I've used 20 crossings this year, you've got to be riding with the fast guys. I've been lucky this year. I've been riding a bit with Mel Pocock, he's got a really good hard-pack track there and riding in Belgium."

'I believe you like the track here (Ottobiano).'

"Yeah, I've been here the last three years. I came at the start of this year with Lee, last year I came with the family and before that I raced the Italian championship here. I really like this track, I've probably rode it more than any other track on the calendar so I've been looking forward to it."

'The next two GP's are in Indonesia, are you disappointed not to be going?'

"Oh, for sure, I'd love to go but it's in my contract that if I'm not in the top fifteen I'm not going. I understand it's a lot of money for the team if you're *not contending for a title; I'm sure it's the same for a lot of the teams."*

'Is the British championship the priority now for you?'

"It wasn't at the start of the year but it probably is now. We've only had three rounds and there's five left so its still possible. It would be good to win and it's important for the team."

Quite clearly there's a difference of opinion between Graeme and some of the team, and for me the answer is a simple matter of communication. By contrast, the Wilvo Yamaha have a team meeting every Tuesday to discuss the weekend; what was good, what was bad and to iron out any disagreements. After the first discussion the riders can leave and the boss briefs the team on the week ahead, travel plans and anything else. I think that level of communication a great idea; it keeps everything in the open and makes everyone feel involved and listened to but it only works if everyone lives close to the team base. With the Hitachi/ASA KTM team scattered far and wide it's just not possible.

The mood under the awning was much more positive as the weekend started. Conrad and Graeme both seemed re-energised. Perhaps it was the public cleansing on Facebook for Conrad or the new suspension settings for Graeme but both went out in free practice and looked fantastic. In free practice Conrad was third fastest, then sixth in the timed session. Graeme was on the pegs and on the gas, railing the bowl turn before pit straight then wheelieing into the next jump; impressive technique and indicative of a man feeling confident. In timed practice he was just a second slower then Max Anstie in fourteenth, although the group is so close that second was six places. Both had good qualifying races, Conrad moving forward to seventh place and Graeme battling all the way for sixteenth. It wasn't their results that were so impressive but their effort and that they were both attacking the track right to the flag.

On Saturday evening I had a beer with Conrad's dad Steve. It was a beautiful summer evening in Ottobiano so the living area where all the rider's campers are parked was filled with barbeque smoke, most people sitting outside despite the mosquitos. Conrad was relaxed as we chatted and revealed to true cause of his unrest. He had fallen out with Jamie Dobb, his manager, mentor and friend, over the issue of control and freedom. The fall-out meant he felt awkward being around Dobb and his family, so he had tried to avoid them which only led to more angst. When he was finally forced to confront Dobb, it was all sorted out and the balance of control and freedom was agreed. It seems incredible that such a small thing could have had such a negative impact on Conrad, his team and his season but the truth is that he is a boy in a man's world, surrounded by authority figures and adults. Despite being nineteen-years-old he hadn't yet acquired the life skills to deal with the situation so tried to avoid it. Teenaged growing pains, nothing more and nothing less. It had been a valuable life lesson for young Conrad; if there's a problem, a conversation sooner rather than later will usually sort things out but never try to run from your problems.

As I chatted with Steve, Conrad was checking social media, relaxed and happy. He may be one of the fastest young men in the world on a motocross bike but he's still just like any other teenaged lad off the track. Perhaps we expect too much of our young sporting stars sometimes.

The next day he was on fire, fastest in warm-up. His start in the first race wasn't great but he battled up to eighth. Returning to the pits his bike cut out. It appeared to be a mechanical problem, and the bike wouldn't re-start so the engine was swapped between races. Another mediocre start, but he was on a charge, up to seventh place when he pulled into pit lane, his sub-frame hanging off. In the rush to change the engine, the top mounting bolt for the subframe hadn't been retightened properly and had fallen out, the sub-frame pivoting on the bottom bolts and being held at the top by the air box connecting boot. There was no way to repair it in pit lane so Conrad was out! He looked dejected, obviously disappointed and frustrated but the team were all supportive; he had done his job and whilst it was unfortunate, things can happen in racing. He was back, fast and pushing hard, and no-one could ask for more.

In the evening I asked Vas, his mechanic, if the DNF bothered him. *"Of course! Always! I can go back many years and I never have a mechanical*

DNF that is my fault. Today, this is my fault. The bolt was tight but not tight enough."

Graeme also had a good day on Sunday. Eighteenth and sixteenth places in the races for eight championship points was his best score of the season and the first time he had scored in both races since the first race in Argentina. His weekend wasn't without drama. His bike also cut out after the first race, spluttering and popping. Without a lot of time to diagnose the issue and fearing it was a mechanical problem the engine was swapped but the new one was doing the same thing. With no time left, Graeme had to use the spare bike. Because of all the suspension testing that had gone on recently they only had one set with the latest settings. BC swapped the forks onto the spare bike but there wasn't time to swap the shock. Ironically, Graeme equalled his best finish of the season with a sixteenth on a bike with an engine "like a f##king animal, it hits so hard" and an old shock setting.

BC had certainly earned his money, and with the British championship in a week's time in Desertmartin he would be swapping everything back around and rebuilding the bike with only a couple of days to do it. He had already taken the head off of the first engine and confirmed to himself that it wasn't mechanical. When the transplanted engine wouldn't run it had to be electrical but he needed to know, just because he's that conscientious that he wouldn't sleep otherwise. Back at the workshop later in the week the cause was discovered; a broken wiring loom. The wire had rubbed through the insulation and was shorting out.

Desertmartin.

For Roger this was the most important event of the year, even more so than the MXGP at Matterley. It was in his back yard, so making a good impression with all the friends, family and sponsors was top priority. The facility at Desertmartin is probably the best in the UK, certainly for the British championship venues. The permanent track has seen investment in the infrastructure to a level that would be comparable to the MXGP venues, with permanent structures, toilet blocks, a pressure washing area and concrete start gate. The site is probably a little bit too small for a modern MXGP but it sets the standard for British championships in my opinion. Six days after the summer solstice, the event was blessed with clear blue skies and twenty-five-degree temperatures, all helping to show the place at its best.

The inflatable air shelter was again in use for the hospitality area, and there was a buzz around the Hitachi/ASA KTM pit all day with the great and the good of Irish motocross enjoying a reunion. Roger's wife Joan was with Ali, keeping the buffet table stocked whilst Roger mingled; tick the hospitality off as a success.

ASA owner Lee Tolan had been racing in the 2-stroke championship but to be honest he was a long way off the pace, and not a very good advert for the team. He had recruited Jack Brunell into the ASA side of the team to replace him on the 2-stroke, and even though Brunell is considered an arenacross specialist it was a good move. Lee also needs to decide if he wants to manage the team or ride, its not possible to do both unless you're Chad Reed or Jeremy McGrath.

On track Desertmartin marked something of a turning point in the season for Conrad and Graeme. They both seemed happy and relaxed but most importantly fast. In timed practice Conrad was 1.6 seconds faster than his nearest challenger despite not getting a clear lap. Graeme was fourth in MX1, 1.2 seconds behind pole man Tommy Searle with red plate holder Jake Nicholls and Evgeny Bobryshev between them.

In the races Conrad was even more dominant, winning the first race by thirty-five seconds with a fastest lap 2.7 second quicker than anyone. The second race was stopped after one lap when Conrad was in fifth; he used the re-start to full advantage, taking the lead on the first lap and winning by over forty seconds. The track was incredibly rough and Conrad picked up a line down the big hill, wheelieing over four large braking bumps then dropping the front wheel into the turn. It was an example of skill that few possess, 'Herlings-esque', indeed no one else was doing it in either class.

When he's happy and 'in the zone', he has the talent to be world champion without any doubt; the challenge for the team is keeping him in that happy place.

Graeme was equally buoyant, his home race giving him extra zest rather than crushing him with pressure. By the second lap of the first race it was Searle, Nicholls, Bobryshev and Graeme. It looked set for a boring race as the four matched each other until lap 5 when Nicholls dropped it, allowing Bobryshev and Graeme past. With twenty minutes gone Graeme was the fastest man on track, passing Bobryshev and setting after Searle, crossing the line about a second behind. In race two he spun on the concrete at the start, ending the first lap in tenth. He charged hard all race to finish in fourth, enough for second overall.

On the podium Graeme was the model professional rider, eloquent and gracious as he thanked the Northern Irish fans and the club for their support, joked about his start technique on concrete and making some points in the championship. *"I honestly think this is the best track in the UK"* he said and the crowd agreed.

Sunny weather always makes things better but it was a very successful weekend for the team and the perfect spring-board for the second half of the season. With neither rider going to the Indonesian fly-aways there was a month to be used wisely. The mechanics would get a short holiday, Ian had some work to do getting all the engines rebuilt to the preferred spec and the riders had time for a bit of rest and recuperation before putting in some hard work before Loket in the Czech Republic.

In the days after Desertmartin, Conrad received an e-mail congratulating him on his riding. The e-mail was sent by the same team manager who had allegedly protested him at the previous race at Blaxhall for jumping under waved yellow flags. Was it a sincere message of congratulations or someone playing mind games? The team took it as the latter. If that is the case it's a shame that senior figures in our sport think its acceptable to be so childish.

Chapter 17

ROUND 12, MXGP INDONESIA, PANGKAL PINANG, JAMIE DOBB – MX AGENT & THE HALF–TIME REVIEW.

Silly season had started early in 2018; it seems to get earlier every year but it's a big topic of conversation in the paddock as people livelihoods depend on securing a deal and it's usually a trickle-down process as the 'big' rider's deals are done first. Much of the conversation is just rumour and gossip but somewhere amongst the chit-chat there is often a glimmer of truth as a confidence is broken. The rumours as of mid-June where thus;

Glenn Coldenhoff out of Factory Redbull KTM to make way for Pauls Jonass coming up from MX2.

Coldenhoff and Tommy Searle both linked to Gebben van Venrooy Kawasaki, a Dutch team with a big money backer. Alessandro Lupino and Maxime Desprey were their current riders so that meant one or both was out.

Jeremy van Horbeek out of Factory Yamaha, replaced by Jeremy Seewer moving across from the factory backed Wilvo Yamaha team or Gautier Paulin if Husqvarna don't re-sign him or Coldenhoff.

Max Anstie out of Factory Husqvarna, replaced by Arminas Jasikonis.

Kevin Strijbos will retire from MXGP at the end of the season, so pretty much everyone linked to the vacant berth at Standing Construct KTM, especially Coldenhoff who had raced for them on a 250.

Shaun Simpson, Arnaud Tonus, Max Nagl, Julien Lieber and Tommy Searle are all said to be out of contract at the end of the year so there could be a lot of moves, but with a big group of riders set to age out of MX2 at the end of 2019, teams could be offering 1 year deals this time to keep their options open for 2020.

It also affects the mechanics. While some stay with the same team for years, some will move with their rider but there are always some that get 'let go' by their team for a variety of reasons. It looked like Vas would be in that category to me. He had been a bit belligerent about the parameters of his job on a few occasions and whilst Ian isn't a man for confrontation, he doesn't forget things like that. Vas told me that if he didn't get a firm agreement from Roger by the Czech GP he would be looking elsewhere. My guess is that Roger will deliberately not say anything as I knew he had already been approached by other mechanics about work in 2019. BC looked more secure. As I had gotten to know him, his pride and work ethic was very apparent and he really cares about the job. He's a total team player and is almost OCD about the presentation of the awning and his bike.... Great qualities in a mechanic that hadn't gone unnoticed by Ian, Howard and Roger. He also prefers the 250's so if the opportunity was offered to work with Conrad he would take it with both hands.

We'll come back to silly season (2018) later in the book (chapter 25) to see how accurate the rumours (and my hunches) turned out to be.

While we were at Ottobiano, I had dinner in the restaurant at the track on Friday with the team. That's the beauty of some of the permanent tracks in Europe, they have much better facilities than the pop-up events, and Ottobiano boasts shops and a restaurant. Most of the teams were eating there, including the Ice-one Rockstar energy Husqvarna team. All wearing their black team uniform, there didn't seem to be a lot of chat or fun going on at their table. One of the mechanics at my table was looking at them and said "everyone who goes to Ice-one turns into a prick. I've known some of those guys for years and now they don't even speak." The team is run by

Antti Pyrhönen, the Finnish ex-GP rider known to be a perfectionist. When Max Anstie had suffered his concussion in Redsand, Pyrhönen had been publicly supportive but I had heard rumours that he was far less supportive or sympathetic in private. He had (allegedly) become increasing controlling, micro-managing every aspect of Anstie's life, even telling him not to smile in public. (That message appeared to have been given to the rest of the team judging by their table in the restaurant.) Anstie's results had been below expectations since his crash but I had noticed that he had been far less glowing about the team lately and I suspected there had been a thawing of relations. In France I heard that Anstie was out of the team at the end of the year, although he denied it when I asked him. I was told that he was growing increasingly fed up with Pyrhönen's demands and took a week off after France; he was already out so what's the worst that could happen? He turned up in Ottobiano and went 3 – 4, tying his teammate for second overall but taking third on the tie-break. With the weight lifted he had his best result of the season, although it was noticeable that Pyrhönen was only cheering on Gautier Paulin and not Anstie. Once the decision is made it makes for a long second half of the season as teams seem to pull up the draw bridge, unwilling to spend money or resources on the departing rider beyond what is contractually necessary, while the riders still have to perform if they are to find a new team. It's like splitting up with your wife/girlfriend but neither of you can leave until the house is sold so you end up living together and suddenly everything she does annoys the hell out of you and vice versa. In private, Anstie had been linked to an HRC Honda deal, with the owner of Garibaldi Honda Racing talking to him before the race, much to Pyrhönen's annoyance. 'Dog in a manger' perhaps?

We were back in the restaurant on Sunday evening after the awning had been taken down and everything packed for an early start, 700 miles back to the workshop in Lommel. Sitting at the next table was Antonio Cairoli and his group, including Marco Melandri from MotoGP, the two Italian legends looked relaxed, chatting and laughing; a stark contrast to the sombre Ice one table on Friday. Cairoli had done the business, winning both races and cutting Jeffrey Herlings' lead to twelve points, the championship had been 're-set' so little wonder he was so chilled. Chad Reed had also been a guest at the GP, it seems to be a regular summer holiday/good will tour for his sponsors. He was in Europe doing some rally car tests, perhaps a hint towards his next career. At the track he was interviewed by Lisa Leyland, the most interesting comment was that he would love to race the MXON as his final motocross event. He's been a 'supercross only' only racer for a few years and it seems to be working for him.

With silly season starting early it's the time of year when managers and agents come into their own. If their rider needs a new deal it's their job to find the best home, a balance of the best possible material (bikes and parts), salary, bonuses and 'fit'.

Jamie Dobb is a riders' agent/manager/representative, but before he was an agent he was a racer competing in America for the all-powerful Pro Circuit Kawasaki team as well as a number of factory grand prix teams in America and Europe, and as the 2001 125 world champion he is Britain's last world champion on a big bike. One of his star clients is Conrad Mewse and whilst Conrad had a two-year deal with Hitachi/ASA KTM UK that included an option for the second year, I spoke with Jamie to find out what he does for Conrad, for the team and to get his take on the motocross 'scene' as it is now.

> ## Jamie Dobb – MX agent
> *"It was very different back in the day when I was racing. Me and Paul Malin (now the MXGP-TV commentator), nobody in the world could get near us but there wasn't the structure in place like there is today. There was a huge difference between Factory bikes and standards bike and we didn't have any of those luxuries. It's a crying shame that I only won one championship, Malin should have won some as well, but we didn't know what we were*

doing. When I was fifteen I turned pro and got third in the British championship then the next year went to the GP's, but I didn't know what to do. I just knew the races were fifty minutes long, so I needed to get to there. I made many mistakes in my past and got taken advantage of, and that's one of the reasons I do what I do today with the riders. On the management side it's very easy to take advantage of a rider and on the other side with the training aspect, so like with Conrad I do all his training which a lot of people don't know.

On the management side I help the guys do the deals and I find sponsors, I've brought sponsors into the team. I do quite a lot for the team, I brought the Husqvarna and KTM deals back to the team, just helping them where they need it. I've worked with Roger for a few years trying to get the team to a good level. It's my contacts and experience that make a difference, it's like anything, I'm not a good mechanic. Some riders try to do their own negotiations, but I can speak to the teams more honestly, and they're gonna tell me stuff about a rider that they wouldn't want to say to a rider. There's agents out there who maybe do it for the wrong reasons, like in football where they don't care about the athletes, but I care greatly about them. I do other jobs to make a living. If my guys make it then great but there's been a number of years invested in them to get them there. The teams want to pay the least possible, you could make more working in McDonalds than some of these riders make but the golden ticket is there if you make it. There are riders who make a good living but if you're motivated by money it's difficult. I was motivated by success, and success brings nice things with it, especially now more so than back then. We need to make stars of the stars of our sport. I'm Britain's last world champion and nobody knows me so trying to get outside sponsors in England... it's just not going to happen unless it's a fan of the sport, but if the guy making decisions is a *rugby fan he's gonna spend his money sponsoring a rugby team, but it shouldn't be like that.*

In Italy, Cairoli gets a lot of sponsorship, he won sports personality of the year last year. When I was world champion they wouldn't even give me a seat there, there was three of us, me, Dougie Lampkin in trials and Richard Burns from world rally, and they wouldn't give me and Dougie a seat. It also goes back to our federation, the ACU, its horrendous.

I made a lot of mistakes, it was trial and error because we didn't have the support. All the guys who've fought for titles since my day, I've trained. Tommy Searle lived with me for three years when he was going for championships, Conrad has been living with me. I'm not a trainer but I bring in the right people to help; I do know what's needed on the bike and I believe I can help with that. We have a trainer and a nutritionist we work with, I've got a core group of people. I wish I could do more but it's not my full-time job, so I do as much as I can. It's my business and it's my passion.

As far as Conrad goes, he's a complex kid like most athletes and everyone thinks they have the answers when really they have no clue, it's my biggest battle, too many advisors".

Roger had made the decision not to send Graeme and Conrad to Indonesia for the fly-away GP's a few weeks before when Graeme was coming back from injury and Conrad was in a slump. With them both riding well now it could be seen as a mistake but the reality is that the decision needed to be made well in advance to allow the necessary time to make all the arrangements to prepare and ship the bikes. With Graeme outside the top fifteen in points, the trip would be at his expense and for Conrad the priority was to keep him in his happy place and not risk any set-backs with long-haul flights, strange food and hot, humid conditions.

Half-time review.

It had been a rollercoaster of a season so far so I asked Roger, and then Howard to give us a half-time report.

Roger; *"We started with Conrad on a high then he lost his way for a few GPs. Graeme was where we expected him to be, top twenty or there-about and he's shown since Matterley that he's getting the intensity in the first few laps of the race but unfortunately he's now dipped off in the last few laps so hopefully in the next few months he'll get the intensity sorted out for the full race. The team set-up has gone OK, Lee has come around to our way of thinking in relation to set up and we've got the hospitality sorted out now for guests coming to the British championships. We use the S.O. Rentals vans to travel to the British and its working out well. The main advantage now at GP level is that we have a new truck driver called Jakke, he's based in Belgium and very experienced doing a similar job for other teams. We've seen the benefit from day one, he's getting on well with the other team members, doing a bit of cooking for them and looking after the awning. The issues we've had with Steve leaving and the riders results are typical of any other team really. Maybe the factory teams don't have the same changes throughout the season but at our level everyone has the same issues. Standing Construct had similar issues for example, we just need to have a strong second half and get some good results; everyone remembers the second half of the year. We have a contract for next year with Graeme and an understanding with Conrad that our team is the best place for him until he's ready to go back to a factory team. In the last few days I've heard some strange rumours that he's going to other teams but as far as I'm concerned he's staying. There's a lot of empty promises that get made but his manager is experienced enough to work out the good teams so I don't see him going anywhere else. We have a verbal agreement with KTM UK for next year but we need to sit down with the factory and see if*

Howard Smith and Jamie Dobb planning for 2019
Photo: Andy Gee

The future? L - R, Ryan ▶ Mawhinney, Cain McElveen and Connor Mullen

Previous victories (clockwise) Ben Watson, 2017 MX2 British champion, Shaun Simpson, 2015 MX1 British champion, and Josiah Natzke, EMX250 winner in Latvia, 2017

we can agree factory material for Conrad, if he gets some good results now that will make it easier. We've already had approaches from a number of other riders but the number one priority is keeping Conrad."

Howard; *"If we start with Graeme, we had a bit of a shock, we thought we had better pace than where we were and with the results not going how he wanted Graeme lost a bit of confidence. He had lots of distractions; went to California, didn't get a house, made lots of changes, did lots of mileage at the beginning if the year and wasn't very settled. As the season has progressed, very up and down and today at Desertmartin is probably the best I've seen him ride all year. Conrad had unbelievable speed at the beginning and does things on a bike that I haven't seen in all my life, but too many outside influences. He's started to settle down and realise what he wants and what he needs but took too long to realise what he has to do. I'm not sure yet if we've found it but we're going in the right direction, it's just unlocking that potential. I think we (the team) left them (Graeme and Conrad) alone to find their own level and only recently got involved to square them up when things went astray. I think it's only now that we will see some massive improvements in the second half of the season. Graeme's done a lot of testing with WP and got the bike how he likes it, got a house, got a base for his family life and it's going well but it's important to remember he's only rode one day riding at British championship level for the last six or seven years. MXGP is two days and it's intense from the start; it's two days flat out riding because Saturday is so important and maybe when it comes to the races he's a bit jaded. He needs to alter his training program to suit. Conrad is just younger and needs to knuckle down and find out what he really wants. Once he starts to believe in himself we've got a real weapon."*

Indonesia provided plenty of talking points, the drama starting when the flight carrying Herlings and Jonass had a near miss when its undercarriage had a problem on landing. Last year the race was ruined by torrential rain so it was moved back a month this year and out of the 'rainy season'. A week of heavy rain threatened to derail the event again but by Sunday the track was in good condition, albeit rutted, technical and sticky, but there were plenty of lines and all the riders could clear the jumps. The high humidity and thirty-degree temperatures were the main hurdle for the riders.

Jeffrey Herlings arrived playing down expectations having not ridden his bike since breaking his collar bone. Was he playing mind games? Its hard to tell but he was second fastest in timed practice then won the qualifying race on Saturday. On Sunday he finished second in the first race before taking the lead in race two and pulling away, a mistake by Cairoli giving him extra breathing room. When Herlings dropped the bike late in the race he was struggling to pick it up, perhaps the first sign of weakness in the injured shoulder. As Cairoli sailed by it looked like an easy win until he too fell a few turns later, injuring his thumb. Herlings remounted and took the win and the overall, an incredible feat by any measure and described by commentator Paul Malin as 'super-human strength'.

In MX2 South African Calvin Vlaanderen made history as he took his first victory in the class. It marked Honda's first MX2 win since Gajser's win at Assen in 2015, South Africa's first win since Tyla Rattray in 2008 and the first time anyone had broken the KTM/Husky stranglehold on the top step of the podium this year. It was an emotional victory for the young man, as tears flowed during his post-race interview and on the podium. Greg Albertyn, Grant Langston and Tyla Rattray are South Africa's previous motocross world champions; could Vlaanderen be the next?

Back in May the Guardian published a feature titled 'Avocado Hand', a light-hearted piece about a 'middle class' crisis due to the increasing number of people cutting their own hand as they tried to de-stone the fruit. What's that got to do with motocross? Max Nagl was the latest victim of 'avocado hand' and required stitches in his left palm making it painful and difficult to hold on to the bars. Anyone know the German word for 'Health and Safety'?

Chapter 18

ROUND 13, MXGP ASIA, SEMARANG, & DAVID LUONGO – YOUTHSTREAM VICE–PRESIDENT.

While the MXGP tour was in the far east, Graeme was at home with his brothers. Plenty of cycling with his brothers provided a great way to recharge and with all three being uber-competitive the cycling was bound to be intense. Conrad was keeping a low profile on social media but getting the work done. A couple of video clips showed him blasting around on what looked like private practice tracks, not as rough or gnarly as he would be facing at the grand prix.

With the second 'fly-away' also in Indonesia all the teams stayed away along with most of the riders. It was still a hike to the next event, a three-and-a-half-hour flight to the central Java island and then a road trip. At Pangkal Pinang last week there were only twenty riders in MX2 that included four locals, with twenty-five in MXGP that also included five locals. I don't want to appear disrespectful, but the local riders were so far off the pace in each group that it was pointless. If this is the elite level then there should be some sort of qualification level necessary to get a licence, not just taking a few wild-card entries to pad the gate. The cost of sending a rider and couple of staff over to Indonesia for the two races was about £20,000 so like Hitachi, many of the smaller teams chose not to go, especially if their rider was out of contention or carrying an injury. I have to say that I didn't make the trip, primarily due to the expense but with the team not going it seemed pointless anyway, so as I watched the race on TV I was keen to see how big the crowd was; it didn't look huge although the Youthstream press release claimed that 'Indonesian fans turned up in large numbers' with even more expected for this event due to it's close proximity to the metropolitan area of Semarang. A completely new track has been constructed for this event so none of the teams will have any data or previous bike settings, adding to the challenge.

It's easy to be critical of the decision to hold MXGP's in these far-flung corners of the globe where there appears to be little interest from the locals, questionable tracks and a lot of expense for everyone involved but there must be a good reason for going. The man to answer this question and many others, is David Luongo, Vice-President of Youthstream, a former professional footballer and the son of Youthstream founder Giuseppe Luongo. I said at the beginning of this book that running a team was a business and it would incomplete if we didn't discuss the role of Youthstream, the company that owns the rights to MXGP and runs the business that puts the whole show together. I met David in his office at the MXGP in Teutschenthal, which coincidentally was the two-hundred-and-fiftieth MXGP under the 'Youthstream' banner. Polite, articulate and focused, he has an air of confidence that you would expect from the boss of a global business.

Founded in 2004, Youthstream have transformed Grand Prix motocross in the last fourteen years. Many of the changes have been controversial; getting rid of prize money, man-made tracks and changes to the paddock area have been much maligned but with the series enjoying its highest ever profile, global TV and competitive racing that seems to have elevated the European riders above the Americans after years of US supremacy, it seems like the vision laid out back in 2004 is bearing fruit. David was happy to discuss all aspects of the business except the annual turnover, which is reasonable but inevitably leads to paddock speculation that puts it in the 30-50-million-euro range. I have no information to substantiate that guestimate but it's not a small amount, that's for sure.

David Luongo – Youthstream Vice-President.

David, could you just explain what it means when you are the rights holder for the FIM motocross world championships.

"Yes, to give you some examples it's like Dorna was in MotoGP or Ecclestone was in Formula 1, we own the rights for the marketing and promotion of the championship. Our aim is to develop and promote this sport world-wide, so our mission is to find organisers, TV, sponsors and to find the way to develop this sport."

When you find a new country or a new organiser who wants to host an MXGP what is the process?

"We have many different ways of making a race. in some countries the government see sports as a tool to advertise and promote their country so when it's like this, they are looking for events that could help the country to be well known, to attract tourists and new people or to talk about their country and have television worldwide, it happened in Qatar and also middle east is a bit like this. Then you have countries who have a strong history, like in Europe countries like Italy, France, UK with a big fan base. Then you have new countries with a huge dynamic of fans for motorsports like south America. When you go there to Argentina, Brazil for example, the people are crazy for motorsports, they are very passionate for all sports like football. And then you have countries where the industry is growing: countries like Turkey and south east Asia and China were the manufacturers sell a big number of bikes. To give you an example, in Indonesia the manufacturers sell more than eight million bikes a year so as a single market it is one of the biggest in the world.

So, we have these major reasons for a country to want to organise a race. Usually, through the federation or through a private organiser we get a request to organise an event. We enter a phase of negotiation, then we send people to inspect the site. We have to check that they can hold all the infrastructure. You can see today how many trucks and hospitalities are present at MXGP events; this infrastructure is very important to the organisation of the race and then there is the location to build the track. We have about five people who check everything, the track, the internet, electricity; if it's overseas, to provide tents, to provide facilities for the press, to provide hotels, where are the airports, this all happens before a race. it's a long process, it can take two years."

Do you consult with your partners and sponsors about the location of races?

"Yeah for sure. We always talk with the manufacturers to know which is the best direction for the industry, and also with the FIM, so it's a tripartite talk, but when it is considering the calendar and location of where MXGP goes we make the final decision as promoter of the championship."

You said how important the infrastructure is for the organisation of the race, can you explain what that infrastructure is, how many people are involved and what you provide for the organiser.

"Youthstream has eighteen trucks and more than one-hundred-and-fifty people. It's a big organisation. When you walk on the track you will see many things Youthstream does; we provide all the boards, many things that raise the level of the presentation like the Sky box and pit lane. For example, the Skybox and pit lane takes more than four trucks and twelve people working on it. Then we have the TV production to broadcast the races live world-wide, we bring three offices, all the bridges, start gate, hospitality. It's a lot of material that provides quality and professionalism of the event. If you watch the GPs since 2000, every year you can see more material, more

colour and more hospitality, and with this we always said we build the platform to promote the event, then the teams and the riders are the actors. We also develop a lot the last year a complete department linked to the sport and to the quality of preparation of the tracks, Rui Goncalves joined us last year to continue on this road. The better the platform, the more the actors can sell themselves to the sponsors and the fans, so this is our mission."

When Youthstream started in 2004 you reversed the philosophy of the organisation by getting rid of prize money and making riders pay to enter. A lot of people still disagree with that policy so can you explain why that happened.

"If we did not do this fifteen years ago we were not able to build this platform. I would just like to clarify that the prize money was paid by the local organisers (not the promoter), and with the extra money the local organisers and promoter have been able to invest in the promotion and infrastructure and work on making MXGP more professional, which I believe is quite obvious when you compare an event from the beginning of the 2000s to today. By making these investments into promotion via television, social network and media it allows the riders to make even more money than ever before. In the three or four years after this decision it was tough, but we only hear talk of this subject today from some old-fashioned thinkers because now all MXGP insiders see the fruits of this decision and are grateful for the professionalism brought through investment and hard work. In motorsports, the top twenty gain money, then you need to find the budget to participate. The only sport where you have hundreds of millionaires is football, and I know that because I was on this side before." (Note, David was a professional footballer before joining Youthstream.)

You have developed a pyramid system for riders coming through from 65's and 85's then the EMX125 and EMX250 championships which seems to be feeding into the MX2 class but in some races such as Latvia the entry list is quite low. Do you think that is just the cost of travelling to those countries?

"I believe it's because it's far to travel. We see for the last four years, every year the entries are increasing. Latvia is not central Europe so it's a bit far for many riders from Western Europe but we also have to bring the European championship there to give the opportunity to riders from that area to take part, this is how Jonass (young Latvian) was able to get into professional MX racing; there are many capable riders from East Europe and they need to have the same chance to be spotted as riders from Western Europe. Honestly, the pyramid is one of the best decisions we made because today the European Motocross Championship is strong with ten races for the kids that follow the world championship so they are used to racing on the same track as the pros, they are on TV like the pros, they are in the eyes of the team managers and part of the pro system so for them when they arrive in MX2 they already speak English, they know where to go, they know the system, so it's a fantastic school for the talented riders. There were more than eighty-five or ninety riders at the first three races, and for sure the further along we go into the season there will be less entries because when a rider realizes they don't have the results they had hoped for at the beginning of the season it's understandable they are not keen to travel too far. But how the European Championships are organised in a way that even if a rider doesn't qualify they still get race at least twice so they don't come and just ride for five minutes and then have to go home. Results are important, but for us and FIM-E the European Championship is above-all a school for the competitors be able to ride on a GP track

because they are the most demanding and technical tracks that exist and where young skilled riders can grow and show-off their talent."
That leads nicely onto the tracks. Some people think the old natural tracks were better and don't like the modern preparation or the man-made tracks like Assen. What is your answer to those people?
"First, what is a man-made track and what is natural? For the French a natural track is Saint Jean d' Angely with elevation and for the Dutch its Lierop which is flat, so it can be subjective. But to come back on circuit tracks like Assen that is an asphalt track that we transform, for us it is very important to attract new people. To do that you need infrastructure because you cannot bring new people that have never heard about motocross to a place where you need gumboots to get around in the mud (which many hard-core Motocross fans don't mind). This is reality, we love this sport but for some people that have never heard about it, it can be overwhelming. For us first it was very important to improve the infrastructure of the organisers, so when you go to places like Teutschenthal and Valkenswaard you will see impressive improvements. But it's also important to have at least three or four races a year where you can really showcase the sport to the sponsors and new fans. So Assen, Imola and Charlotte (when we went to the USA), are places where teams can bring potential sponsors like a banker or someone that will go not as a passion but for a show, just like you can go to a football game. We see that it works because we get the biggest number of spectators to these events, so it's not that we want to have half the season like this, we are passionate about traditional motocross, my father gave his whole life to motocross and I love it too, I was born in this sport, we just need to have some places where we can attract people that would normally not go to a motocross race without certain comforts. An important aspect as to why man-made tracks are valuable to the

World Championship is due to the fact that motorcycle evolution over the last years, especially concerning the suspension and electronics, have significantly increased the speed. For this reason, we have had to work very hard to reduce the speed keeping in mind the value of the sport, technique and the show, and this can be done only by creating obstacles and technical sections to considerably reduce the speed. Today the world and technology advances extremely fast and therefore we always face big challenges to adapt the Motocross tracks because for us the main issue remains the safety."

There are twenty races this year, are than any plans to add more races?

"No, it's a good number. With the MXoN it's twenty-one, it's a very global championship where we touch many markets so for us we want to consolidate the championship, to have better races, better infrastructure, and to always raise the level. For example, in Spain we have a new organiser and already the quality of organisation is premium, for us this is the next target to raise the level of organisation. Our goal is not to increase the number of races, it's to increase the quality of the races. In the US, riders are competing in 29 official events, while the MXGP riders are participating in 20."

We are going to China in 2019 but are there any other new countries you are looking at?

"South America, we are negotiating with a second country and we have been talking with Australia, we would like to bring MXGP back there. The two last historical markets where we would like to go is Australia and Japan, both are important to the manufacturers and for the fans but we're still in preliminary negotiations. We have twenty races with twenty-five organisers demanding to have an event so it's a very good sign. In 2004 it was twelve. It shows in one way that this sport is very dynamic, we want to maintain with twenty but

it's always a good sign when you have more demand than available races."

The MXoN is in the USA this year (2018) and there have been American GPs for the last few years. There seems to be more co-operation with Youthstream and MX Sport in America now, working together to promote the sport.

"You are right, cooperation with MX Sports is very constructive and we are on the same line now. Now to make more races It's up to the market to decide. We already tried to have the US MXGP in many locations and the best number of fans was in Charlotte. It was a very good event but also very expensive. Now for the MXoN we know it will be a great success, we already have pre-sales up twenty-five percent on the best previous MXoN event which was Maggoria, so it's very positive. Also, we see the response of the fans and the industry. Together with MX Sports we will have to evaluate the future of the US MXGP; we have to be sure that the US riders will participate, that it's useful for the industry and that it's craved for by the US fans, now it's too early to decide."

The provisional calendar for 2019 was published in the week between the Indonesian GP's. It's worth pointing out that there are usually some changes to the first draft but a few things jumped out. MXGP of Great Britain at Matterley Basin again but on March 24th! Expect a mud-fest if that date is confirmed. Two new fly-aways to Hong Kong then China (on Wednesday 1st May) are among six fly-aways. It is a truly global world championship but it will take a considerable budget just for travel costs. Many of the smaller teams are already struggling financially and the 2019 schedule could push some over the edge.

The support classes will also be racking up the mileage, for example the EMX300 championship has seven rounds including the Czech Republic,

Russia and Turkey while the EMX250 class will have at least nine rounds including Russia and Latvia two weeks apart.

Finally, the MXON will be held at Assen on the completely man-made track built on the road racing circuit; that should really upset the old school 'natural track' brigade.

Back to Semarang, and the track was well received by the riders. New, purpose build, hard-packed red clay with some huge jumps. It was another fast layout and didn't get very rough but the main challenge came from the track watering, turning parts of the track very slippery particularly in the early laps of each race with riders in each class caught out. Shaun Simpson had picked up an infection and flew home, while Arminas Jasikonis was battered from a crash last week so the already depleted gate was another two down. MX2 was hit even harder with fifteen riders in race two that included four local wildcards. The limited numbers didn't seem to dampen the racing though; KTM's MXGP hard men battling injuries, Cairoli in a lot of pain with a damaged left thumb lost a few points to his teammate Herlings with his still healing collar bone who managed another win and finally gave a small insight into his motivation each week.... To beat Cairoli while he is still at the top of his game.

One change that seemed to happen in Semarang was a cluster of penalties for not respecting waved yellow flags. Strijbos, Guillod and Searle all docked ten places in the qualifying race, Nagl and Coldenhoff docked ten places in race one. Its not a bad thing if riders are continuing to jump dangerously when waved yellows indicate no jumping but there has been some inconsistency with marshals getting carried away, frantically waving their flag when a stationary flag was sufficient.

In MX2 KTM teammate Jonass and Prado ended the weekend tied on championship points. While Jonass kept the red plate by virtue of more race wins it seemed that the momentum had swung in Prado's favour. In the overall championship table, Graeme was overtaken by HRC fill-in rider Todd Waters, dropping to 27th. Does that make any difference? Realistically none whatsoever, it's all about the British championship for Graeme where he is a title contender but in MXGP it's more about personal achievement and getting experience for another go next year. Bonuses stop at fifth place so there's no money at stake. For some riders championship momentum at this time of year is everything; those looking for a new deal. Coldenhoff confirmed he was moving to Standing Construct KTM for 2019 so that was one less place available for riders like Shaun Simpson who had been told he would not be re-signed at Wilvo Yamaha. Missing another GP was the last thing he needed particularly as he was overtaken by Tommy Searle in the championship. Both riders had missed GP's through injury, Searle had missed six and Simpson four but Searle was riding back into form just at the right time. It's surprising how short team managers' memories are, no one remembers the early season races if the late season results are good.

During the rider interviews they all said they were looking forward to going home, back to their routine and familiar food and surroundings. The hotel life is OK, but just like when you go on holiday it's always nice to come home. Was the Indonesia trip a success? If you asked Youthstream you would get a resounding 'yes'. The presentation in Semarang was first class with the track and facilities only receiving praise, except for the watering carried out by local track staff that need educating not to turn the jump faces into icy death traps. With a claimed 47,000 attendance, the grandstands looked full and there were long queues to get in, so if you consider what David Luongo said previously then it's a great business decision to bring MXGP to the bike mad far east markets, both for Youthstream and their partners who make and sell bikes, parts and clothing. If you're an old school purist who thinks there should be forty riders on the gate you will probably disagree, but the MXGP tour will be back again in 2019, you can be sure of that.

Chapter 19

ROUND 14, MXGP CZECH REPUBLIC, LOKET, LISA LEYLAND – THE FACE OF MXGP–TV & DISASTER IN DUNS.

There was a two-week gap after the Indonesian fly-aways, necessary to allow time to get all the infrastructure back to Europe. The week was filled with Brexit news as Boris Johnson and David Davis resigned from the cabinet over Prime Minister Theresa May's negotiating position, the headlines soon replaced with coverage of Donald Trump's visit to Britain. There was plenty of other sport for the sports fans to watch, Wimbledon tennis, the football World Cup and the first week of the Tour de France with a show-case stage to Roubaix that included 22km of cobbles, (the infamous pavé) on Sunday.

At the Sachsenring in Germany, the ninth round of MotoGP saw Marc Marquez take his ninth consecutive pole at the track, (the 48th in the premier class and the 76th pole of his career) and turn that into another win to remain unbeaten at that track. His career bears comparison to Herlings, as he has been the dominant riders of his generation and like Herlings, he's ruffled the feathers of the established stars, most notably Valentino Rossi, with his aggressive riding and 'never-give-up' approach. He's got a big personality and his rivalry with Rossi has seen them clash on and off the track, every incident making the headlines. But it's Marquez' riding style that has influenced the whole MotoGP paddock in much the same way as

James Stewart's 'Bubba scrub' changed motocross; everyone has had to learn the new techniques, elbow sliding and rear wheel steering. It's almost Darwinian; evolve or die. Maybe that's the beauty of all sport, it's ability to constantly refresh itself as techniques and equipment designs evolve and track designs change. However dominant an athlete or team is in any given era that domination is bound to end as a younger, faster gun comes through; it's the circle of life in team colours.

The decision not to go to the fly-aways meant the team had something of a summer break. BC went home to spend more time with his new baby, Minty visited his mate, Vas went home to work on his house while Ian had time at home. *'It was nice to have some time off, it's the first time I've had time off in the season since………. I can't remember when. You think you've got time to catch up but it just goes; we've only got one free weekend until the end of the season and there's some long trips to Bulgaria and Turkey, it's difficult trying to plan how we're going to do it, and the MXON for Graeme'.*

The free weekend was filled with national championships in Germany and the Zwarte Cross festival in Holland, one of the biggest race weekends of the year as it runs alongside a music festival and the last round of the Dutch masters. At home, Graeme spent a few days with his family in Northern Ireland that included doing a track day with his brothers, Graeme riding a 600-super-sport, Glenn on a 959 Ducati and Andrew on a 1000cc Suzuki. The different displacements meant to uber competitive Irwin boys couldn't have a fair race so how could they decide once and for all who is quickest? Simple, run the "Fastest Irwin Challenge". The event will take place after the season and be comprised of a day racing motocross, a day racing super-moto and a day racing short-circuit (road bikes). With support from Alpine Stars, the Hitachi team, KTM and the BBC interested in making a TV program it could be good for moto-cross, motor bike racing and Northern Ireland. It remains to be seen if it will actually settle to argument about who is the fastest Irwin.

Next stop was Scotland to stay with BC and train. Graeme wanted/needed race time to hone his race-craft so a wild card entry to the MX Nationals at Canada Heights was the ideal race for him to face enough competition to keep him on his toes but also build some confidence. Taking pole in qualifying, 1.16 seconds faster than his Maxxis British championship rival Jake Nichols was the perfect start to the day. 3 – 2 moto finishes for second overall was enough to keep his mechanic BC happy before he headed to the workshop to get the bikes ready for Loket. Graeme was left frustrated as the mixed displacement classes meant he was stuck behind the fast-starting Mel Pocock (riding a 250) for a few laps that allowed Nicholls the chance to build an unassailable lead. From there it was across to Belgium for more sand riding accompanied by Minty and suspension testing with WP. That might seem like a strange decision with a hard-packed track next but most, if not all of the GP riders train in sand all the time for technique and fitness, only using hard-packed tracks for bike set-up. The testing was positive as Graeme had been unhappy with the rear shock all season and finally WP identified a solution. *'We found a little problem and fixed it... I hope. I feel like we're making improvements'*.

The Czech Republic round would be the start of a twelve-week run to the end of the season with just a single weekend off in September so it means three months hard work for the mechanics with little opportunity for time off. For the riders an injury now could be costly with no time to recover. Unfortunately, Conrad was the victim of a freak accident that put him out of action for Loket. Riding at a public track, he crashed into a fallen rider, taking the full brunt of the impact in his leg. The impact had caused a large haematoma but more seriously an x-ray revealed that he had dented his femur, as the leg had taken the full impact of the crash. He was lucky that the bone wasn't fractured but the advice was emphatic; *'complete rest for week or you'll probably end up unable to ride for a few months'*. With the MX2 championship long gone it was decided that he should rest as ordered and try to be fit for the British championship in Scotland a week later. As Ian put it, *"the British championships are the priority as we can still win that; in MXGP we just want to get the best results possible for Conrad, the team and KTM".*

I caught up with Conrad a few weeks after the crash and he told me *"I was doing my second moto of 30 plus 2, I came over a big jump and there were tow bikes in the track. I landed literally into the bikes so there was nothing I could do. It was a big crash; the bike came over and landed on my leg quite hard. I had a massive haematoma on the top of my leg and we thought that was it but I couldn't walk so after a couple of weeks I went to my physio. She started doing stuff to it, then cancelled all of her days work and took me to hospital. The x-ray showed I had put a dent in my femur. That obviously put things back, I couldn't do a single thing. It was quite tough to deal with, I couldn't do any fitness or cycling".*

TM was absent from Czecho, their 450 rider Nagl was injured but the surprising news was that they had sacked their MX2 rider Samuele Bernardini. A press release was suitably vague and politically correct with Marco Ricciardi Team Manager saying *"The path made up to last year with Samuele was very satisfying, with ups and downs but in the end we always achieved the goal, our goal was to bring Samuele to conquer the top five of the MX2 in this is his last year in this fantastic class. I wish Samu to find his dimension and work hard to honour the great talent he was given."*

The paddock rumour was the Bernardini had got a new girlfriend and had lost his focus on training and practicing, with TM growing increasingly exasperated by his lack of effort and results. He had been with the brand since 2013, winning the EMX300 championship in 2014 and finishing eighth in the MX2 championship in 2016. 2017 was wrecked by a mid-season injury and his 2018 season had been inconsistent, lying fifteenth in the championship. He had not gone to the two Indonesian rounds but whatever the truth behind his sacking, it was an unusual time to let your only MX2 rider with only six relatively cheap European GP's left, and especially with such a long history. Something had obviously gone badly wrong with the relationship. Almost before the ink was dry on the TM press release there was another announcement from ATES4-TESAR Yamaha to say they had recruited Bernardini for the remainder of the season. He would be moving up the 450's in 2019 so it was potentially a make-or-break opportunity.

Loket is a hard-packed track and one of the more 'old-school' venues with elevation changes and a 'natural' feel than many of the modern tracks. Television doesn't do justice to just how steep the hills are as the camera seems to 'flatten' the track but TV coverage is one of the main areas that Youthstream have improved the most since they took over. The races are broadcast live around the world, along with MXGP-TV on-line. Lisa Leyland is the 'face' of MXGP-TV. While ex GP racer and MXON champion Paul Malin does the commentary, Lisa co-hosts the TV studio show with him but also covers all the rider and team features, plus start line interviews before the races and post-race reactions from the winner. In a nice switch of roles, Lisa became the interviewee to tell me what she does.

Lisa Leyland – the face of MXGP–TV.

Lisa, how did you become the TV presenter for Youthstream?

Before Youthstream I studied media, journalism, TV and film at university, so I always knew I wanted to get into this line of work. I did some odd bits of film and TV, I did the travel channel and things like that just to get experience. I met someone when I was doing that in 2008 who knew someone that was looking for a presenter for motocross. I hadn't done much in sports, but I did some reading, checked out the website and thought it was something I could be interested in, so I sent my show reel to Youthstream, had an interview and got the job.

You were here from the start of Youthstream's TV production, has your role evolved over that time?

Yeah it has. I did it for a few years then left so I haven't been here all the way through. I came back in 2015 and couldn't believe how much it had changed. For starters in 2008 there was no social media, at least not like it is today. Now it's a huge part for all the riders, team, media and journalists. We weren't live on Saturday for the qualifying races, we were only live on Sunday for MX2 and MX1 as it was then, and we didn't have all the support classes so in terms of my role it's a lot more involved now, there's a lot more to do and it's a lot busier. How does the weekend show get planned? Is there a production meeting in the week? I notice that you always have your notebook in your hand when you're interviewing riders so it looks like there's a lot of thought that goes into it.

I get here on a Thursday, then we have a TV meeting, not just about my work but what support classes are here, if the academy is here, what channels are broadcasting and any special media events. In terms of my work, I do all my note myself. When I'm interviewing the guys on the grid I see what happened in qualifying, but I also go on their social media. You can get so much information, even personal stuff that you can throw into a question so I write that down. I already know who I'm going to interview so I just have back-up notes.

You have a great rapport with Paul Malin, do you plan your interviews? *Paul does loads of prep for his job. Our roles are completely different because he's doing live commentary but he knows the sport inside out. He used to race so he's looking at it from a different angle to me. With the studio show we have a script that he's done because he acts like a producer for the show, but we get on great as friends as well as colleagues so that makes a difference, we know how each other work.*

When you're doing the live interviews during the races it seems like you try to 'spread the love' so that you're not just interviewing Herlings' team manager every week. How do you decide who to interview during the race? *Generally, we try to interview all the manufacturers and teams but it is hard sometimes because the sport is dominated by Red Bull KTM; they're the ones at the front and that's where the story is. If the cameras are following a rider, with the pit lane interviews I have to interview the team of that rider, it's quite spontaneous. If the cameras are following Jeffrey and Tony which is often the case it makes sense to interview a member of the KTM team and tie it all together. I try to mix it up with the start line interviews.*

I'm smiling now as I'm thinking about this question. You did a pit lane interview with Ian from Hitachi KTM in Redsand when Conrad was battling with Prado. Ian is very quiet at the best of times and he just gave you one-word answers which probably makes your job quite difficult.

It's just part of the job (laughing). There're the guys that I interview all the time, they've had their media training and they know what to say in front of the camera. When I interviewed Ian, his team were having a good race and the cameras were following Conrad so it made sense to interview him but some people are just shy in front of the camera. For me it's not a problem, sometimes when I interview the riders, especially the young ones they get really nervous, they just see a camera and freeze but you just deal with it.

I know you probably shouldn't have a favourite but is there anyone you find really easy to interview?

I don't really have favourites as such because I think in my role it's important to remain neutral but obviously I've known some of the guys for years and interviewed them a lot. Shaun Simpson is so easy to talk to, always accommodating for us, always got a friendly and even if he's having a bad day he's smiling and makes it easy for us. Tony (Cairoli) is so used to the cameras, Max Anstie is so animated, I ask one question and he can talk for fifteen minutes, he's a great guy.

Are there any developments in the pipeline for expanding MXGP-TV?

No major changes are foreseen at the moment but I think social media is going to be the key. This year we've started to do the Instagram stories on MXGP, that's new and it's just a way to get behind the scenes.

Thanks Lisa.

You're welcome!

With Conrad missing the race it was bitter-sweet for his mechanic, Vas. His family home is about an hour and a half away from Loket so his family and friends were at the event to see the man in action. Without a rider he had time to chat with them in the hospitality area, but he would have preferred for them to see him in action, spinning wrenches. BC had a relatively easy weekend, the only drama being a leaking gear shaft seal and a stripped thread in the clutch case that required a quick heli-coil. Graeme felt positive, the new suspension settings would hopefully cure his handling issues. Sixteenth in free practice, fifteenth in timed practice and sixteenth in the qualifying race was his best Saturday at a GP. It could've been better as he battled with Evgeny Bobryshev for eight laps before crashing and losing four places. Afterwards he said *'the Russian roadblock..... we hit a few times but I just couldn't make the pass stick. I was trying everything to get by, went wide and lost the front end.'*

Ian was impressed with Graeme's riding; he looked aggressive and while he was battling Bobryshev they had pulled away from Gautier Paulin. The teeth on the front sprocket had started to hook so there was no doubt that he was twisting the throttle hard. I had a look at the burns on Graeme's back; he said they were no longer painful but the skin still looked very dry, tight and red to me, and still needed dressing to protect it when he was riding.

Unfortunately, Graeme's starts in the main races remained the weak link in his arsenal. Starting in the mid-twenties, he had to battle with the wild-card riders which saps time and energy. 'Sending it' over the big triple jump was a bold move that got him up to twenty-first place but no points in the first race. Second verse, same as the first as he was again squeezed going into the first corner although he did manage to grab the final point in twentieth. A pragmatic Facebook post the next day conveyed his feelings. *"I'm working so hard and just so frustrated that I couldn't show it in the races. But this weekend has been good in some respects and we are definitely starting to go in the right direction - just two bad starts killed it. There's nothing I need to change now about my preparation for the races,*

I'm training hard and it will all come together."

Behind the scenes the team were being uncharacteristically proactive with their plans for the next year. Although Graeme had a two-year deal, it turned out that Conrad's deal with KTM meant that there was a possibility that he could be moved to another team, or even the factory team. It was highly unlikely that KTM would force such a move against his wishes and he seemed completely happy with the team, but it doesn't hurt to have a plan 'B' so possible replacements were being considered.

Ian had also been approached by four mechanics putting the feelers out. I asked if that was unusual at this time in the season. *'Not really, some teams might be cutting back or the mechanic losing his rider. The four that have approached me are quite young, the reality is that not that many people can do the job, it's not as easy as just turning up wearing a team shirt.'*

There was some tension building again between the mechanics; Minty had been moaning and it was starting to grate on the others. He had previously annoyed Jakke by picking fault with some omelettes that Jakke had cooked for the mechanics. I don't think he realises he's doing it but the affect can be quite demoralising which is the last thing that is needed at this stage of the season. Jakke had told him to 'f##k off and cook his own' while BC had a word about his negativity. It may seem petty when you read this but when you spend so much time in each other's pocket there needs to be harmony otherwise you soon end up wanting to kill each other!

Roger had been busy too, pushing KTM and Milwaukee for their commitment so that he could plan for next year. I picked up whispers of a third rider coming to the team but I couldn't get either Roger or Ian to talk..... yet! Jamie Dobb was also at the GP, not really surprising as he represents a number of riders. With Lommel just two weeks away it was anticipated that a few more deals would fall into place then and even if they weren't made public agents like Dobb would be aware as 'seats' got filled. The situation is dynamic; for example, I heard from a very good source that Gautier Paulin had been offered another contract with Husqvarna as expected but with a huge pay cut. Everyone had assumed he would be staying at Ice One Husqvarna but the story in Loket was that he was incensed by the offer and looking elsewhere, opening the door for Max Anstie to stay after being told he was definitely out the door just a month before.

Another more interesting rumour from the team's point of view concerned their sponsor/partner Lee Tolan. While I was interviewing riders for my regular report for www.dirtbikerider.com I was told that Tolan was definitely splitting with Hitachi and running his own team next year. The rider was quite emphatic although he had no connection with the team, but was this the first sign that the marriage of convenience was about to end or just another silly season rumour? If true, what would happen to Graeme? Lee was only interested in the domestic championships and Graeme's MXGP support came from Roger so a 'divorce' could lead to a custody battle. Roger was also the link to KTM and it seems most unlikely that they would have the budget or desire to support a breakaway ASA team.

Duns

The next round of the British championship in Duns might offer some information.

After the mini heatwave with record temperatures recorded around Britain and hose pipe bans put in place, the weather broke in the days before the Maxxis British championship arrived in Scotland for the sixth round, with gusting winds and thunderstorms shutting Edinburgh airport and lashing the east coast track.

Almost as soon as he arrived at the track BC was back in the van and heading for home 86 miles away. This wasn't for cosy night by the fire but for an engine swap. Graeme and he had decided that he could get better starts with the more powerful engine so BC was off to his workshop rather than doing it at the track. I chatted with him on the phone as he was driving back, his enthusiasm for his job is incredible. There was no hint of annoyance at spending a Saturday evening working on his race bike and the chance to grab a few minutes with his kids was a bonus. He said he would rather work on the bike in his own workshop even if it meant extra driving. The team had already approached him about continuing to work with them for 2019 and I felt pleased for him, his relentless hard work was noticed and appreciated.

On Sunday morning the hard-packed circuit was in prime condition despite the rain, although shorts and sun cream had been replaced by jeans and winter jackets. Conrad again took pole but only two tenths of a second clear while Graeme was on fire, 2.27 seconds faster than Bobryshev, Searle and Monticelli. The latter three were all faster than Graeme in Czecho but he seems to get some extra self-belief in the domestic series.

Unfortunately, qualifying was the highlight for the team as the event turned into a disaster. Rain started before the first MX2 race and didn't stop. Conrad was forced to pull into the pits for goggles after getting completely filled in. He worked his way back up to eighth before a crash dropped him to fourteenth at the flag.

Graeme's race lasted just three corners as he was hit from behind. The impact bent the rear sprocket and chain guide, causing the chain to derail and rendering his bike unridable. At that moment all prospects of defending his title evaporated; when the day was over he would be 47 points behind Jake Nicholls and 35 behind Bobryshev with only three rounds left. Between the races the conditions deteriorated and spectators went home, soaked by the driving rain that had left standing water around much of the track as a fog also rolled in making visibility across the track tricky.

In the second MX2 race Conrad came from a long way back after a dire first lap. With mud obscuring the race numbers it became difficult to identify the riders when the live timing failed. Conrad battled through the field to finish second as the unheralded Jay Hague took his maiden victory in horrendous conditions, the lap scorers somehow able to keep track of the places. Conrad was happy with his riding, catching Hague by nine seconds on the last lap but ultimately a second short. He was magnanimous afterwards, "Jay is one of my best mates so I'm happy for him to win. It was nice for me and him to go one-two, I know how hard he works and how much him and his family put in".

It had become a battle of survival but when the fog got worse it left the organisers little choice but to cancel the final MXY2 youth race and the second MX1 race. BC was fuming; it meant there was no possibility for Graeme to redeem himself and claw back some points. Roger wasn't happy, especially when he received some information later that suggested another team manager had influenced the decision to abandon the second MX1 race, (the same team manager that had interfered at Blaxhall) because he was concerned that his rider would lose points in the muddy conditions.

If there was a bright spot it was that Conrad had retained his championship lead although it had been cut from 31 points to just 23 points. On the ASA side of the awning, Lee Tolan's MX2 rider Michael Ellis had his best results of the season with a seventh and thirteenth, although that was small consolation for Roger.

I spoke to Graeme after the race to get his thoughts.

You were 2.27 seconds faster than anyone in qualifying, including GP guys like Tommy Searle, Bobryshev and Monticelli that you seem to battle with at the grand prix. Do you come into the British championship races with a different mindset?

"No. If you look at Ottobiano and Loket, we've been good and turned over a new leaf. We've been testing with WP and found a problem that I've been complaining about all year and fixed it, that made a big improvement to the bike but to be honest I've been working really hard. When I go to the GPs I don't know the tracks as well as some of the tracks at home but in Loket I had good speed all weekend. On Saturday Boby was holding me up until I crashed. I'm still building confidence but I don't think speed has ever been my problem, it's just been hard to show that at the GPs sometimes but hopefully we can show it for the rest of the year."

Has the approach got to change now?

"Before Duns we were still in a really good position. We've got the speed to win so the championship overall was still within our grasp. Now we need mistakes from other riders. There's still three rounds left, six races so it's

not over until its over. I can't believe I'm still third, but I need to win races and everyone else to have a bad day, that's why I really wanted the second race to run at Duns. I know it was about rider safety and I know they made the right decision, Gareth Hockey is a ballsy guy and he's not afraid to run tough races like Weston and he doesn't cancel easily but I understand why they cancelled. But for me I would've loved it to run."

Next weekend we head to Lommel. Is that a race that you look forward to or just want to survive?

"I'm really, really looking forward to it. it's the track where all the hard work shows and I've definitely put the work in. Me and Mel (Pocock) have been going there all season, looking for tougher tracks. You can't prepare for this race in a week or two or three, there's a lot of work goes into it. I wanna be top twenty in qualifying then go for it in the races and be top fifteen, that's my plan."

The bikes were washed off and loaded into the sprinters for the long drive back to the workshop in Belgium. At least next weekend there wouldn't be any driving, the workshop is at the back of the Lommel track.

Chapter 20

ROUND 15, MXGP OF BELGIUM, LOMMEL, SHAUN SIMPSON'S PERFECT WEEKEND & HAWKSTONE.

Belgium has a long and illustrious place in motocross history with many legendary Grand Prix tracks. Namur is probably the most famous track, with the huge citadel and fortifications atop the hill before the narrow decent down through the woods onto the road where Hakan Carlqvist stopped to chug a beer on his way to winning the GP in 1988. The Citadel track is now a tourist attraction, consigned to mx history but the most imfamous track has to be Lommel. The deep sand circuit near the border with Holland is like a home race for most of the paddock as the epicentre of European motocross. Most of the GP riders, teams and industry suppliers are based in the area (the team workshop is next to the track along with Rockstar and Revo Husqvarna), but it is the Lommel track that holds the key. On any given day you will find European championship and GP riders pounding out laps; it's the best way to get the bike time they need on the most brutal and unforgiving track in the world. If you can survive here you can ride anywhere. The track has plenty of history; way back in 1981 it was the venue that started the American domination of the MXdN as it was then when they won the Trophee des Nations for 250cc bikes in the deep sand, then the 500cc MXdN the following weekend in Germany. For

Hitachi KTM it is the site of their best weekend ever at an MXGP when Shaun Simpson dominated in 2015. His incredible story of that weekend is coming up shortly. It was part of an amazing weekend for the Brits as Max Anstie won the MX2 class and Brad Anderson won the EMX300 class.

This year the week didn't start quite as well for the team as BC was bitten by the guard dog at the workshop. It was quite a nasty bite on his right leg that drew blood so BC got some antibiotics from the local pharmacy. Unfortunately, he turned out to have an allergic reaction that caused a severely upset stomach and nausea. *'I don't feel like I can fart with any confidence'* was my favourite quote on Friday as he rushed to the bathroom.

Saturday was hot...32 degrees, which made for some pleasant conditions for spectating and chatting but less comfortable for racing. The awning was full on Saturday morning with lots of Brits making the trip to Lommel for their annual GP weekender. Roger was at the race and had given instructions for extra hospitality as he was expecting a number of special guests and sponsors, plans already developing for next year. There was a good buzz. A blast from the past also showed up; Steve 'Hendo' Henderson was back from Thailand, already bored with retirement. It was too good to miss the opportunity to give him some abuse, "Hello homeless, quick someone take a photo of Hendo smiling". He was in good spirits, "of course I'm smiling, I'm in the happy side of the awning". He had no plans to look for another full-time mechanic job but said he'd like to be a practice bike mechanic just to keep occupied. Despite all his protestations last year it was in his blood and like most of us have found, it's hard to walk away from this sport.

While we all love the sport, I said right at the start that running a team is a business. If more proof of my theory was needed, Carglass Honda is that proof. Set up to compete in the EMX250 championship with Dutch rider Freek van de Vlist and Brit Steven Clarke, the team looked the part with a big truck, big awning and all the team paraphernalia. Clarke is a very likeable journeyman pro. I don't mean that with any disrespect, as he's achieved a lot. 2005 85cc world champion, 2007 Loretta Lynne 250A champion and 2014 EMX250 champion, he's raced in America, Australia,

Europe and around the world as a sort of 'gun for hire', having fun and making a great living. Always positive and professional, it's hard not to like him. I had interviewed him a few times for my dirtbikerider.com column and it was clear to me that there were problems with the team (slow bikes and not delivering what they had promised) but Clarke was always discreet, once telling me 'I'm a professional, I'll make it work'. By late July the team had collapsed and I would finally get the truth. Set up by team owner Peter with team manager Patrick, it had started well but the pair had only run a small amateur team in Holland before and were out of their depth. Patrick had set up deals with sponsors and suppliers but most of the agreements were not written down, and even where there were contracts they weren't followed up. The pressure soon built and Patrick quit. Peter tried to carry on but without all the information (because much of it was in Patrick's head) the end was inevitable. There was money available but no sponsors were ever sent an invoice so they never paid the money promised, and rightly so. Without an invoice there are all sorts of tax and money-laundering implications. Clarke was quick to stress that Peter had paid him up to the end, but the team had no-where left to go and so it folded. To me it seems like basic business to document agreements, get contracts drawn up and signed, and most importantly to invoice your customers, in this case the sponsors are your customers buying advertising space on your truck, bikes and riders. Without money coming in no business can survive for long, it's called cash flow and has been the downfall of many businesses.

Lommel seems to be an important race for all the riders, many hoping their hard work will be rewarded at the toughest, roughest track of the year. The undisputed sand master is Jeffrey Herlings and during Saturday's sessions he put on riding clinic. Almost 3 seconds quicker in free practice, his mechanic then lined his bike up early for the start of timed practice but was beaten to the front of the queue by Max Anstie and Harri Kullas. When Herlings arrived, he positioned his handlebars in front of Kullas who didn't protest. When they were released by the marshal at the end of the pit lane, Herlings darted ahead of Anstie and on his first lap put in a blistering time five seconds faster than anyone. As he came past the back of the mechanic's area he was given a thumbs-up and pulled off the track. Cairoli eventually closed the gap to 1.18 seconds with Febvre 2.55 seconds behind, but the time wasn't the important bit, it was Herlings' display as the Alpha male, pushing in front of Kullas, getting to the front and in a single lap demonstrating his dominance. If he was a lion he would have sprayed his musk over the whole group. During the qualifying race he took the lead on the first lap and cruised around but still winning by sixteen seconds. I say cruising because his fastest lap was two seconds slower than he had gone in timed practice but he was still sixteen seconds ahead in a twelve-lap race.

Saturday couldn't have gone much better for Conrad and Graeme. Conrad was second in free practice and third in timed practice. In the quali race he ran in third for half the race before his fitness started to tell and he lost a spot. His leg was 80% healed but he had taken complete rest for three weeks, losing a bit of race fitness as a consequence. Graeme was also in a confident mood. Fifteenth in timed practice boosted him further and despite a poor start he worked his way from twenty-fourth to sixteenth, much more in line with his pre-season expectations for himself and his pre-race goal. It reflected under the awning, the atmosphere was so happy and positive. It was a stark contrast to the dark days in Portugal when everyone was demoralised and down. Of course, the sunshine helped but it was the rider's performances that had made the difference, both riding to their limit and delivering results that everyone could feel pleased with. Hopefully it would continue on Sunday.

Riders, mechanics, trainers, teams and sponsors all work towards one goal; winning. A few riders achieve that goal, some more often than others, but the history books are full of great riders that never won. The reasons are complex but in simple terms they never put all the pieces of the jigsaw together on the same day. On the 2nd of August 2015, Hitachi KTM rider Shaun Simpson put the pieces together, with a dominant victory at the Belgium MXGP, at the roughest, most brutal track on the calendar, Lommel. It was a near perfect weekend but came so close to disaster. It's one of my favourite stories, told here in Shaun's own words.

" Shaun Simpson's perfect weekend.

"I was riding for Hitachi, Dad was my mechanic, and my brother Stefan was doing my suspension and John Volleberg was doing my engines. Things were going well, we started the year solid in Qatar, Argentina was good. There were a few guys out, Villopoto looped out, and Nagl was leading but got injured, but I was consistent. I had a fifths and sixths overall and was pushing, Maggoria was good and I just missed the podium. We were on a roll, feeling good with the bike. We'd done our pre-season testing and training, then more testing and kept getting the bike better every two or three GPs. We had more information from the year before, it was the same bike so we started with that, we were just doing our own thing, I was doing a lot of work on my own bikes as well, dad was doing the race bike so I would do my practice bike, wash it, filters and stuff and we've always built the race bike together on the Wednesday or Thursday before the GP. We were always short of time and often I'd go practicing on my own or with a mate. With the workshop being at the back of Lommel I would get changed there and ride around to the track, do a moto then ride back, refuel and have a drink then ride round and do another 40-minute moto. Leading up to Lommel I was doing that two or three times a week for about four weeks, so I had 12 forty-minute motos in the bank. I hated 50% of them, the track was hard, the practice bike was a bit of a dog, I'd been working all morning, maybe late the night before, sometimes I'm riding round thinking 'there's gotta be an easier way, maybe I could have this afternoon off', but I always felt a sense of accomplishment after I'd finished it. We could drive home that night at ten o'clock after doing the race bike thinking 'Lommel's in a couple of weeks, it'll do me no harm'. Dad was always a believer of 'toughen you up', it's not easy. I remember one time; the foot peg spring broke

half way through. I fixed it then went out and finished my moto, where I could've said 'I've done twenty minutes, that'll do'. I remember on that lead up, Febvre and Paulin were there just about as much as me, but my speed was good. Dad would come sometimes and even he said I looked good, launching the jumps a bit further. Looking back at now, launching the jumps and landing on the next bump meant in the race when I was launching the quad I just felt good on my bike, the confidence was there. We probably had our focus set on Lommel without really knowing it. I'd rode there well before, I had a podium behind Cairoli and DeDycker in 2014, it was close to home and the workshop and we didn't have time to drive elsewhere so I practiced there a lot.

We had a weekend off just before Lommel and I remember going to a festival with my mates, I even had a beer or two and it felt really relaxed. I was doing what needed to be done and I was enjoying it; there was no big pressure from myself, dad or the team, it was just go and put 100% effort in, that was never questioned especially working with my dad. If I put in 95% he would see it and even if I'd finished in say fourth, if I wasn't giving 100% I'd get a bollocking. It wasn't about the results it was about the effort, race to the flag.

The routine wasn't perfect, working late, grease on my hands, I could hardly fit in my training but that was what we had to do to go racing, and the results on a Sunday were good so it was working, it was good times.

On the Friday I had to do some TV and photos with Youthstream because of the podium the year before. I'd had my hair cut and it all felt good, that 'look good, feel good' thing. It was a bit hectic, but nothing fazed me.

What started the series of good event was when I went out on track on Saturday. Within two or three corners, the bike feels mint, simple as that. It's weird how you just get a reaction that quickly.

I rolled a lap, then whacked in a fast one, in the pits, checked my sectors, back out, bam, do the quad. It was as easy as that, no real thought went into it. We ended the session in first which was the goal. The bike felt fine, suspension good, and it just started that air of confidence that you want from a weekend.

I wasn't fastest in timed practice, so it wasn't the perfect weekend (he was third in timed practice) but I won the qualifying heat, I can't remember the details but it was sweet.

I had to go to the press conference and had a few pulls with interviews. Villopoto was at the press conference as an invited guest. All that takes about an hour and by that time dad had washed the bike and found something wrong. He'd made the decision to go back to the workshop and I was going home to get away from everything and I remember feeling super guilty about leaving him to do that work while I went home to relax. I felt that bad, I even drove round to the workshop with Rach to see him before we went home. No other rider/ mechanic relationship would even make you feel like that because it would be 'that's my mechanic, bike's gotta be done, I'm going home', but that wasn't my thing. Not one part of me felt nervous, I trusted him 100% and if he thought there was a problem he'd have it fixed even if he had to work all night, I just felt that I should have stayed with him, even if it was just to chat to him. A couple of our friends from home were there with him so I could leave them to it and go home."

(Note. When he was washing the bike, the rear wheel wouldn't spin. It turned out to be a bearing in the gearbox that was seizing up. Dad, Willie worked until the small hours, stripping the engine completely and replacing the faulty bearing. Whether it would it have lasted the race we will never know but Willie told me that he couldn't take the chance, he couldn't live with himself if it had failed and Shaun was injured as a consequence. It would have been easier to simply put a spare engine in, but this was the race engine.)

"I got up on Sunday and the sun was shining. I put on some shorts, had my breakfast and just felt relaxed. As we were leaving the house I just knew we were gonna have a perfect day. I just felt it. I don't know at that point if I thought it was gonna be a 1 – 1, or if I was just gonna win the GP, I never doubted it. I've read loads of books on phycology and telling yourself you're gonna win and it hadn't worked for me before, and it hasn't worked for me since but that day.......... I felt it. I wasn't telling myself, I didn't tell Rachel or my dad, but I just felt it. As we left the house we took a selfie on the drive.

I went out for warm-up and in the first corner the bike stopped. I pushed it back and dad was 'what's wrong?' It turned out to be the woodruff key, it had sheered, and the flywheel had just moved. There was an element of panic then, everyone was getting worked up for me, other riders and teams looking but I wasn't bothered. I just walked back to the camper all clean and set my gear down and put that same stuff back on for the first race. It wasn't the perfect morning but maybe that was part of the recipe. Perhaps if I'd gone out and got fifth my mental state would've been knocked, or maybe I would've gone pole, we'll never know.

Some people psych themselves out before Lommel. I knew the motos would be tough and I'd have to ride at a hundred percent, but I could do two 40-minute motos with my finger up my nose, I'd done hundreds. Coming to the race I knew my starts were the only thing I had to worry about, once I got around the first corner I would be fine. I was on the inside and if I made a reasonable start I'd be OK and that's what happened in both motos, I think I was about third and fifth. I think I passed someone for the lead over the quad on the first lap which was the easiest lap to do it because it was all brand new. I don't remember much about the first moto, I just got a gap and managed to win it.

The quad was one of the easiest jumps I'd done, even though a lot of people rave about it. All you had to do was come out of the corner absolutely flat out and just hook fourth as you're at the bottom of the take off and send it.

Between the races everyone wants to congratulate you and tell you you're gonna win. The announcer told me a guy in the V.I.P area had said if I did the quad every lap he'd give me 250 euros, and he's giving me the cash as he's telling me, so I'm riding back to the truck in my riding gear with 250 euros in my hand, and the same deal for the second race.

Dad was happy, but it was more work for him.

The second race wasn't as simple. I didn't get the hole-shot but I'm putting in lap times that I know I can go to the end. Paulin is checking out, doubling stuff into corners and I'm thinking 'holy smoke, I can't do that', and watched him going up the track. After a few laps I started catching him and I've watch it on TV, Villopoto was talking to Malin and completely unaware as I changed my line and just rode around the outside of Paulin for the lead. His plan was to hole-shot and just charge balls-to-the-wall for five laps and get enough gap to hold me off, but it didn't work. I had been honest with myself because I knew I couldn't match those times without falling off a cliff later, and if I did that we might both end up third and fourth or something. After three laps I started smiling because I knew his plan hadn't worked. When I passed him, I knew there was no possibility that he would pass me back because he'd spent that energy in the first laps. I started doing the stuff he was doing on the first laps but then you're into the last ten minutes and you start overthinking stuff in case you throw it *away. I stopped doing some stuff, then I cased the quad and had a stupid tip-over crash. I just got a bit off line and landed in a soft bit. I picked the bike up and again, watching the TV Paul Malin was 'saying will he do it again?' but there wasn't even a question in my mind, I'd been doing it all weekend.*

It was quite a surreal moment, my first 1-1, and I'd done it in such good form, I'd even won the heat race which is quite a big deal because I haven't won that many races. There were lots of friends and family there. We had a photo afterwards. At the press conference there was so much respect from Paulin and Febvre, and I remember saying that the only other guys I saw putting in as much work as me were these two sat next to me, so hard work pays off.

The moments that followed were weird. Monday just went back to normal, we had to wash the bike, prep some stuff and on Tuesday we were going to Unadilla to do an AMA National so instead of being able to live off of that moment it was straight away, cap that because now we're going to do something we've never done but wanted to do for years. That turned out to be a fantastic weekend and I just missed the podium there, but that's a whole other story. There was so much cool stuff going on that I probably didn't enjoy all the social media comments and write-ups that were going on that I could've lived off for weeks."

The perfect weekend didn't happen for Hitachi/ASA KTM this time as Jeffrey Herlings owned Lommel, a level above everyone else and emulating Shaun's great performance four years previous but that's not to say it wasn't a successful weekend for the team. Graeme had his best grand prix so far finishing fifteenth and fourteenth in the races for thirteenth overall. He matched his stated goal but more important was the manor in which he did it, battling until the end and regaining places. You can only ask a rider to give their best effort and he had done that. In the press release after the race Graeme said "Obviously, this weekend I had two of my best results this year and it feels like it's been a long time coming. It's strange trying to be happy with a 15th and a 14th because we always want more". That statement encapsulates the problem for almost everyone on the start gate. The depth of talent is so good and a good start so important that whilst finishing fifteenth might not sound like much, it's a fantastic result in the context of the competition. I talked in chapter 6 about realistic goals for Graeme; a fifteenth-place finish in every race so far would put him fifteenth overall so finding that consistency could be something to work towards for next year.

Conrad also had a successful weekend with sixth and eighth finishes. Like Graeme, he had given 100% and looked like the Conrad from the start of the year, smiling, happy and racing well. Roger was happy too, telling me *"this place has always been good to us"*. There was a big British contingent in Lommel and plenty of them wanted to see Conrad for a selfie or an autograph. When things had quietened down on Sunday night I asked him about his weekend, any lingering problems with his leg and if he felt that he had put all the mid-season doldrums behind him.

"My leg still isn't fully recovered, it still gives me quite a lot of pain and obviously this isn't the nicest track to be banging out motos with a sore leg. I asked the physio what the situation is, will riding make it worse and she said I won't make it worse, it will be very painful. I said that's fine, I can deal with the pain as long as I know I'm not gonna make it worse. It's all sorted out with Jamie, I'm back with him and having a lot of fun. I know I'm doing my work properly. It was a bit of a tough stage this year, I know I was in the wrong, I didn't like to admit it at the time but when I look back I can see it. I was trying to do the things a normal eighteen or nineteen-year-old kid does, trying to enjoy my life too much for the sport that I do. Now I know that was the problem and I won't fall into that trap again".

There was other feel-good news for the Brits as Mel Pocock won the EMX250 overall and Max Anstie was on the podium in third place in MXGP.

Roger had a busy weekend, a couple of meetings and one sneaky meeting that no-one was supposed to know about with a potential third rider/replacement for Conrad if he went elsewhere. It was all top secret but what it indicated to me was a feeling in the paddock that you have to be riding a KTM or Husky to win. Lots of silly season news/rumours/gossip was going around but what seemed to be playing out was a race to the bottom as riders desperate to secure a ride were offering to race for lower and lower salaries, some even offering to ride for free if they could bring their own clothing deal and other private sponsors, and stories of some trying to 'buy' a ride by bringing big financial sponsorship to the team. That scenario is good for the teams and OK for the riders with big personal backing but for quite a few it could spell disaster.

Finally, a race truck up-date. At the start of the year there was a problem with the suspension air bags leaking, so they were replaced but only on one side to keep the cost down. As a result, the trailer hadn't been tracking properly and had worn out two tires on one side. While the bikes travelled to Hawkstone in the vans, the truck went in for new suspension bushes and two tyres!

Hawkstone.

Round 7 of the Maxxis British championship was at the legendary Shropshire circuit, Hawkstone Park, once home to the British GP. The summer heat wave had again given way to heavy rain overnight that fortunately abated before practice but the venue seemed to have lost its aura. The crowd was sparse, I'd be surprised if there were more than a thousand people there, and the entry list in every class couldn't fill the gate. In the 'good-old-days' a British championship race at Hawkstone would have forty riders on the line in the main races, with half regularly competing in grand prix; it does make me wonder what has happened to make it so unattractive to teams and riders.

The day started with Ian hobbling around in some discomfort, his knee giving him jip. A steady procession of riders called by to speak to Roger about the possibility of a spot on the team for next year, just like in the MXGP paddock the British lads also need to secure a ride. There were some interesting proposals and offers to bring financial packages to the team but some riders come with too much baggage regardless of the package or potential results. Conrad had done an interview in the week suggesting that he was considering various other options which I think gave other riders the impression that a place would be available on the team. Roger had his secret 'iron in the fire' so even if Conrad went elsewhere the team had it covered but I think it was just Conrad 'playing the game' in order to get an improved offer, basically better material from the factory, (read – factory engines). That seemed like a strange request to me as his best results had come using the semi-factory engines or the team's own Volleberg engines, but the factory engines are said to be a big advantage off the start. The contract on the table was the same as this year and the only thing that would potentially increase the offer would be a string of GP podiums.

On track Conrad again took pole position in qualifying and Graeme looked good, ending fourth fastest in MX1, but it came at a cost. He had compressed a disc in his back during the second race at Lommel the previous weekend, and when he jarred it during qualifying he was in agony. It was doubtful that he would race but Graeme is a tough cookie and managed a strong second place, harrying race leader Jake Nicholls for the whole race. He needed to be helped off the bike after the race but again suited up for race 2 where some luck finally went his way as he inherited third place on the final lap when Bobryshev crashed, enough for third overall and keeping Graeme in the title hunt albeit losing another 5 points to Nicholls. Clearly in pain, the ACU doctor was called over. Nothing life threatening but complete rest would be needed, putting his participation in the next MXGP in Switzerland in doubt. Roger was pragmatic, telling Graeme to do as the doctor said and if that meant missing a GP then fine.

While that conversation was going on, Conrad was in Shrewsbury Hospital. After a convincing win in race 1, forty-one seconds ahead of second place he was on a high. His dad had offered a bribe/bet/inducement before

◀ *Shaun Simpson leading World Champion Romain Febvre*

Podium pie ▶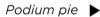

◀ *The Simpson Army celebrate*

Custom helmet paint for the MX1 2015 British Champion ▶

the race; £10 per second lead. Conrad had kept charging, earning a handy £410 from his dad, so no wonder he was smiling. The smile disappeared in race 2 when he clashed with championship rival Josh Gilbert off the start as the Honda rider got a better launch out of the gate and moved across to block Conrad. It was a legitimate move that forced Conrad to shut off but a hundred meters ahead more trouble was waiting for him, a first-turn crash sending him over the bars. Restarting in last place he was shaking his hand but worked back up into the points before crashing again and retiring. The first-turn crash had caused the injury but adrenaline got him going again until he could no longer hold on; it looked like ligament damage to his left hand so without any further delay he went to hospital to get a scan. If ligament damage was confirmed it would almost certainly mean surgery and the end of his season, just as he had started to get his mojo back.

Conrad still led the championship but his advantage had been cut to fifteen points, and Graeme was still third and had closed the gap to second place to just thirteen points with six weeks until the penultimate British championship round at Foxhills, but as the team packed up 'uncertainty' was the word of the day. Would Graeme and/or Conrad be fit for next weekend and the MXGP of Switzerland?

Chapter 21

ROUND 16, MXGP OF SWITZERLAND, FRAUENFELD–GACHNANG, SOCIAL MEDIA & SAMANTA GELLI – YOUTHSTREAM PRESS OFFICER.

There were some logistical headaches for team co-ordinator Ian Browne. Going to Switzerland was easy enough but it was the start of a month-long trip with three back-to-back grand prix in Switzerland, Bulgaria and Turkey. Plans were well advanced before the riders threw Ian and the team a curve ball at Hawkstone, injuries putting their participation in doubt. Even if they missed Switzerland, it was on the way to Bulgaria, which was on the way to Turkey, so Ian had to carry on with the assumption that they would be making the trip.

Turkey required a visa for all the team members, not a problem because you could apply on line but to take the race truck they needed a special permit. Jakke had to take the invitation from the club hosting the race to the Turkish embassy in Brussels along with all the details and paperwork for the truck to get the permit. They would also need a carnet for the bikes and spares. A carnet is a form that declares that the bikes and parts aren't being imported, merely transported through the country. It requires the frame numbers of the bikes and details of all the spares carried. The visa and carnet had already been obtained after Lommel.

After the Swiss MXGP the race truck would immediately head for Bulgaria. The direct route is overland through Hungary and Serbia, but because Serbia is outside the European union it creates extra headaches and delays at the border, going in and going out. It's not too bad with the correct paperwork but if something is missing or incorrect expect long delays and a big headache. There are routes further south through Croatia, Montenegro, Albania and Macedonia, or further north through Romania, but neither route is advised as Albania and Romania are both poor countries and fraught with potential security problems. Civil unrest and protests about government corruption in Bucharest, the capital of Romania only added to the potential danger. The alternative route is down into southern Italy to Ancona, take the ferry across to Greece then there's still a long drive across Greece into Bulgaria. Jakke seemed unperturbed and planned on the shortest route through Romania in order to get to Sevlievo in the time available.

From Bulgaria it's a relatively short hop of about 500 miles east to Turkey but then it's a four-day drive back to the base in Lommel. Because of the distance and the carnets required the team need to put everything they need in the race truck to last for the three events, bikes, spare engines, wheels, plastics and spare parts for every eventuality.

The mechanics would drive to Switzerland then return to Belgium. They would then fly out and back to Bulgaria and again to Turkey. That sounds easy but getting the right flight times was very difficult, and getting direct flights even harder, and expensive. They would need to be at the track in Bulgaria on Thursday in order to get the awning up and start preparing the bikes. Getting everything packed away on Sunday evening would be hard but if they couldn't get a flight until Monday it would be almost pointless flying home as they would be back at the airport on Wednesday to be at the track in Turkey for Thursday.

The cost of taking another vehicle, fuel and hotels was about the same as flying, but at least flying gave the mechanics a bit of time at home rather than sitting in a van, it just took some organising.

Booking flights, hotels and hire cars takes a while but it's easier now than it's ever been, thanks to the world-wide-web. The internet has transformed all of our lives and a vital part of any business today is their on-line and social media presence. In the good old days, printed brochures and leaflets gave potential customers all the information they needed but in the modern world most people go straight on-line and look for the company's website. Social media is also an integral part of modern life and used in the right way it can be a fantastic tool for sharing information, getting your message out, building brand awareness or just publicising a good news story. Most of us use Instagram and/or Facebook as an easy way to share a post, usually about a holiday or night out, its so easy. When you're using those platforms for business it's a little bit more important to think carefully about what you post and make sure you're presenting your brand in the best way. Just about every rider and team in the paddock is on social media (it's often in their contract that they have to post regularly and share team press releases), and if they're not doing it themselves they probably have a press officer doing it on their behalf. There's a whole industry grown up where people make a very good living from their blogs and endorsements. Some of the 'stars' of reality TV shows have gone on to make millions just for promoting products on their social media. Referred to as 'influencers' by advertising types because of their ability to influence their 'followers' to buy a product, it's the new way to promote or sell a brand. In the context of MXGP, the riders are the influencers so how they use their Instagram page is important. Dean Wilson is considered to be one of the best proponents, posting something virtually every day when he wasn't injured and Ken Roczen took it to a new level with graphic images of his arm surgeries and recovery and Adam Cianciarulo's vlogs are hilarious as they're authentic; they capture his spontaneity and sense of humour, while away from motocross American President Donald Trump has used Twitter to get his message out, by-passing all the usual press protocols that would sanitise his words. Like him or loath him, it's a very effective way to express your opinion in less than 140 characters. At Desertmartin I filmed Conrad wheelieing downhill over some big braking bumps and posted it on my Facebook page, The MX reporter. Within a week it had over 29,000 views, by far the most for any of my posts, because it was shared and re-shared by people with a lot of followers. It was a great bit of technique by Conrad but more importantly shows how wide a post can travel, and the reach of social media.

Samanta Gelli is the Youthstream Press Officer, working behind the scenes, herding the winning riders to interviews and press conferences on race day, facilitating media events, publishing on the Youthstream pages and much more. Always busy, but always helpful and accommodating, I managed to get her to sit down long enough to tell me about her role and the importance of social media to MXGP.

Samanta Gelli – Youthstream Press Officer.

Samanta, what is your role in Youthstream and how did you start working in MXGP?

I work for Youthstream as the press officer. I have a degree in economics with a specialisation degree in marketing. I used to work in a marketing consultancy in Florence which was cool but my ideal job was a bit different; I missed travelling and I needed something more creative. Some of my family were involved in motocross and that's how I heard about this opportunity. I started in 2013 as the assistant to the previous press officer and had the chance to learn many things. I think the important thing here is to understand how the world is running because we are like a big circus travelling everywhere so step-by-step I learned a lot. In 2014 I got this position.

Can you explain what are the responsibilities of the press officer in Youthstream?

Being the press officer in the motocross world championship is not just sending press releases and taking care of accreditation. I take care of all communications going on digital platforms, that includes MXGP.com and MXGP-TV. I take care of the general overview and strategies for social media, and I'm happy to say that we are growing a lot....... Not only thanks to me (laughing). When you do something and you can see the results are positive of course you are happy. Since last year I am more involved in TV as well and I work a lot with Lisa and the TV Crew on the content for interviews and videos. While when we go to the races I have to set up the media centre and take care of the accreditations for the international media.

Just looking at social media, Youthstream post a lot of content but so do a lot of the riders, teams and journalists. Do you monitor what gets posted?

It does feel like I'm always on line because I have to monitor what is happening. I am very lucky because I have another guy with me called Kyle who is taking care of that and posts everything for us on social media. This is really helpful because I'm not saying you need to be there 24 hours but most of your day, especially at the races sometimes it is very busy.

The last two years our social media platforms have increased a lot, on Facebook, Instagram and YouTube, so that means that the championship is growing in that way and we have some new markets as well. We have some interest from people who are not really hardcore fans of motocross. When I started we had a target of people who go to the race or watch MXGP on television, so they were already fans of motocross. Now we can go outside, like in Moto GP for example.

You can see how the paddock has changed; this is one of the few sports where a kid for example, can meet his hero, have an autograph and attend many other activities in the paddock. We show this on social media, not just the winner or who is fastest in timed practice. We show the atmosphere and the activities. In Indonesia for example, we put a lot of things about the opening ceremonies. We had a fantastic atmosphere and the city welcomed us in an amazing way so this is something that we like to show. They were dancing in national costume with no shoes on the track when the riders were lining up; when you see this atmosphere, you can feel the change that motocross is doing.

Do you offer and guidance to the riders or teams about what they should post?

We did some media lessons for the riders in Argentina and showed them a presentation of what we did in 2017 and gave some guidelines. For us the riders are very important of course as well as the sponsors. With the journalist, we are always open to discuss about our line and ideas but then, they are managing their platforms with their way, which is very good, we do have a lot of Medias following the MXGP and they all have their own particularities. With the riders and sponsors we do many cross promotions. I am always in contact with them, often for simple things like which hash-tag we will use during the weekend. For example, we just launched the MXGP video game so we're doing many promotions with the riders on that.

You just mentioned that journalists sometimes have a different point of view. If someone is critical of Youthstream or an event, do you just monitor that or would you speak to them?

My idea, also for the staff I work with, is that communication is always the best way. So, I will never send an e-mail saying I don't like that. It's your point of view and I can do nothing about that, but for sure either by e-mail or face to face I would explain our point of view or how something could be written in another way. This is how I am with all the people I work with; just let it go is not a good way, just complain is not good either. Have a nice polite conversation is the best way.

Looking at the future, the calendar is out for 2019 with some new races in China and Hong Kong. These are massive markets so will you be doing something different for those events, maybe Chinese language on social media?

For sure we are planning something but we are looking for something specific on social media because in China they do not have Facebook, so we continue to promote these events on our platforms but we are looking at other platforms to use also. We are working to have not only posts in Chinese but some different social media for that market. For sure it's a huge market but with the social media we have at the moment we cannot reach them as we wish. I'm quite sure with one event in Shanghai and one event in Hong Kong, and a different social media platform we can reach a lot of people.

Just thinking about the different countries and markets that MXGP goes to, are there differences in what people like around the world and do you adjust your content to meet any differences?

Yes of course, what I can say is for example Indonesia is one of the easiest, they love motorsport so much that they will 'like' whatever you post. Then countries like Argentina and Brazil, they like action, so when we post action videos they are the first to 'like' them. European countries are more specific we have to put the correct picture or video footage with good and customized writing copy.

It seems to be easy to make a post for Facebook which it is if you're doing it for your private profile but on a business profile it takes time to get it right. For example, when I make a promotional advertising post it takes at least fifteen minutes to do it. We use analytics and monitor everything. We look where the GP is and our calendar, we have a strategy for that and when we are at the race we want people to feel the atmosphere that we feel on site.

"

Social media can also be very destructive and damaging. Tommy Searle has spoken about his displeasure in reading the negative and hurtful comments around his selection for the MXON but unfortunately there are some idiots who think they're clever posting their insulting nonsense. Conrad had received some stupid comments about his mid-season troubles, so I asked him if it affected him. "Not really, not everyone is going to have a good word to say about you. It's obviously not nice when people are slating you when you know you're trying your best, if an injury puts you out you can't do much about that; I try to deal with it as best I can. Regarding Tommy, I think he has every right to be annoyed, people take it too far. It's alright for them sat at home commenting on everything you do. If they were in my situation, or Tommy's situation then fair enough. Those people watch a boxing match and think they're Anthony Joshua (laughing), it's the same in every sport".

Ironically, the Hitachi/ASA KTM website and social media pages could use a refresh. The link to the team's own website no longer works, instead taking the reader to KTM UK and the Facebook page has random posts from events but the 'about' section ends in 2014, and there is no information or links to the currents sponsors or team members. Without regular up-dates, links to current sponsors, features, current team member profiles and information, the sites look poor, but more importantly it's a big opportunity to showcase the team, products and sponsors that is lost. As with everything it comes down to budget, but the bigger teams and businesses understand the value of the various electronic platforms and use them fully. KTM UK prepare the race reports and press releases in-house but there are smaller teams with much better social media profiles............C+, must do better!

Driving down to Frauenfeld I got a call from Roger to let me know that Conrad wouldn't be racing. The Hawkstone crash had broken his left index finger and it would be three weeks before he could ride, ruling him out of the three back-to-back GP's. It was bad timing for Conrad if he was trying to raise his stock but also because he was just starting to come good after his mid-season doldrums and really needed to keep the momentum going. For the team and Conrad it would be all about winning the British championship now. Graeme was also in the wars after Hawkstone. He had received chiropractic treatment in the week and ridden on Wednesday to test his back which seemed OK but it was a long way to take the race truck to Bulgaria and Turkey with just one semi-fit rider so Roger had decided to review the situation after the Swiss GP; if Graeme had a good weekend and his back held up then Roger would send the team to Bulgaria, if not then the team would return to Lommel and Graeme would have time to get his back problem fixed, returning at Assen with Conrad.

Just to add to the injury woes, Ian had spent the week in hospital and was also missing from the paddock. His knee had become so painful that he couldn't walk, forcing a visit to A&E where he was admitted and kept in for treatment to a Baker's cyst. It would be the first time he had missed a race in years. Fortunately, he had made all the necessary arrangements for the trip to Switzerland already but Jakke, BC and Minty are experienced and know what to do. Vas had decided to go home, which left the trio a bit short-handed putting the awning up but the paddock in Switzerland is tarmacked so it wasn't really a problem.

BC was left in charge but no sponsors were expected so it was a fairly easy GP. The BOS team were making headlines, announcing that they had parted company with their star rider Jordi Tixier and hired Jean-Jacques Luisetti to manage the team. Luisetti was BC's boss at CLS Kawasaki didn't waste any time, signing Tommy Searle for 2019 and approaching BC to be his mechanic. BC had already been approached by another team, an indication of how well he is thought of by team managers. Was he considering the offers? "Of course," he told me, "I listen to everyone and see what's on offer. I like it here and Roger has been good to me but you've got to take the best offer for you. It's not all about the money but I have got bills to pay. If they match the money and give me Conrad I'd stay. I want to be with someone where I've got a chance to win." That wasn't a slight against Graeme; BC has a great relationship with him but he prefers working on 250's and is very competitive so working with Conrad with a real chance of MX2 podiums next year and a British championship was very appealing.

Some things can't be planned for, like the fridge/freezer packing up in the truck. With most of the food ruined it meant a trip to the local supermarket and also the nearest electrical store for a new fridge on Friday. Other things are avoidable, like BC leaving the roof vent open when it was pouring with rain, leaving him with a rather damp bed.

Graeme arrived on Friday with his wife and daughter but seemed resigned to missing Bulgaria and Turkey. An M.R.I. scan had revealed the bulging disc that was causing the surrounding area to be inflamed. It really needed rest but he was determined to see how it felt in the race conditions. "It's Ok when I'm riding but if I get a little twist it goes into spasm, then I tense up and everything is tight. It needs a deep tissue massage to release the muscles which is painful at the time and it's agony the next day. I know it's a long way to take everything to Bulgaria and Turkey, and with Conrad out it might be better to get my back sorted out."

Heavy rain on Friday had made the track very wet for the first EMX groups out on Saturday but but by the time the MXGP riders were out conditions were perfect but with some very deep ruts already formed. Graeme put in his fastest lap on the last lap of free practice, his back seemed to be holding up. Starting the qualifying race in twenty-second, he picked off a few riders including a feet-on-the-pegs, inside rut pass on HRC rider Todd Waters; nothing wrong with his technique. The real test would come tomorrow in the two 30-minute-plus-2-laps races.

Sunday dawned and the feeling was positive, Graeme's back was holding up and warm-up went well as he put six laps in. Unfortunately, more bad luck was waiting for him in the first race. A good start in fifteenth spot and a fighting first lap would be undone as he crested the finish line jump. A rock smashed into his face, punching a hole through his top lip and bending two teeth back. He would pull out immediately, riding straight back to the race truck, his face, shirt and bike now covered with blood. With his lip gaping he was taken to the local hospital where he was stitched up, the swollen and bloody mouth looking like the worst Botox job ever.

It was a case of Deja-vu for the team as Josiah Natzke had suffered an almost identical injury in his MX2 debut at this track a year ago. Fate and a random rock had made the decision; there was no way Graeme could race with a bad back and facial injury so the plug was pulled on the next two events. Trucks aren't allowed on Swiss roads on a Sunday night so there was no rush packing up, the Jakke would leave for the workshop in the morning instead of the long journey east.

Chapter 22

Round 17, MXGP Bulgaria, Sevlievo, Bob Buchannan's midnight run & Brooke, Milly, Jill and Joan – MX WAGS.

With the Hitachi/ASA KTM UK team missing in action it seems like a good opportunity to highlight how the smaller teams cope. Owned, financed and run by Bob Buchannan, GL12 gets its name from the Gloucester postcode where Bob lives. The sport needs more people like Bob; he's all about the racing with no desire for fame or fortune. His story about the first trip to Bulgaria was too good to miss so instead of Hitachi/ASA KTM's weekend, here's GL12's Bulgaria experience.

Bob Buchannan's midnight run.
If passion and desire was enough to win championships then Bob Buchannan would have a trophy cabinet bursting wide open. The owner of the under-dog GL12 team, Bob is a staunch advocate of two-strokes, competing in the British two-stroke championship and the European EMX300 with Mike Kras and EMX250 with James Dunn, both racing 250 two-stroke KTMs. With no financial backing, Bob runs The Goggle Shop and uses the income generated to buy the bikes and fund the racing program. It's a 'hand-to-

mouth' operation but he makes it work. I was standing with him a Hawkstone during the second race when Mike Kras clinched the British two-stroke championship for the second time but what no-one knew was that his race bike had blown up in practice and he was racing an old practice bike that might not last the race. Bob was physically sick with nerves during the race, it means that much to him! If I ever win the lottery I'm giving some of it to Bob but that's a different story.

When the Swedish MXGP was cancelled Bulgaria was added in its place, along with a round of the EMX300's. For GL12 this was catastrophic to their budget, there were no funds for the long, expensive trip east so Bob had to think outside the box to make it happen. He told me about his first trip to Bulgaria and what was planned for this year as we sat in the paddock in Switzerland.

"They introduced EMX300 series in 2014 and the very first date was Bulgaria. My heart sank but we had to go; we'd all been shouting about getting this series going and it would look very remiss of us not to go. It was following Arco, in Italy, and the best way to go was from Ancona on the ferry to Ignoumenitsa in Greece so we doubled up with the bikes and went across. The ferry was about 600 euros each way. No one knew what to expect, I had Lewis Gregory and we turned up with a stock 250 Yamaha and a pipe. It was horrendous, soaking wet and the bike weighed about twice as much with all the sticky mud. I think we got tenth overall but we did regroup and win the next round in Talavera. Bulgaria is a beautiful country, very clean and tidy; the people have got no money but they've got a lot of pride, all the houses were immaculate with flowers outside and were freshly painted.

In those days there was a lot more togetherness in the paddock. I always drove with PK, that was Dixon's driver and Steve Turner had Jacky van Doorn so we were all at the races together and all had to be back for a British championship. The easiest and safest route is back on the ferry but it would take four days. We looked on the map, Serbia and Macedonia were a no go, I think they were still fighting at the time, or Romania, Hungary and Germany. Romania wasn't really playing with Europe at that time but we thought we'd give it a go. We all filled up with fuel at the last garage in Bulgaria so we could get through Romania without stopping, and I sat Sophie in the front seat with a stack of Monster caps and a low-cut top.

We got to the border and there's queues of lorries so we drove up the outside to the first border guard. The guard goes to Sophie's side and we explain 'motocross in Hungary' and give him a cap. He waves to his mate to let us through but we had the same thing with another two guards. The last one wanted to get in the back and I thought 'sh#t, we've had it, he wants to check the bikes' but he just didn't want to take a cap in front of the cctv cameras.

We were now in Romania! The roads were horrendous, the tarmac had bermed up in the corners. In the middle of the night Jacky wanted to stop for a pee so we pulled over, but we had pulled into a brothel and they're all run by the mafia there. We floored it out of there but I had cramp in my leg so I'm stood up driving and trying to sort my leg out!

We got to the Hungarian border at day break and the look on the border guard's face was just disbelief. They went through all our paperwork but they wouldn't accept that we were in campers, they wanted carnets so that took a bit of sorting out. I got back into Belgium on Tuesday morning and put a picture of the sign on Facebook; the first three comments were 'fake', 'that's impossible' but we had saved two days."

Tell me about this year, what is the difference between going to Sweden or Bulgaria?

"Well for a start its 600 euros each way on the boat. Sweden is a 24-hour drive, we had sensible EMX rounds apart from Russia and then they give us Bulgaria. It's a stand-alone round although we have got the EMX250 in Switzerland before it."

You've been a bit creative to get there, tell me about that.

"I can't bring the shop to Switzerland because of the border controls and it's pointless taking it to Bulgaria because it's such a poor country so I had to think of another way to fund it. When they announced the date, everyone thought the same thing, 'how am I gonna get there?'

I put up a Facebook post and spoke to a few people about taking their bikes. I had about eleven who said yes but in the end I'm taking four bikes to cover my costs."

The interesting one that you're taking is Brad Anderson, your main championship rival. You helped him get to Russia last year when he wasn't able to go and told me then that you would rather lose the championship honestly than win it because Ando couldn't get to a race. That's quite an unusual point of view.

"I've helped Brad out for years. People have said I'm stupid but I'm not. It's a fair compliment that they trust me to take his bike because they know I wouldn't tamper with them, it's not in my nature. I don't use team orders, it's the fastest rider who wins and that's what a championship should be, not the rider who can afford to go. Why shouldn't Brad win the title if he's faster all year than Mike Kras? This year he hasn't been, Mike has been better but we had two DNF's at Matterley because my bikes let him down. Without those DNF's Mike would be winning hands down, but the championship has to be decided on the track, not in the bank accounts."

So, will it be another midnight run this year?

"That depends on Matt Smith (Josh Spinks' sponsor). He has a guy that sorts the ferry crossings and according to him we're crossing both ways but as I'm sat here I've only seen the confirmation for the outbound crossing! If he hasn't sorted out the return then it will be another midnight run but Romania has tamed down a bit since before."

The two mechanical DNF's at Matterley had been costly for Kras, now twenty-seven points behind Brad Anderson. The pair had consistently been the fastest and when Anderson injured his knee it looked like Kras would simply ride off with the title. But Ando is a tough competitor and overcame the pain, capitalising on Kras' misfortune. With two rounds left Kras needed to win every race and the hard-pack if Bulgaria wasn't his strong surface. For Ando, third place in each race would be enough even if Kras won every race, but anything can happen in racing so it was game on.

The distance and cost of getting to Bulgaria was obviously affecting other riders and teams. Just fifteen riders had entered the EMX300 class and twenty-seven entered the EMX250; there wouldn't even be any need qualifying. Even those figures flatter the truth as a couple of local wild-cards had entered, one of whom was over thirty-seconds a lap off the pace! The MXGP (26) and MX2 (25) entries were also lower than usual. Some could be explained by injuries, as with the Hitachi/ASA KTM riders, but I'm sure if the race was in Belgium or Holland Roger would have been more willing to send Graeme and maybe even Conrad if he could ride. At this stage of the season though, if you're not in contention for a top five or even a top ten finish, it's very tempting to save the budget needed for the long trip and prepare for the last big push from Assen onwards.

The hillside track is an old-school, hard-packed circuit, blue -groove in many of the acceleration areas. Blue-groove is a term given to tracks where the dirt is almost like concrete, causing the bikes to wheel-spin and lay rubber down creating a blue line, typically found in Italy southern France. With modern track preparation ripping and watering the ground you don't see it much anymore. The thermometer was in the thirties for the EMX300 riders, who faced a mixture of blue-groove and slop as the track was watered before their races. Kras won the first race but despite a bar-banging dual in the second race, championship rival Brad Anderson took the race win and overall, holding his advantage at twenty-seven points with one round left. Bob didn't get the win he wanted but at least the racing was good; firm but fair. I said at the beginning that running an MXGP team is a business but if the GL12 team was run purely as a business it would've stopped trading long ago. But for Bob and his loyal group of supporters it's still the sport that's most important, and he proved that by taking his competitor's bike to the race. The final round was a month away at Imola and anything can happen in racing; a crash or mechanical failure for Ando in the first race would leave everything to play for. Bob isn't the type of bloke to wish misfortune on his competitors but you just know that on that long drive home he must've been rueing his own bad luck at Matterley.

And it was a long drive home. The school holidays meant the ferry back to

Italy was fully booked but it was still preferable to a solo midnight run through Romania. Matt Smith's travel agent had arranged a stand-by ticket which meant a 24-hour wait in the port until a space could became available, even then the process was only eased by slipping a 50 euro note into the stand-by ticket to help the loading guy with his decision making. A twenty-three-hour drive back to Holland to drop off bikes before the final leg back to Gloucester, Bob got home at midnight on Thursday, four days after the GP.

MX WAGS

Changing the subject slightly, they say that behind every great man is a great woman, and being a professional athlete takes a lot of dedication, desire and usually support from your family and partner, and likewise for the managers and team owners providing a platform for the stars to perform.. We've all watched TV programmes about the footballers' wives and girlfriends; life is one long round of parties, designer shopping and champagne while their millionaire boyfriends kick a ball about. But is it the same for the motocross WAGS?

Without turning this chapter into 'Hello' magazine, I decided the best way to find out was to ask the 'other halves' of three MXGP riders about the reality of life as a motocross WAG, and the team owner's wife. Brooke Irwin, wife of Hitachi/ASA KTM UK's Graeme Irwin, and Milly Sears, soon to be married to Ice One Husqvarna's Max Anstie, Jill Cairoli, wife of nine-times world champion Antonio Cairoli and Joan Magee, wife of team owner Roger Magee, share their stories.

Brooke, Milly & Jill – MX WAGS.

Graeme and Brooke live in Kent with their daughter and are the only parents in this interview. With another child on the way so Brooke hasn't been to as many races as she would like this year. I spoke to her at Hawkstone park and asked about balancing family life with racing.

Brooke. "When it was just British races I came to all of them, and we planned to go to all the GPs but it just didn't work out. It's hard to travel with a two-year-old and taking her to place after place is taxing. If we fly we have to pay for a ticket for her, and sometimes it's easier for Graeme to travel on his own and maybe share a room with his mechanic. It can be rough getting her up at six in the morning for an early flight. I let Graeme do his thing. A lot of the time he's away in Belgium all week and I'm at home with Summer. We put her in nursery this year, we made the commitment to do that. We have a different dynamic because I'm from California, I like to go home and visit my family. It's not like footballers' wives; it's more like trying to make it through Tesco without your kid losing it and make it home, I don't get to do any designer shopping.

When Graeme is at home he tries to be in dad mode but he's very involved in what he's doing and wants to do his best. He gives it everything from the time he wakes up until he goes to bed, he's very, very busy. When we come to the races we help with lunch and waters, stuff like that, but as Summer gets older she's much more active and just wants to play in the mud. I have to be there making sure she doesn't get hit by a bike. She knows when daddy is racing and cheers him on but then sees another kid and just wants to go play, or she sees a dog and she's gone."

Milly's situation is different to Brooke's, living in Belgium and travelling to all the races with Max. I spoke to her before the MXGP in Switzerland over a diet Coke (it was too early for Prosecco!)

Being a professional MXGP rider is a different kind of life to a regular nine-to-five job but how is it different for you than if you were married to someone with a regular job?

Milly. "It's hard to plan anything. I couldn't plan anything for Max's birthday because the team decided to go testing for three days, the same thing happened on my birthday, things just change at short notice."

Any professional athlete has to be very focused and self-disciplined so they probably don't want to do things that a regular guy might, everyday things like going to a restaurant or a club.

Milly. "They have to be selfish and to be honest I do struggle with that sometimes but when they do well you forget and it's worth it for those rewards".

Max is leaving his team at the end of the season; how does that impact on him and you?

Milly. "That can be hard, you have to be positive. In real life if something wasn't going well in your job there are processes or maybe an HR department but with racing things can change if you get a bad result and that can be hard to see. I can't stop eating because I'm anxious (laughing). Max is really good at staying positive although he does sometimes say 'why does nobody want me, what have I done wrong?'. I don't have a job anymore so what affects Max affects me too. It's not like I can say 'we'll be Ok because I still have my job', our lives are totally together".

You had a good job in England,, working as a P.A.. Was that a big decision to give it up and move to Belgium?

Milly. "Obviously it was a joint decision. It wasn't possible for me to move here and keep my job. It's worked out well because I'm able to put all my efforts into supporting Max. I do everything for him so all he has to worry about is riding. I would like to do something in the future though. I've been his P.A. for two-and-a-half years, it works well for us because he goes to the team every day and I get all the travel booked, and make sure his life runs smoothly. All he does is come home and get his gear ready for the next day. Max doesn't even know how to make a cup of tea, you can ask him. His dinner is on the table, all his washing, I just make sure he doesn't have to think about anything".

Max has had a couple of injuries; how do you help him deal with the time on the couch?

Milly. *"Last year when Max injured his knee that was easier to deal with than the concussion. With the concussion I really didn't know what to do because you can't see it. The first few days afterwards we were having dinner and he looked really funny and was being a bit weird but he was saying he was fine. It's hard to deal with."*

You're into your fitness so do you train with Max, at the gym or cardio?

Milly. *"I did try training with Max but it doesn't work, I do a lot of classes".*

So far it sounds like a pain in the ass, but there must be some good points to being a motocross WAG.

Milly. *"Sometimes I moan that I don't see my family or friends much but then I think I could be doing a crappy job. We get to travel around the world, which is really cool and we've been to some amazing places, Argentina was so beautiful. We have lots of friends in the paddock and say hi to everyone. There's no-one I would try to avoid.... Well maybe two but they know that. It's no different than working in an office really."*

Jill and Antonio Cairoli married at the end of 2017 after being together for twelve years. They met through motocross when Jill's father and brother were racing but her parents weren't keen on their daughter dating an Italian motocross racer (Jill is from Holland) so it took a while before the couple got together. She had a good job and her parents didn't think motocross would offer a secure living, but she's happy with her decision.

Jill. *"I made a really good choice, he treats me like a princess, he's a really, really good person."*

I see you at every MXGP, often at the start with his helmet and water. How do you see your role supporting Tony?

Jill. *"That's a really difficult question to answer because it's so much that I do, and you can't explain it in a few words. I do everything around him to take the work away from him. Before e had RedBull hospitality I would cook, I make his drinks, get everything ready at the races. Then at home I help with the financial parts and book keeping. I gave up my job but I am Dutch and we have a working mentality so I said 'OK, if I stop my job I want to do the things for you.' We also have our own brand, RACR, so being at the races is just a small part, during the week is the really work, the weekend is easy."*

The Italians love motorsport and riders like Antonio Cairoli and Valentino Rossi have a much higher public profile than any rider in Britain, more like David Beckham whose fame transcended football. Can you and Tony go out for dinner without fans wanting a selfie?

Jill. *"The Italian mentality is very enthusiastic. In Holland people would say in a quiet voice 'there is Antonio Cairoli' but in Italy they're on your table, taking selfies, giving you their baby to hold; that's the Italian mentality, they are very out-going. In a way it's nice. We worked for it for a long time and we've grown into it together, him becoming more famous so it went smoothly."*

Do people recognise you without Antonio? Have you become like the Posh and Becks of Italy?

Jill. (laughing) *"No, we are not like that. Sometimes people recognise me but its nice. Of course, I accept it especially during the week, but sometimes at the races it feels like a lot of eyes are on me. I feel the pressure of not showing emotions; if I smile too hard they would say something, if I'm angry they say, 'Oh she's angry because he didn't race good' so I just try to be nice to everybody."*

Do you have plans for a life after motocross? Tony just signed for another two years with KTM so you have at least two more years in the paddock.

Jill. *"The life after motocross isn't coming because he keeps continuing and he does such an amazing job, I don't know how he does it. He finds the motivation again and again; he's like Valentino, its their life, they are special and motocross is his family. But of course, in a few years there will be retirement but Italians live day-to-day so we don't really talk or think about that yet. He's not ready, he feels that he can win the championship still and he will do everything to try to win again next year. He knows already a few things he can be better on."*

I think Valentino Rossi, Chad Reed and Antonio have shown that age can be an advantage and you're not too old when you're twenty-five.

Jill. *"Exactly, if you have the motivation that's everything, and of course if you can be healthy it's really important."*

Would you and Tony like to have a family, maybe a baby Cairoli to be in MXGP in 2040?

Jill. *"Yes, but for us it's after motocross. Tony really wants to race on a high level still. Being a boyfriend or a husband of someone is a totally other responsibility than being a father. Maybe doing a sport like this makes you realise that you need 100% focus for racing."*

Roger and Joan Magee have been married forever. When Roger started the team in 2004 he probably didn't imagine it would turn into the factory supported effort it has become. Joan isn't a motocross fan but as she put it *"to when you enlist, you've got soldier."*

Can you talk about the early days of the team, what it was like and how it's changed?

Joan. When it started it was much more of a family atmosphere. That did cause some problems with the boundaries getting blurred but it was fun. It's become a lot more professional now.

Are you involved with the day-to-day running of the team?

Joan. No, that's Roger's department. I help with the hospitality sometimes but it's Roger's baby. People don't understand how much of his own time he spends running the team. He's always talking to the sponsors and trying to arrange new ones. He also has dialysis three times a week so he does a lot of work while he's having it done. He's got so much drive and he's very determined. He's very loyal to the people in the team, the riders and sponsors and he just wants to make sure it continues every year. I think sometimes people under estimate him but you wouldn't want to cross him.

Do you come from a motocross family or is it just because of being married to Roger?

Joan. I didn't know what motocross was until I met Roger. He was riding then and when the team started all of our family holidays revolved around motocross, going to the grand prix. I've stepped back a wee bit in the last few years and we have normal holidays now but we've had some lovely times and met some lovely people.

Have you got a favourite memory or a special moment?

Joan. There are too many to pick one. Some of our riders have been like our children and we've had so many good times. I'd have to say Howard and Ali have become very close friends, they've been there from the start and done so much for Roger.

I know that Roger has got a big collection of old bikes and all the team bikes from over the years. If he wanted to put a special one on display in the hallway of your house what would you say?

Joan. Absolutely not! I can be just as determined as Roger (laughing).

While the MXGP in Bulgaria being held in thirty-five-degree heat, the MotoGP in Britain was washed out. After the summer heat wave, torrential rain at Silverstone meant the races were cancelled for the first time in over thirty years. Silverstone had invested a lot of cash resurfacing the track and ironically it was the new surface that was causing the problem; very slippery, bumpy and not draining the surface water fast enough. It was a bad day for everyone as the many spectators lambasted the organisers on social media. Graeme was a guest at KTM with his family, catching up with friends like Jack Miller who had visited him in Redsand but with no racing it was a day in the Redbull hospitality suite, drinking through a straw as his mouth was still too swollen and sore.

MENU
Podium pie, champagne,
glory and gold

Elliott Banks-Browne, ▶
Brit MX2, 2012

◀ *Elliott Banks-Browne, BritMX2, 2013*

Jake Nicholls, Brit MX1, Culham 2017 ▶

◀ *Jake Nicholls, Brit MX2 2010*

▲
Josiah Natzke, EMX250, 2017,Latvia

▲
Kevin Strijbos, Brit MX1, 2012

Chapter 23

ROUND 18, MXGP TURKEY, AFYONKARAHISAR & DRUGS TESTING AND WADA.

Sometimes it feels like big sporting events happen in a parallel reality to the real world, carrying on regardless of political or economic issues. Perhaps it's because events like an MXGP take so much advanced planning and organisation that it's just not possible to change at short notice so short of a war breaking out the show goes on.

As the MXGP circus rolled into town, Turkey was gripped by an economic crisis as its currency had crashed, losing 45% of its value over the year on international currency markets. American sanctions, economic mismanagement by President Erdogan and cheap international loans were all being blamed but the President's bullish response wasn't helping to calm international nerves. As a NATO member and the most easterly European country with borders to Syria, Iran and Iraq, Turkey is strategically important to the west so all eyes were on the unfolding crisis.

For tourists and the visiting motocross teams the devaluation of the currency meant there were some bargains to be had, eating out and shopping. Graeme and Conrad were focused on a return in two weeks at Assen and another four-week run that included two MXGPs, two British championships and the MXON for Graeme. Conrad had gone very quiet, getting on with his training without any hoopla while Graeme decided to enter the last round of the MX Nationals for some practice under race conditions. It paid off as he took two race wins and a nice confidence boost. Without much team news to discuss it seems like a good opportunity to discuss the thorny issue of drugs in sport.

In America earlier this year, Factory KTM rider Broc Tickle had failed a random drugs test. As the MXGP riders are also under the jurisdiction of the F.I.M. and the testing regime of WADA, I've included the Broc Tickle case as an example of how draconian the process is. I'll state my position now; I'm strongly against taking performance enhancing drugs, but the current system of enforcement goes against all the principles of natural justice in my opinion, guilty until proven innocent.

Drugs testing and the World Anti-Doping Agency (WADA).

The issue of performance enhancing drugs in sport is a world-wide problem that affects every sport from Curling to NFL football. It's perhaps understandable in physical sports like American football or cycling that athletes might be tempted to seek an easy gain or just some help recovering from an injury but a positive test before the winter Olympics was reported widely and although the athlete was not officially named, sources confirmed reports in Russia that Curler Alexander Krushelnytsky was found to have Meldonium in his urine, quite shocking as curling is far from physical. Meldonium is used to treat heart attacks and increases blood flow.

Drugs testing in motocross has been with us for some time since the F.I.M. signed up to WADA. The World Anti-Doping Agency was set up as an independent testing agency in 1999 with the aim of eradicating drugs and doping in sport. James Stewart is probably the highest profile racer to fall foul of WADA, but the issue came up again this year when Redbull KTM's Broc Tickle tested positive for a banned substance, Methylhexanamine, at the San Diego supercross on the 10th of February. It wasn't until two months later, on 13th April that he was informed via e-mail and prohibited from racing with immediate effect. The F.I.M. press statement at the time simply said:

The Fédération Internationale de Motocyclisme (FIM) has advised US Supercross rider Broc Tickle that he is provisionally suspended pursuant to Article 7.9 of the FIM Anti-doping Code. The decision to provisionally suspend Mr. Tickle was taken following the receipt of a report from the WADA accredited laboratory in Cologne indicating an Adverse Analytical Finding of 5-methylhexan-2-amine, a specified substance under Section 6 (Stimulants) of the 2018 FIM Prohibited List, in a urine sample collected from him at an in-competition test carried out by the FIM at the round of the Monster Energy AMA Supercross, an FIM World Championship held in San Diego, California, USA, on 10 February 2018.

Mr. Tickle has the right to request and attend the analysis of his B sample.

Mr. Broc Tickle is provisionally suspended with effect from 14 April 2018. He is therefore barred from participating in any Sports competition until further notice (Art. 10.12 of the FIM Anti-doping Code). Under Article 7.9.3.2 of the FIM Anti-doping Code, Mr. Tickle may request lifting of his provisional suspension.

Under the World Anti-Doping Code and the FIM Anti-Doping Code, the FIM is unable to provide any additional information at this time.

Information was scarce but, in an interview published on Transworld mx on 16th of April, team manager Roger Decoster confirmed that the team had very little contact with the FIM in Europe and no clear information from the FIM officials located in the United States. Tickle only had only two working days to lodge an appeal and because he was notified late on Thursday evening, Friday would be counted as one of those working days. As part of Aldon Baker's training program there was concern that other riders could have also taken something, even if it was inadvertently, although everyone involved with the team thought that Tickle was innocent, and Baker is a strong advocate of clean living and minimal use of dietary and nutritional supplements. The substance concerned turned out to offer a short-term boost similar to drinking a cup of coffee so it seemed illogical that anyone would jeopardise their career for such a small effect. On 27th of April, Tickle issued the following statement.

As has been widely reported, on April 12, 2018 I was notified by the FIM of an alleged Adverse Analytical Finding for 5-Methylhexan-2-Amine, stemming from a random urine test on February 10, 2018, directly after the San Diego Supercross Event. The notification from the FIM was a complete surprise to me because I have never, intentionally or negligently, ingested any prohibited substance, and specifically, the alleged substance I allegedly had in my system on February 10, 2018. I have never cheated, doped, or tried to better myself by taking the short way; nor, has anyone around me offered or provided to me any substance that is prohibited by the FIM Anti-Doping Code. I have worked too hard throughout my career to put my career at stake by taking any prohibited substance.

I am devastated about this allegation, and really frustrated with the process. The FIM has been less than professional with me regarding timeliness of communication, disclosure of information related to my Sample A test, and request to Test Sample B. After much delay, the FIM finally has informed me that the soonest that my Sample B will be tested is May 16, 2018*, the receipt of results and supporting lab documentation undisclosed. In addition, the soonest I will receive the lab documentation associated with Sample A is 10-15 working days from April 15th, 2018.

At this point, I have filed a Request to Lift the Discretionary Provisional Suspension imposed, but have little faith in this process as it is based solely on written documentation. The soonest that I will have a full-blown hearing regarding this allegation will be months from now. I have discovered that the FIM is an organization that possesses ultimate power — to suspend a professional athlete with the stroke of a pen, without any process, opportunity to defend, and no supporting evidence. Consequently, the FIM eliminates the athlete's source of income, and consequently their financial wherewithal to defend themselves with what little information is provided, all while refusing to timely communicate, and disclose evidence. To say that the process is unfair is an understatement.

Despite this disproportionality, I will do everything possible to fight this allegation, clear my name, and continue with my career. Should anyone have any information that may be relevant to my case, please contact my attorney, Brian D. Harrison at harrison@harrisonlegal.net. Thank you.

*Interestingly, shortly after filing of my Request to Lift the Provisional Suspension, the FIM advised me that they contacted the Laboratory to change the date for Sample B testing to May 9, 2018; however, no information was conveyed as to date of receipt of such test, or the lab documentation associated therewith.

I have to say that I fully support the goal of eradicating doping and drugs cheating in sport, for a number of reasons. Firstly, I want sport to be fair with the athlete that has worked the hardest and has the most talent succeeding. Secondly, we have to protect athletes from unscrupulous team, agents, managers and sponsors who are happy to risk the young athlete's health for short term gain by making them take dangerous drugs and thirdly, we have to protect the athletes from themselves if they are tempted to take the easy route and cheat, although the third point is controversial in itself. Known as 'the Goldman dilemma' after a study by US Physician Bob Goldman that offered them sporting success at the cost; they would die five years later. About half said they would take the magic pill and that has precipitated the belief that most athletes are so focused on winning, that they would trade long-term health problems (or even death), for short-term glory: a kind of live-fast-die-young, trade-off. There are a couple of problems with the original research that was done in 1984. Firstly, times have changed so attitudes move on, and secondly it was only 198 athletes which statistically is a very small sample. With a sample that small and a carefully phrased question you could produce whatever outcome you wanted. One of the authors, Associate Professor Stephen Moston (Department of Psychology, CQ University) said: *"The story of the Goldman Dilemma has grown with each retelling, with a succession of authors adding their own interpretations, twisting the story to fit their own preconceptions and personal theories. It is used to justify strict anti-doping controls, to protect athletes from themselves. Basic privacies and rights have been cast aside, all to safeguard athletes from their baser instincts."* (Source - http://www.medianet.com.au/releases/150427/)

However laudable the goals, the process must be fair and transparent otherwise it is no better than burning people accused of being witches in the middle ages. Tickle's case raises a number of concerns for me, and don't think that this is an American problem, any MXGP rider could be in the same boat.

1. Why does it take over two months to test the sample?

2. Why is the rider banned from riding immediately? Surely there should be a hearing to weigh the evidence with the rider innocent

until proven guilty. The F.I.M. statement says 'provisionally suspended' but there's nothing provisional about it, the rider is suspended immediately.

3. The information needs to be available immediately to the rider and team so that they can defend themselves or admit guilt without delay.

4. Any ban needs to be proportionate. There should be a different punishment for serious attempts at cheating than for the accidental use of something like an inhaler or cough medicine.

For Tickle the consequences of being found guilty go beyond getting banned from racing. KTM have a clause in the riders' contracts that if they are found using banned substances and barred from competing they have to repay KTM their earnings and he would be sacked. Tickle hasn't exactly been setting the world on fire with his results, and with the knowledge that he risked losing all his earnings and a factory ride, it seems crazy that he would deliberately take the substance.

That also brings up the use of T.U.E.'s or Therapeutic Use Exemptions. These allow athlete with a bona fide health issue to use medication in prescribed doses, for example asthma medication or to treat hay fever. Whilst the idea is good there have been allegations of the abuse of T.U.E.'s whereby an athlete will get the team doctor to diagnose them as asthmatic when they are not, thus allowing the use of asthma medication that opens the airways and gives a performance advantage. Team Sky and Sir Bradley Wiggins were accused of such practices and whilst they vehemently denied the charges, such practices are certainly against the spirit of the rules if not the letter of the rules.

There are rumours of riders seeking to gain an advantage in this way, indeed James Stewart was banned for taking Adderall without having correctly submitted a T.U.E. I'm not suggesting that he didn't need the drugs for genuine reasons but by failing to submit the correct paperwork he was deemed to be guilty and banned for sixteen months. It's difficult to substantiate any of the rumours as obviously people are very secretive about such activities if they are using T.U.E.'s.

Testing takes place after the races with riders picked at random, but each year a number of riders are selected as part of the registered testing pool. These riders can be tested at any time and must indicate one hour per day when they can be tested at a specified location. Failure to comply with a test or failure to be at the specified location when WADA officials turn up can also be punished by a ban. In the aftermath of the Tickle case, Jason Anderson said he had been taken from a restaurant to a hotel to give a sample. This seems at best heavy handed and at worst an abuse of authority with no respect for the athlete concerned.

The Hitachi/ASA KTM team have first-hand experience of the system from 2012 when Natalie Kane was riding for the team, then called the HM plant/KTM UK team. She was a 'registered rider' and had to start by filling out an extensive on-line form. She also had to give her location at all times. She told me *"It's hard to know where you're going to be all the time. If it rains or the weather changes you might want to go somewhere else, but you can't go until you've told them. They want to know where and when you are every day not just the weekend. You had to log in and change it every day if your plans changed. One time they came out when I was training (at a track) and wanted to take a sample there. I was escorted by a woman medical person to the toilet, she led me to the door and waited outside the cubicle. I was also tested at three GP's. I was always tested if I had a good race, they were watching me and if they thought I had a good race they would test. I had to go with them to the port-a-loo behind the podium and give a sample before the podium presentation. I've never cheated but it is stressful knowing that even if you took some cough medicine there could be something in it. I have asthma, so I had to send them a doctor's note and I always carried it around just in case. I was only on the light inhaler but even that would have been illegal if I hadn't told them. It lasted for a year and when it ended I didn't even hear from them to say thank you and it's over, they just disappeared".*

On the 15th of May Tickle was informed via e-mail that his 'B' sample had also tested positive. Keep in mind that this was two months after the sample was taking in San Diego and a month after he was suspended. He issued the statement below and his frustration is obvious.

Today, via e-mail, I was notified by the FIM that testing of my Sample B allegedly confirmed the alleged results of my Sample A test; however, as of today, neither the FIM or the laboratory has provided any supporting evidence for the alleged testing results. In addition, the FIM informed me that, Article 3.3.1 of the FIM Disciplinary and Arbitration Code, Mr. Anand Sashidharan has been appointed by the Director of the International Commission of Judges (CJI) as single judge to "deal" with case before the International Disciplinary Court (CDI). Mr. Sashidharan is the same person that presided over Mr. James Stewart's proceedings. Now that my case has been formally identified with the CDI, perhaps the process will proceed in a professional manner so that I can finally begin to defend myself. Their system presumes my guilt and presumes their supremacy all while hindering, impeding, and delaying an athlete's ability to discover evidence to argue against both. As I stated before, I have never, intentionally or negligently, ingested any prohibited substance, and specifically, the alleged substance I allegedly had in my system on February 10, 2018. I have never cheated, doped, or tried to better myself by taking the short way; nor, has anyone around me offered or provided to me any substance that is prohibited by the FIM Anti-Doping Code. I have worked too hard throughout my career to put my career at stake by taking any short cuts. I will do everything possible to fight this allegation, clear my name, and continue with my career. Should anyone have any information that may be relevant to my case, please contact my attorney, Brian D. Harrison.

The next day Tickle was sacked by KTM and the press release simply read;

It was released today by the FIM that Broc Tickle's initial positive test from San Diego Supercross was confirmed by the "B sample" test. As a result, KTM Motorsports hereby makes the painful decision to terminate its agreement with Tickle, effective immediately. Roger DeCoster, KTM Race Director SX/MX: "We've had a good relationship with Broc over the last six months and he was a great guy to work with. However, KTM's strong company policy gives no room for any other solution but to terminate the contract. We wish Broc the best in the future."

Tickle did a video interview on Transworld MX where he seemed resigned to getting banned but none the wiser as to how he had ingested to substance. He was pragmatic about being sacked by KTM but determined to clear his name and reduce any ban as far as possible.

As is his rite, he applied to have the 'provisional suspension' lifted pending the full hearing. It was denied on the 20th June as one might expect, with no further comment from the F.I.M.

At the Ottobiano MXGP a number of riders were called in for random testing, including the HRC riders Tim Gajser and Todd Waters (filling in for the injured Brian Bogers). When Waters was giving his sample, the official (allegedly) handed him the paperwork for Gajser. He obviously pointed out that it was the wrong name, but Gajser had already been and gone. Stories like that don't exactly fill me with confidence about the reliability of the system.

I've included this in the book as a case study because it could easily happen to any rider in the MXGP paddock, a spurious test result and their career is over before they ever get a chance to defend themselves. I'm not talking about letting deliberate drugs cheats off, but a chance to explain yourself is part of natural justice.

WADA need to improve their procedures, transparency, communications and speed because now they appear to be no better than a bureaucratic judge, jury and executioner.

In the parallel universe of professional cycling, Chris Froome tested positive for Salbutamol after stage 18 of the 2017 Vuelta a Espana (Tour of Spain), an asthma drug. The issue was that the amount exceeded the permitted dose and gave an "adverse analytical finding". Unlike Tickle, Froome was allowed to carry on competing as Salbutamol is a 'specified substance' rather than a prohibited one, meaning Froome was allowed the chance explain the test result and continue racing in the meantime. He would also win the Giro d'Italia (Tour of Italy) in the spring of 2018, although if he was found guilty he would be stripped of the Vuelta and Giro titles. There was some controversy just before the Tour de France when the organisers moved to stop him competing under article 29 of its own rules which states it "reserves the right to refuse the participation in – or disqualify from – the event, a team or one of its members whose presence is liable to damage the image or reputation of ASO or those of the event" as he was still under the cloud of investigation. Team Sky appealed to the French Olympic committee's court of arbitration and in the week before the Tour started the UCI (cycling's governing body) came to the conclusion that despite Froome having exceeded the permitted dose for asthma drug salbutamol in a 24-hour period, the explanation provided by the rider and his team, alongside 'significant additional expert evidence', gave sufficient grounds to have the original finding overturned.

A simple Google search will throw up numerous articles on this case, among the more interesting are about the mitigation that could be used for the adverse finding; pharmacokinetics (how drugs pass through the body), the effects of dehydration, urine density, the effects of exertion as well as the severity of his asthma at the time. The key difference between this case and Tickle's is that Froome was allowed to continue racing while the facts were gathered (which seems like a much more reasonable approach) and he also had the full support of the Sky team and their experts throughout. Had he been found guilty he would have been severely punished, and rightly so but Tickle was presumed guilty and hung out before any process had taken place. The F.I.M. need to examine their protocol in my opinion; why couldn't Tickle be allowed to finish the supercross series and race in the AMA Nationals until his case was heard? I edited the final book manuscript in early October, eight months after Tickle's positive test and six months after he was informed and "provisionally suspended", yet I still can't include an update, verdict or conclusion to the story!'

Cleared to start the 2018 Tour de France, talk turned to Froome making history if he won the Tour, joining cycling legends Jacques Anquetil, Eddy Merckx, Bernard Hinault and Miguel Indurain as the only men on five victories. The world's most famous drugs cheat, Lance Armstrong had won seven before his cheating was discovered but his results have now been expunged from the record books, his

> only legacy being that seeking an advantage by taking drugs won't be tolerated in any sport. As it turned out, Geraint Thomas would win Le Tour and Froome would have to wait another year to join the legends with five wins.
> In December 2014, Motocross Action Editor Jody Weisel wrote an interesting article on James Stewart's case and a few other riders that have failed drugs tests. You can find it at https://motocrossactionmag.com/amp/10-things-you-need-to-know-about-james-stewarts-doping-case/

With no support classes scheduled for this event it may as well have been a fly-away. Set in the middle of now where, it was difficult to find flights that landed anywhere near the track so a five-hour car journey was a nice little sting in the tail. When I looked at booking the trip, most of the flights were indirect, took a very long time with stop-overs and were expensive. The trip to America for the 'nations was cheaper and quicker!

It was too far from most of the tourist destinations to get a package holiday and hire a car for a day trip to the GP. The event was launched with a very professional presentation at the MXGP of Trentino where Giuseppe Luongo assured the assembled team managers and journalists that the organisation would be first-class, so it seems like a shame to use a venue that was so far off the beaten track that it was always going to be difficult and expensive to get to for teams and spectators alike. Even the packages put together by the organisers (which were very tempting) were still expensive in my opinion. Ultimately though, the sanctioning fees still get paid and the TV cameras focus on the battle at the front and any battles just behind so even if there's only fifteen riders on the gate it still makes good TV viewing. The low number of riders that entered in Bulgaria didn't get any better for Turkey, just twenty-three riders entered in each class. Even that figure was flattering as there were four local wildcards in each class that had no right to be there in my opinion, thirty seconds a lap off the pace, it was like the Indonesia rounds all over again. you have riders that are that much slower they create a safety hazard as they are unable to do most of the big jumps and just get in the way of the genuine GP riders, who were lapping them after three laps. To me it would make much more sense to offer the top ten in the EMX250 class a free entry and assistance with travel expenses to give them some experience and exposure rather than putting local rich kids out there.

In the MXGP class Jeffrey Herlings all but wrapped up the championship with two more wins that took his points lead to ninety-five with just one hundred points available. Only Cairoli had a mathematical chance to catch Herlings but a fifteenth or better in the first race at Assen would be enough for Herlings to be champion. Romain Febvre took a hit in timed practice that saw him taken to hospital, a concussion ending his weekend. He had only just returned to his old self after a concussion sustained at Matterley Basin in 2016; that injury seemed to hamper him all the way through 2017 although he did struggle with bike set-up issues too. Knowing about Max Anstie's experience with concussion I hope Febvre takes the necessary time to recover properly but with fifth place in the championship to defend and the MXON looming you know there would be pressure to race if possible.

In the first MX2 race, KTM teammates Jorge Prado and Pauls Jonass crashed into one another as they battled for the lead. Both riders were unhurt but it could have taken them both out of the championship hunt. Lisa Leyland interviewed both as they lined up for the start of race 2 and they were both keen to play it down as a racing incident but Jonass said he had hurt his knee and Prado was a disappointing seventh, looking decidedly de-tuned. I would've loved to be a fly on the wall in their respective KTM trucks after the race!

Chapter 24

ROUND 19, MXGP OF THE NETHERLANDS, ASSEN, FOXHILLS & THE ASA PARTNERSHIP

Assen is the event that best illustrates Youthstream's ideas for taking MXGP forward and attracting a new audience. A completely man-made track is constructed on the start-finish straight of TT-circuit Assen, also known as 'the cathedral of speed'. Thousands of tonnes of sand are trucked in and shaped into rollers, jumps and turns. With a huge covered grandstand and giant TV screen, it gives the spectator an experience that is far removed from standing on a muddy slope peering over track fencing. A huge paved paddock area and plenty of permanent on-site facilities make it feel much more inviting to the less hardcore fans. It also embodies everything that is wrong with modern MXGP if you listen to the 'old-school-natural tracks-were-better' gang. On the weekend before Assen, the Vets MX des Nations was held at Farleigh Castle. It's the biggest twin shock and evo event in the world, attracting riders from around the world for a nostalgic trip down memory lane, and in fairness to them, some great racing. Farleigh Castle is the perfect venue for a twin shock and evo meeting; grassy, off camber turns and a few small jumps set on a gentle hillside with all the history that comes from being the home of the British 500 GP in the 70's and 80's. Beautiful autumn weather only added to the ambience as I watched with an old friend. *"I'd come here every week"* he said, *"proper moto-cross on a proper track."* We discussed the merits of venues like Assen and although he hasn't been to an MXGP for years he wouldn't concede that modern track design has progressed. *"It's just jumps, nothing technical like you get here."* I guess it's just a matter of personal preference and not really an argument you can win if the other person's mind is set.

There's obviously a market for the old bikes and evo/twin shock meetings but modern bikes have evolved and riding techniques progressed, so they need different obstacles to test them. It's also worth remembering that the infrastructure needed today simply wouldn't fit in some of the old tracks like Farleigh. It's always good catching up with old friends and check out the painstakingly restored bikes, but it's not MXGP and I prefer Assen to Farleigh. Behind the grandstand there's a massive covered bike park and a storage area for leathers and helmets, trade stands, food vendors and decent toilets; the place is set up for bike fans.

Graeme and Conrad had both recovered from their recent injuries and were hoping for a strong performance at the two remaining GPs and British championship rounds, but in Assen all eyes were on Jeffrey Herlings who would almost certainly clinch his first MXGP championship in the first race. The Dutchman is already a legend in Holland, often making the mainstream TV and newspaper headlines and only beaten in terms of public profile by his Formula 1 countryman Jos Verstappen. There would be a big partisan crowd wanting to see their man seal the deal. He had turned twenty-four on the Wednesday before Assen so it could be a double celebration.

Roger was in Assen with his own deals to finalise so I asked him to bring us up to date on Saturday morning.

"KTM have made us a formal offer for a number of riders about two weeks ago for bikes and a spares budget so we know that's set. There's a couple of omissions, they've cut back on the WP support package for the grand prix so we'll have to find some more budget for that. The number of bikes etc has been agreed but there's another rider that's come into the equation in the last ten days so we might modify that but it looks like we're ready to go. Negotiations with the main sponsors have been going pretty well over the last couple of weeks and it looks like everything is gonna be

put in place a wee bit earlier this year."

There are rumours flying around about your rider line-up for next year, would you like to confirm them?

"It looks like its going to be Graeme Irwin and Max Anstie on 450's, and Conrad Mewse and Bas Vaessen in MX2, but until it's signed we don't really know for sure."

So, you're planning on expanding the team to three or even four riders?

"I think it could be a combination of both. We hope to retain Graeme and Conrad but we need to secure some additional funding if Graeme wants to do the fly-aways. The second MX2 rider will come on board and it's onwards and upwards."

I've heard that you want to keep the existing staff, Jakke, BC, Vas and Minty but presumably you'll need additional mechanics for the new riders.

"There's additional mechanics that we were approached by back in Lommel and we think we will probably end up with at least one of those mechanics, maybe two. We will also have an additional practice bike mechanic which we didn't have this year. We just have to sort out the logistics when everything is put in place but until we've got the jigsaw together we can talk about it but we need to see who's gonna be living where and what their expectations are. It depends if Conrad is going to be in the UK more than Belgium and the second MX2 rider is in Belgium more than the UK; it's how we plan for that."

Changing the subject slightly, the calendar for next year includes six fly-aways and is going to be very expensive. There's a lot of talk in the paddock about the costs and logistics; what's your thoughts about it?

"Youthstream have said this is where we're going but they haven't given any indication of costs. The non-factory teams are making representations to Youthstream today with regard to 2019 and there's a number of items on the agenda to discuss. The non-factory teams aren't happy with the additional cost but they obviously want to continue doing all the GPs but there has to be some give and take regarding what S.E.L. (Youthstream's travel and logistics partner) charges."

Is there a danger that some of the teams are getting priced out?
"Effectively that's what is happening, that's why the grids at some GPs haven't been what they should be. Surely they should take that on board and have a reasonably full grid with riders of the right calibre. Its also the safety factor; its dangerous to have a mobile road block out there."

I also wanted to ask you about the partnership with ASA and whether that will continue for next year.
"It might be better to discuss that after Foxhills because we don't really know how that's gonna work out. We don't really know if we can get the additional funding for Graeme to do the fly-aways so it depends which way we structure with four riders. Whether we continue with ASA is really up to him (Lee Tolan). I think if he gets more of what he wants in relation to Graeme then maybe he will continue but time will tell."

Jamie Dobb was representing Max Anstie in negotiations with the Factory and Roger, trying to secure factory material and support for Max to run under the Hitachi awning. If they could pull the deal together it would be huge for Roger's team and with Bas Vaessen joining in MX2 it would be one of the strongest teams in the paddock.

Team co-ordinator Ian Browne was less enthusiastic about the prospect. Running four riders is a huge undertaking which is why most teams only run two or three; it just takes so much work, money and resources. Then there's the simple practicalities like having enough space for the mechanics to work at the workshop and under the awning, living space in the race truck for another two mechanics and the vans and logistics involved.

Anstie had looked at racing in America but really wanted to stay in MXGP and the prospect of securing him was enticing for Roger; he's a genuine podium threat, great with the fans and would be a strong favourite to win the British championship. Roger, Howard and Jamie Dobb spent most of the weekend in small huddles. Robert Jonas, the boss of KTM (but no relation to the MX2 rider Pauls Jonass), was also back and forth as phone calls, offers and counter-offers were exchanged. Roger's negotiations with his two main sponsors, Milwaukee and Hitachi, were virtually concluded and over the weekend the deals with Anstie and Vaessen were agreed with contracts set to be signed at the next MXGP at Imola in two weeks. It wasn't just the bikes and factory support from KTM; Anstie came with sponsorship from Fox clothing and they would come on board as a team sponsor, not only for race gear for all four riders but the team's corporate wear for the mechanics and team staff. As the premier clothing brand in the paddock this was a real coup; a fantastic sponsor to enhance the professionalism, presentation and image of the team.

Jeffrey Herlings duly won both races and clinched the championship as expected, and with two great rides Anstie grabbed third place on the podium making his imminent arrival at the team feel even more sweet.

Graeme and Conrad had less successful weekends with each managing to shoot himself in the foot, metaphorically speaking of course.

Conrad had had plenty of time since getting injured at Hawkstone. He looked fit and had been back on the bike getting plenty of practice and said he felt confident coming in to Assen after a great ride there in 2017 and really believed he could get on the podium. In the qualifying race he was running second until half distance when Vlaanderen passed him but he still finished a comfortable third. With Dixon Kawasaki reportedly still wanting to sign him, he had asked for additional salary if he finished on the podium. You can't blame him for trying to maximise his wages but after the lacklustre season so far I thought he was lucky to be offered the same deal again let alone ask for a pay rise. 9 – 16 race finishes for eleventh overall were very disappointing numbers that certainly didn't help his cause. The second race was particularly damning as he lost about eighteen places in the first lap. A great jump out of the gate put him in about third place but as the pack dived into the sharp-right first turn Conrad hit the brakes rather than dive inside and fight for his place. With riders streaming around the outside of turn one to put themselves inside for the left-hand turn two, Conrad was shut out, ending the first lap in twenty-first place, shades of Portugal all over again. After going through all the growing pains throughout the season this seemed like déjà vu and not in a good way.

Shaun Osmond didn't hold back with his opinion. *"If he thought he was worth more money for finishing on the podium today then he rides like that Roger should reduce the offer by the same amount. That second race was appalling."* And no-one in the camp disagreed.

Graeme's 20 – 17 finishes were less than he hoped for but scoring in both races for the fourth time this season was good. However, he had made a comment in the week that he intended to finish his motocross career at the end of 2019 and go road racing in the British Super Bikes championship. It may seem like an innocent remark but why would Roger continue to invest in a rider who would be leaving the team and the sport, particularly when he had a faster rider joining the team. Anstie hadn't been under-handed in any way, if anything his due diligence was impressive. He had phoned Graeme amongst others, to find out what the team was like to ride for. Graeme had told him that he had been given everything he had asked for and Shaun Simpson said he had his most successful years whilst riding for them. Max Anstie is close friends with both Simpson and Conrad so probably knew quite a lot about the team already but Graeme seemed oblivious to the fact that his position in the team was likely to change. I asked Graeme if he was concerned about Anstie joining the team and he said he thought it would be good to have a fast teammate to practice with and that hopefully it would mean more resources for the 450 side of the team. Maybe Roger hadn't told him that without more funding his MXGP schedule would be reduced as Max would be getting star billing.

Foxhills.

From the deep sand of Assen to the hard-packed clay of Wiltshire, the swooping Foxhills track couldn't be more different. Earlier in the year the MX Nationals cancelled a meeting at the track stating that it wasn't of a sufficient standard to hold their race. It appeared that this criticism had spurred the owners into action and some improvements had been made, more soil added to the rock-hard ground. The weekend would be potentially pivotal for Conrad; with Josh Gilbert fourteen points behind and Mel Pocock just fourteen points behind in the championship he couldn't afford any mistakes. What had looked like a walk in the park for Conrad at the start of the year had come unravelled at Hawkstone and with just four races left he needed something to salvage his season. Graeme wasn't mathematically eliminated from the championship but he would need horrendous bad luck to befall Jake Nicholls who was fifty-two points in front. Evgeny Bobryshev sat in second just thirteen points ahead of Graeme so second place was still a realistic target.

On the Thursday before Foxhills, a storm started brewing both metrologically and metaphorically. Jake Nicholls appeared on Mel Pocock's Instagram post riding at the re-vamped Foxhills track. The ACU prohibit practicing at a British championship track before an event so understandably Pocock, other teams and riders wanted to know what Nicholls was doing there. Clerk of the course, Chris Warren, was emphatic that it was all above board, even having a dig at Pocock. Gatedrop.com published his statement which said

"There was one rider invited and he was invited for a press day to get some publicity pictures and videos were taken and forwarded to the Swindon Herald to coincide with some adverts that come out today and tomorrow. That rider was Jake Nicholls. I'm not stupid I know the rule book, I wrote it I think! It was definitely not the full track, he rode round probably 25% of it.

To be honest I am desperately trying to get this track right in time for the weekend in 60mph gales and Mr Pocock is not helping me. I can assure you he (Nicholls) did 25% of the track photographs and videos were taken to appear on the Swindon Herald FB pages to coincide with our adverts. It's what every organiser does to try and get people to come through the gate to watch people like Mel Pocock so he gets sponsored rides and makes a living out of motocross."

If Warren and the ACU thought that was the end of it they were mistaken. I was told that at least two team managers had protested, not against Nicholls who was only doing what he was told, but against his Buildbase

Honda team, owned by Dave Thorpe, and the ACU. Predictably the on-line world was quick to voice a variety of opinions about the 'press day' that all became moot-points the next day when the organising Langrish club took the "bold decision" (their words in a press release) and cancelled the meeting due to "the heavy rain and driving winds forecast for the southwest". With no championship meeting it didn't matter who had ridden there in the week, or so the ACU may have hoped but the story was far from over. I'll let Roger explain.

"We're most disappointed that the ACU have taken this decision. We've got flights, hotels and hire cars in place and they don't think about the impact on the teams. I've made my feelings known to the ACU today that the meeting should be re-run after the Weston beach race. The decision to cancel favours some teams and not others; you could say it favours us with Conrad 14 points in front but Graeme still had an outside chance with four races left, a slim chance but anything can happen and we already lost one opportunity at Duns when they cancelled race 2. These decisions seem to have a common denominator; Dave Thorpe seems to be instrumental in at least two; the protest at Blaxhall and the second race getting cancelled at Duns, and now Foxhills. I don't mind about the press day, we're not criticising Jake but press days are usually local riders, and there are a lot of other top riders that live a lot closer than Jake but no-one else got invited. The press day was supposed to be for the Swindon Herald Facebook page but I've searched for it and don't think it even exists. The ACU wasn't receptive to rescheduling Foxhills but I'm writing to them tomorrow to suggest that they run the final round at Lyng as two days so that everyone still has four races. I don't agree with double points for the last round, we just want an open championship without any scandal."

Within the paddock community the suspicion of skulduggery and alleged undue influence exerted by Dave Thorpe was being openly discussed with the further allegation that a few individuals with vested interests were putting their own bank balance before the interests of the sport. The on-line conspiracy theories started almost immediately about the reason for the cancellation; *'the ACU cancelled to dodge the protests', 'the track wasn't ready', 'my mate lives near there and it hasn't rained all day'* were just some of the things I read. If the meeting had run the track may have been muddy, it's not a track that handles rain as well as a sand track, but the way the ACU handled the 'press day' with Nicholls was either naïve or incompetent (you can't just bull-shit your way out of it when you've broken your own rules and been busted on social media), and even if the decision to cancel was the correct one it was a public relations disaster. As it turned out the weather wasn't anywhere near as bad as forecast and just to prove the point, Hitachi/ASA posted pictures on Facebook of the track taken on Sunday morning with a tea-light candle perched on the gate and the caption *"Photos taken this morning proves that the cancellation on Friday was very premature – very little rain and not enough rain to blow a candle out!! More answers are required for the REAL reason that the round was cancelled."* The reaction was predictable with multiple comments criticising the Buildbase team and the ACU.

With the meeting cancelled, I called ASA owner Lee Tolan to get his reaction. His main focus was on the British championships so he was less than pleased.

"Firstly, for them to take the round away would be unfair for anyone who's got a chance of salvaging some points, I would say that because Graeme needs points but there will be other people too. It just doesn't feel like a proper championship if they do away with the round, we already lost a race at Duns. There's a lot of money and time been invested this year; money is one thing but time and effort is another thing. I run a scaffolding business with fifty blokes and it doesn't take as much time and effort as the team, so for someone to take away a round just because someone was riding at a track that they shouldn't have been is completely unreasonable for all the sponsors".

"Do you think that's the real reason it's been cancelled?"

"I don't know. I've never heard of a British championship being cancelled

because of the weather so early, they normally get you all there and run a block before they make a decision. If the weather turns out to be that bad you'll say it's a good call but if it's not that bad it's a bad decision. The riders can get around and it makes the championship more exciting because anyone can win. I don't think the weather is the thing. Jake riding the track in the week, when he was invited by the promoter is supposed to be the reason why because people been making a noise about it but unless they publicly make an announcement saying that, we'll never know. It's easy to blame the ACU but speculation can get a lot of people in trouble so we've just got to go along with it."

What's your preferred solution to this? There is really only one free weekend at the end of October so time is running out to rearrange the event.

"The two-dayer at Lyng sounds like the best option, even if they just ran MX1 and MX2 on Saturday. For us, Graeme wants to redeem himself and win races. We've got Graeme who needs the points and Conrad who doesn't so we could say let's wrap it up quick and win the MX2 but that's not what it's about."

I really wanted to know if the partnership with Roger was a success from Lee's perspective. There had been some teething problems at first but we were nine months in, so it was time to ask some questions.

> ## The ASA partnership.
> Right from the start I think there was a difference of opinion about how the partnership between Roger's team and Lee's ASA set-up would work. Lee had a vision of raising the professionalism of British Championship motocross and would run the British championship effort, providing the race truck and awning for the British championships with the articulated race truck used for MXGP. Lee supported Michael Ellis in MX2 and later Jack

Brunell in the 2-stroke championship as well as jointly supporting Graeme with Roger. Conrad was not part of Lee's deal but would use the awning at British championships. It seemed that Roger viewed him as a sponsor rather than an equal partner but was happy for Lee to be the team manager at British championships. The mechanics would turn up with the bikes in Sprinters, use the work space under the awning then leave, so I was interested to understand how Lee saw his role. Ian was the team co-ordinator and ran things on a day-to-day basis which included the preparation before each race and both Roger and Lee also seemed to have an entirely different expectations about the hospitality side of the team. I asked Lee to talk me through his experiences.

You told me one of your goals was to raise the image and professionalism of the British championship paddock with a race truck and awning rather than sprinter vans and pop-ups. Can we tick that off as mission accomplished?

"Definitely. We've had a lot of positive feedback but I feel we could've done better in some areas. Just the way we presented some of the graphics, I approved it all quite late and it was forced a little bit. We didn't have time to try out different awning set-ups but it's just me being particular. We've had good feedback, what did you think of it?"

I thought the truck and awning looked great but one thing I wanted to ask you about was the lack of hospitality. There hasn't been a hospitality space under your awning and I remember at Culham when it was wet and cold, standing with one of the team's sponsors who puts in a lot of money and he couldn't even sit out of the rain. If I was spending my money on the team I would've been very unhappy. You ended up with Steve Fry bringing his camper and doing the hospitality alongside your truck."

"We knew in the beginning that the awning would only take four bays

so the plan was for Roger to arrange the hospitality so I left it to him. There was a cup of tea and sandwiches at Culham but you're right, it wasn't ideal. I agreed with Roger that I would provide the facilities for the bikes. I understand that it wasn't good if a sponsor was left outside."

Moving on to your riders, how would you assess their performances this year?

"I accept motocross for what it is. Let's start with Graeme Irwin, I know that he gives 110%. He's had a terrible year but its not for the want of trying, that's why I wanted to invest in him. At Hawkstone he could hardly get on the bike with his back but he pulled off a podium, I was ecstatic. I'd said to him that there's no pressure from me if he couldn't ride but he pulled it off, that was the best time of the year for me.

Conrad has got such a talent but he's had his ups and downs. He's Roger's rider so I don't know much about what's gone on so I can't really comment on him.

Michael Ellis was a bit unnoticed but he's got talent and has been chipping away. I'd been watching him and they approached me when we were setting up this team so we gave it a go. He's made the top ten at the last few rounds and I think he's got a lot more to offer. I've been more excited by him, watching him develop and grow to be honest, feeding him the right information for his confidence and to feel at home."

You were riding in the 2-stroke championship but at Desertmartin you put Jack Brunell on the bike and stopped riding. What was the reason?

"I was just over-worked. At the beginning of the year it sounded like a fantastic idea for me to ride, represent my own team and be involved, it was just living the dream really. I know I'm not a pro rider

but I could compete in the 2-stroke championship; I don't want to discredit them but it's not the same calibre as MX1 and MX2. But I was so tired after, trying to organise the team, ride, pack everything up after then go to work the next day, I just thought I can't keep doing it. It was an easy decision to put Jack on the bike, let a pro do more justice to the team than I could. After I took a step back from riding it meant I could enjoy the team a bit more, be there for Graeme on the line, go down with Michael and show them my support; I couldn't do that when I was riding."

You've mentioned to me a couple of times how much work it is running the team but which aspect is the most demanding, either timewise or mentally?

"It's not that it's hard, it's just trying to run it, and run my business and the track at Mill Lane. Everything comes back to me for decisions so it's a lot of stress when its combined with my full-time job. The amount of money it takes as well."

You told me previously that there were some teething issues initially with the 'two-team' arrangements, your ASA side at British championships and Roger's side, but things like the hospitality at Culham just seems to be a communication issue. How has the overall experience been? It sounds like there have been some learning points along the way.

"Well........ the season has not been the one I was sold. Graeme signed with me to do the British championship but we didn't have a manufacturer. Graeme had spoken to Honda and also JK Yamaha offered him a ride. He said how would I feel about him riding for them in the GPs and me in Britain? They would supply bikes and parts and we would do our own venture with their bikes. It looked like a done-deal but near the end I noticed a couple of things that weren't right

and to cut a long story short we ended up not doing it. Roger had called Graeme and offered a deal, we agreed what we were going to pay and it was agreed that he would ride for Roger in GPs and me in the British but it didn't go how we agreed. I never saw a bike, they got prepared at Roger's place and turned up. My name was supposed to be title sponsor on the bike and in the programme at GPs as Hitachi/ ASA KTM but it wasn't. It did start to fall apart and we stuck a plaster on it and got through. There was a point where I was gonna pull out, I said to Graeme this isn't what I signed up for, it looks like you're riding for Roger and not me. Even after Culham everyone thought it was Roger's deal and I didn't know how it was gonna affect me, I just felt like all the effort I had put in was being ignored. I felt deflated and disheartened from it all, Roger's been in the game a long time and I suppose I wasn't getting what I wanted out of it. I guess I was looking for gratitude for bringing a new team to the British championship but it was being dismissed, even when you asked me the other week you called me a sponsor."

But you just referred to yourself as a title sponsor and that was how I referred to you in the text. I understand that you own the truck and the British championship side of things but with the team you're a title sponsor as in Hitachi/ASA KTM UK.

"That's how sensitive I am about it. I felt like someone else was taking my glory; that might be selfish on my part but I love motocross so much and all my effort and all my hard-earned money has been put into this team, I wanted it to be my little thing."

Do you think it would work better if you re-named your team as Lee Tolan Racing so it was Hitachi/LTR KTM UK?

"I suppose it wasn't thought about properly. You asked what I've learnt from these experiences and the reason I'm where I am today

is because I've made mistakes, nothing's been easy but I've learned a lot. I went into this the wrong way and I've come unstuck with a few things and had a bit of a reality check with the way things got done. I feel like people have made promises that they haven't kept and with the amount of money I've spent I haven't got what I wanted out of it, but I had to maintain my word to Graeme. If I had pulled out and told Graeme to carry on with Roger....... I couldn't do it because the one person I was doing it for was Graeme so I couldn't pull out for my own selfish reasons, I would've been walking away from him. We've had a good year with some bad luck but I have enjoyed it and learned a lot."

The 64,000-dollar question is, will the partnership continue next year? And if so in the same form or re-badged?

"We're negotiating very soon. I'll take what I've learned this year. I would like to have my own team but I can't get a deal with any manufacturer. They're all tied up and none of them are going to entertain a new team and I don't want to put the amount of money that's required to pay for everything. I can pay wages, I've got the truck and everything there to run a good team but you need so much money to run someone like Graeme and I'm not prepared to put that amount of money in, it just gets out of control. You need help from a manufacturer and then the other bits and pieces can be picked up."

It sounds like you want to continue but change a few things.

"There's lots of things I want to change but that's just my thoughts, it's all down to Roger. It's got to be a joint venture; there's things I definitely need and other things I've got movement with. It is gonna need a sit-down conversation, I've got a figure but I want to be involved. Graeme knows what's going on and the worst thing that can happen is that I walk away and he doesn't get any money for the British championship".

If you can't come to an agreement with Roger would you insist that Graeme still rides for you?

"Graeme can do what he wants, we're friends and I've told him he's got to do what's best for him so if it doesn't work out he could stay with Roger or come with me but I would like to keep it the way it is, iron out our differences and work together."

That sounds positive, you can learn from your mistakes and move on.

"Exactly, I'm learning all the time. Someone asked me why I'm doing it and I didn't want to say. But I love it and I want the credit for it, I want to stand back and be proud of what I've created but I didn't know that at the start. I wanted to do a team, do everything right, it should be easy to do everything properly and that's what I tried to do but it just didn't work out exactly as I wanted it, there was someone else making decisions and spoiling what I wanted to do. To make everything easy there need to be two people but you need to be on the same page and in the real world that doesn't always happen so you've got to make it work. For me, I've got to be realistic about what I want and with the experience I've gathered this year I hope to put that right next year. I've learnt about myself this year and I just want to be part of it, I love it so much.

It just depends on the amount of responsibility and the amount of money being put in. If the numbers get silly and I don't see the value in it, that may be the only thing but I'm willing to negotiate. I don't want to put years on myself but if I was a bit older I could probably enjoy it a bit more and not get so stressed about the things that bother me".

Without wanting to provoke an argument it only seemed fair to put some of Lee's points to Roger and give him the chance to reply. Roger was forthright as ever, *"Lee doesn't really seem to fathom what it really takes to keep a motocross team on the road for a full British and World Championship season. Yes, his contribution to the team has been valuable overall, but I really do believe he has had more coverage and recognition for himself and ASA than even he anticipated, as ASA has always been named in the team title by MXGP commentator Paul Malin. The ASA logo has also been prominent on ALL of the team riders' bikes, and not just Graeme's. That being said, I really do hope that Lee continues his support for Graeme and the team. At the end of the day, there is no "I" in team and we must all remember that in order to keep a happy, strong, focused and successful structure to the benefit of all."*

Anyone who thought running a team is easy has hopefully changed their mind after reading this book but if you needed more evidence of what a roller-coaster it can be here it is. Earlier in this chapter I told you about the negotiations with Max Anstie; it seemed like a deal had been agreed last weekend and everyone was excited about acquiring such a marque rider, the contract would be signed at Imola. When I asked Roger about it in the mini interview he said, *"It looks like it's going to be Graeme Irwin and Max Anstie on 450's, and Conrad Mewse and Bas Vaessen in MX2, but until it's signed we don't really know for sure."* Those words turned out to be wiser and more prophetic than I realised at the time. Amongst all the on-line chaff about Foxhills, Gatedrop MX posted on Saturday evening *"We are hearing that Britain's Max Anstie may have finally secure himself a ride in MXGP with Standing Construct KTM."* My heart sank as I read it; Gate drop are good moto journalists with their finger on the pulse and reliable sources. I sent a screen shot to Roger with the caption *"Fake news I hope."* Roger replied immediately. *"Doesn't seem to be – just found out a couple of hours ago as we had made him a good offer but I think he met Mathys (owner of Standing Construct) and got rail-roaded into signing – probably with the assistance of Monticelli money."*

It appeared that Anstie had taken the decision without negotiating or consulting his personal manager, Jamie Dobb, who had a longer-term strategy in mind for Max at Hitachi. Standing Construct is a good team with a base in Lommel and had already signed Coldenhoff and Monticelli so Max would have strong teammates in a team solely focused on the 450. You can't blame a rider for taking a 'better' offer but sometimes more money in the short term isn't the best choice in the long term. The deal was on the table and he had made his decision. It was a blow for Roger and the team but as he had said, *"until it's signed we don't really know for sure"*. It felt like more Déjà vu to me, the episode with Davy Pootjes that played out over the MXON weekend last year at Matterley only a more significant loss this time with Anstie.

On Monday the ACU put out a press release in which the British championship series manager, Stuart Drummond, stood by the call to cancel Foxhills due to the weather and confirmed that *"with no provision to re-run the Foxhill round, the 2018 championship will now conclude at Lyng on the reserve date of October 14."* That decision meant Graeme's quest to retain his number one plate was over; fifty-two points behind Jake Nicholls with only fifty points available from two races at Lyng. A ninth place in the first race at Lyng would secure the title for Nicholls (only Bobryshev could catch him but was thirty-nine points behind) although Graeme and Bobryshev would fight it out for second in the championship. It was an unsatisfactory end to Graeme's title defence; he had shown immense toughness and determination at Blaxhall to overcome the pain from serious burns sustained in practice and again at Hawkstone when he was barely able to ride but the DNF and cancelled second race at Duns had been the fatal blow in the points chase. Nicholls had been fast and consistent, winning five of the eleven races so far. He's a great rider whose own career has been dogged by injury, not least the dislocated hip that ended his MXGP aspirations last year so I'm pleased for him, a worthy and well-deserved British Champion, assuming he got the job done at Lyng.

The social media recriminations rumbled on all week. MX Vice ran in interview with Thorpe on the Tuesday in which he said the promoter had asked Nicholls along and the team were happy to oblige. Whilst his words were conciliatory, there were still plenty in the paddock enjoying his discomfort. He had phoned a number of team managers, riders and associates looking for support and I'm told he was given short shrift by all of them, most still ready to stick the knife in and get revenge for his previous alleged trouble making. Roger didn't believe Thorpe's comments, telling me *"he says that Buildbase always like to support the Clubs where they can also advertise their sponsors - if so, why was Jake Nicholls at the alleged Foxhill press day for Foxhill with a plain black Alpine Stars race shirt, devoid of any Team sponsors."*

Thanks to all the sponsors, we couldn't do it without you

Chapter 25 - Round 20, MXGP Imola, silly season wrap-up & the season reviewed.

Like Assen, Imola is part of Youthstream's plans to take MXGP to more spectator friendly venues. The iconic motor racing circuit would host the third MXGP in Italy this year. The hard-pack track was created at the start of the start/finish straight using the banking inside the race track and crossing the tarmac to a big paved area on the outside. It was a bit of a jump-fest but it did offer good viewing for the partisan crowd. Herlings may be the world champion but Cairoli is the superstar in Italy, mobbed by fans at every opportunity.

Silly season wrap-up.

The silly season moves that we mentioned in chapter 17 had mostly been finalised with the majority of the MXGP riders' new deals confirmed, including a few surprises.

Jeffrey Herlings and Antonio Cairoli would stay in their respective sides of the RedBull KTM team as they chased their tenth and fifth world championships respectively.

Pauls Jonass had been expected to move into the Factory Redbull KTM 450 team but instead went to the Ice One Husqvarna team alongside Arminas Jasikonis, two young guns with talent and ambition.

Glenn Coldenhoff was out of Factory Redbull KTM (to make way for Jonass we thought) and moved to the Standing Construct team to replace

Kevin Strijbos. Valentin Guillod was also let go by the team, replaced by Ivo Monticelli. That was a surprise to some but he was rumoured to come with a substantial cash input for the team which seems to be an increasing trend; the premium rider gets paid and the supporting rider pays the team. As discussed in the previous chapter Max Anstie was a late addition to make it a three-man 450 team.

Tommy Searle had been linked to Gebben van Venrooy Kawasaki but ended up at BOS alongside Evgeny Bobryshev as the team became a Kawasaki backed outfit. Gebben kept Alessandro Lupino after a strong season for the Italian and signed Benoit Paturel to replace Maxime Desprey. After Paturel's acrimonious split with BOS that played out on social media at the start of the year and a mixed bag of results with Marchetti KTM, it was a surprising signing but hopefully he will feel more at home back on a Japanese brand.

The MX Panda, Clement Desalle, and Julien Lieber would remain at Factory Kawasaki while HRC Honda stick with Tim Gajser and Brian Bogers who returned at Assen after missing the whole season with a complicated ankle injury.

Romain Febvre is joined by Jeremy Seewer who moved across to Factory Yamaha from the factory backed Wilvo Yamaha team. Wilvo promptly signed Gautier Paulin from Husqvarna and kept Arnaud Tonus for another year. Like Bogers, Tonus had not ridden all year, in his case a double shoulder injury had kept him out so both riders were very lucky to have the continued faith shown by their respective team managers.

Graeme Irwin stayed with Hitachi/ASA KTM UK and Shaun Simpson signed a late deal with a new team born out of a split by the ifly/JK Yamaha team. The team would race KTMs but had not announced the team title when I spoke to the manager in Imola.

Jordi Tixier found a home with the VHR KTM team. After two years of injuries and getting dropped by BOS in August he had looked to be heading out of MXGP so it was a welcome life-line.

That still left some big names without a home for 2019. Jeremy van

Horbeek said he would retire if he couldn't find a suitable team 'rather than risk his life on inferior equipment' but by Imola was offering to ride for no wages if he could keep his clothing deal. Maxime Desprey had agreed to race in the French Elite championship rather than GPs, while Kevin Strijbos, Max Nagl and Valentin Guillod had all been subdued by injuries and looked like they would disappear from the MXGP paddock. It's a harsh world sometimes.

* * * * * * * *

The weekend in Imola was probably the most eventful weekend of the season for the team, both on and off the track. The Foxhills recriminations rumbled on as a few people called in to talk to Roger. It transpired that even within the ACU there were officials who had had enough of Thorpe's influence and a certain official. There would be a new regime for 2019 with the ACU motocross committee taking over the running of the Maxxis British championship from ACU Events, with more transparency in the decision making. The proof would be in the pudding as the saying goes but with the championship in crisis it could only be an improvement. Even Roger was surprised by the reaction.

Max Anstie called by to apologise to Roger and Howard personally. I didn't ask about the details of the conversation but they were impressed that he was man enough to come over, explain his decision and apologise for wasting their time. His integrity left the door open for a future relationship and went some way to soothing the pain of disappointment.

Conrad and Bas Vaessen both signed new two-year contracts to race in MX2. After all the back-and-forth it was good to get the riders signed. It meant another mechanic would be taken on to work with Graeme and there would be a re-shuffle with BC working with Conrad and Vas working with Bas. The rationale was that BC could mentor Conrad, Vas and Bas both lived in Lommel and knew each other so it seemed like a good fit and the new mechanic (a young, French guy) would benefit from working with the experienced Irwin.

Roger was still working to close some other deals that would raise the profile of the team. A new race truck was being discussed with a bigger awning, new back-drops and flooring that would really enhance the appearance of the team, giving it a real factory feel. The deal with Fox for riding gear and corporate clothing was agreed, despite Anstie not being on the team. This was a very prestigious brand to get on board, both for the riders and the overall look of the team.

On the track the weekend had the potential to be an anti-climax as Herlings had clinched the MXGP title at Assen and when Pauls Jonass announced in the week that he was having immediate knee surgery to repair damage sustained when he jumped into his teammate at the MXGP of Turkey and would not ride, it meant Prado was the MX2 champion. But racing always has the possibility to throw up a surprise and when Cairoli's back wheel broke through a berm on the pit straight during qualifying, the bike high-sided the Italian into the tarmac next to the track. He was in a lot of pain and would miss the race on Sunday.

The enigma that is Conrad continued. Sixth in timed practice, he picked a start gate about ten places from the inside for the qualifying race and was then jostle back through the first few corners before ending up on the floor in turn five. Twenty-third place put him on the outside half of the gate for the main races as the riders lined up from the inside. He would again end up on the floor at the start of race one, this time in the first corner, telling me after that he had *"kept it o all the way into the turn, aiming for the berm around the outside but I lost the front end."* He actually got a good start in the second race but seemed like he hadn't 'switched on', coming around at the end of the first lap in twenty-first place. A frustrated Vas (his mechanic) fumed in the pit box. *"F##king come on! He was eighth there (pointing to the first corner), tenth there (pointing to the second corner) twelfth there! He loses five places there, boom, boom, boom (more pointing and plenty of arm gesticulating)."* Vas's frustration was understandable. Conrad would manage to pass a few riders, getting to eighteenth but his last lap looked more like a sighting lap than a race, even his dad was pi##ed off. There would be a lot to work on through the winter!

Graeme started the weekend in a great mood. He had found the settings he was happy with and through Saturday he was consistent, nineteenth in free practice, twenty-first in timed practice and twenty-second in the qualifying race. There was intermittent smoke coming from the bike in qualifying so BC stripped the engine on Saturday evening and found that the piston was worn. *"No stress"* said BC, as everything was checked and rebuilt.

Sunday was a beautiful day, the late Italian summer meant it was T-shirt and shorts weather. Graeme was pumped to be going to America for the MXON and throughout the paddock there was a relaxed atmosphere, most of the championship places were set and everyone just wanted to get the day over, it had been a long season. Twentieth in the first race was good, he had passed eight riders on a track that had become quite blue-groove and one lined, just another 30-minutes-plus-2-laps race and it was over. If only it was that easy. On the first lap of race 2 as he was approaching the big monster double-jump he clashed with another rider, the impact sending him out of control and flying through the air. Off the bike, he landed between the jumps like a rag doll. The incident happened out of sight of the team so when he didn't come around Ian immediately went to look for him. In the confusion of the race, Graeme was taken to the medical centre but because of the language barrier the team got the message that he had been taken to hospital. While they were trying to establish which hospital, Graeme arrived back at the race-truck in an ambulance, most unhappy that he had been left in the medical centre. He was in a lot of pain with what would turn out to be a dislocated right wrist and broken scaphoid. He got his phone and the ambulance took him to the local hospital with BC following in their hire car. With no one able to speak English at the hospital there was more confusion and delay as they tried to re-set his dislocation without any pain relief. Finally, BC and Graeme convinced the hospital staff that Graeme needed a general anaesthetic before his dislocation was finally re-set but by this time BC had been ordered to leave the ward. BC said *"when*

I looked in the cubicle where he was, two people were holding him and two more were pulling on his wrist. It's a good job he was out cold. They said he would be out for at least three hours and discharged after about four hours so I went back to the track to carry on packing up." BC's phone was nearly flat so he left it in the hire car while he and the team packed everything into the race truck for the long drive back to Belgium. *"I was conscious of the time and thought I had plenty of time, so we went to the Red Bull party to celebrate the KTM double world championship. Graeme turned up about an hour and a half later and went f##king mad!"* He had come around from the anaesthetic and walked back to the track, about one and a half miles. He had called and texted BC but with the phone charging in the car BC hadn't heard the calls.

Graeme told me his side of the story. *"When we got to the hospital they wanted to re-set my wrist but I was in so much pain. A nurse was trying to re-set it and I was telling her to stop. BC was giving his motivational talk saying, 'go on, he's not a pussy'. When they had enough of him they sent him out and there were seven of them pulling on me before they knocked me out. When I came around they had unplugged the drip and heart monitor and my x-rays and notes were just on the bed. They said I had to stay at least another hour and a half but it was already late and I had a six o'clock flight from Milan which was three hours away. I knew I didn't have time to stay another hour so I was calling BC. I called Minty, Vas, everyone, eventually Ian answered but he was at his hotel which was miles away. I called BC twenty-six times and in the end I thought f##k it and walked out. I still had my riding gear and knee braces on but no boots. When I got back to the track there was no-one in the truck and I knew where BC would be; when I walked into the Red Bull rig his face just dropped, he couldn't believe I was standing there. I just said, 'come on we gotta go' and he threw his drink down and we left. He'd had a few drinks so I said 'f##k that you're not driving', so I was driving the hire car with one hand and BC was being Braveheart and shouting 'Freedom!' all the way to the airport. When we got to the airport they were saying I couldn't get on the plane if the cast was less than four weeks old so I'm telling them 'sure it's fine, we flew over last week with it on, it's been on six weeks.' It was just a relief to get on the plane."*

Graeme told me the story from his hospital bed in Northern Ireland, after the second operation to put things right, with Roger by his bedside. *"I told you it was a good story"* said Roger.

BC was less forthcoming, mightily embarrassed that he had left Graeme in the hospital and gone to the Red Bull party. *"It's shite, I feel so bad about it. I hope you're not putting that in the book."* Sorry mate, it's too good to leave out.

Graeme's injuries turned out to be far more serious than first thought, more than just a dislocation. The scaphoid was shattered and there was soft tissue damage to the wrist that had caused compartment syndrome, causing the arm to pump up would. The injuries were similar to the well documented injuries suffered by Ken Roczen in his crash with Cooper Webb in 2017. Graeme's would require three surgeries and need at least three months to heal.

It was a terrible way to end his MXGP season and with the MXON only five days away it meant disaster for Team Ireland, but we will come to that in the next chapter.

The season reviewed.

Over the weekend I had asked Conrad, Graeme, Roger and Howard to same question; Has this season been a success? It's a very simple question with a more complex answer depending on your perspective and how you measure success.

Conrad.

(Interviewed before the qualification race on Saturday.)

"It's been a success in some ways and I've experienced things that

haven't benefitted me. Obviously I was in fourth or fifth in the world championship early in the season so it was a great start for me with a new team and new bike but then its just been injury after injury. Not big ones but niggly little ones that have made me miss rounds and not perform to my best, and now we're at the last round and it doesn't feel like I've done much of the season. It's been difficult but I've found a team that I really gel with and I'm happy to be staying with them for the next two years. I had a lot going on at the start of the season that was affecting my performance but we got that all cleared out and I feel free now. I'm not getting great results because I haven't been on the bike that much but I'm enjoying myself, laughing and joking, and I can spend some time at home with my family. I'm loving doing my job at the moment and it feels good to have a smile on my face while I'm doing it. I've got that last British championship at Lyng, hopefully it all goes well there and we don't get any more bad luck and I can wrap that championship up then I'm doing Weston beach race for the first time so I'm looking forward to that."

Graeme.

(Interviewed before he dislocated his wrist on Sunday.)

It's been a bit of an epic fail. The season has been rough. Its not that I've been riding bad, we started the year off winning the first round of the British championship, we had some bad luck at Canada Heights, a small crash but I couldn't get the bike started then I ended up with the burns at Blaxhall. That was a really serious injury; I could ride after but it took a lot out of my body. I got things turned around a bit at Desertmartin but my back was bad at Hawkstone. Duns was a disaster. I qualified two seconds faster than everyone and thought 'OK, let's get this championship going' then I bent the chain guide and had a DNF which was so unlucky and they cancelled the second race. I was looking forward to Foxhills, it's a good track for me and

I felt like with four races to go I could still do it but they cancelled it because of a spit of rain so now there's no way I can win. I don't want to sound awful but I wanted to win it, no one remembers who came second. I wanted to defend my title this year and I didn't do it. In the GPs I didn't know where I was at in the beginning. I've learned so much, the biggest thing was learning the tracks. I maybe took my time too much on Saturday instead of going out and getting them dialled in free practice. I'm in shape now and can do every lap of every session. Everyone is so fast but someone asked me recently if I feel like I belong here and I do, for sure. I'm used to the tracks at the British, I know where all the bumps are but the tracks at GPs, I've had to adjust to them. It's OK riding them but racing them is different. Lommel was a success, that was a good weekend. I've had a lot more available to me (parts and set-up), the biggest thing has been not worrying about what other people are using. Just because it works for Jeffrey Herlings doesn't mean it'll work for me and once I started saying what I wanted I think we came on a lot with the bike. At the start of the year we had a choice of two engines; one was really fierce and one was more mellow. I went with the mellow one because it was easier to ride but we realised that the other one is faster and I can get better starts. Next year I think we need more testing before the season and crack those little things that you can't do during the season. I didn't tell anyone but I broke a wee bone in my hand in December so we didn't start testing until the end of January. I wouldn't go to California again.

Roger.

(Interviewed on Saturday at our Hotel.)

"It's been a success in that I think we've got a better overall team in terms of the mechanics, and everyone bonding and getting on. I think we've upped our presentation this year with the new awning and

generally with a good look. The bikes have been excellently prepared; in fairness the previous mechanics did the same but the small things come together, bring Jakke into the team as our truck driver has been a real bonus. Like every season there's been some highs and lows. The early GPs, like Conrad at Redsands but then got into a bit of a downward spiral. Graeme started where we thought he would but didn't make as much progress as we hoped but we have to factor in the severe burns he suffered at Blaxhall which could have ended his season. He was coming back to form then got hit in the mouth in Switzerland which set him back again. It's been a bit of a roller-coaster but the future looks bright if we can get all the pieces of the puzzle together in the off season and come out swinging in 2019. We're negotiating with our existing sponsors and hopefully later in the year we can announce some quite different sponsors that haven't previously been involved in motocross. We've been innovative and aren't chasing the same sponsors as everyone else so it's looking well for the future. We like to be loyal to all our sponsors so hopefully we can reach an agreement over the next few weeks."

Howard.

(Interviewed on the way to the airport on Monday.)

"For me it's been disappointing. We started with high hopes and great expectations but never really gained momentum and pushed on. Hopefully everyone has learned something this year. The results have been some good and some bad; the riders set high goals for themselves which in all honesty haven't been met in the British or at GP level. I think Graeme got himself a little lost with bike set-up, he was pushing hard at the beginning of the season but the results didn't come and he's had a tough time with the burns and other injuries. Conrad show moments of brilliance but frustrates the f##k out of me. Someone with that much talent is top five without any

> *effort, top three with a bit of effort and if he really got his finger out he could have a proper crack at the championship so I hope he's learnt from this year. Hopefully with a proper structure in place next year from the start we can have a better year."*

It's impossible to write about the 2018 MXGP season without mentioning Jeffrey Herlings. When he clinched the championship at Assen you could've forgiven him for taking his foot off the gas and tucking in to the Big Mac and fries he had been craving all year, but this is Herlings; ultra-competitive and motivated. It had been a record-breaking year as he became the rider with the third most wins at 84, behind Cairoli on 85 and the retired Stefan Everts 101. His stats this year are incredible; 17 MXGP victories including 15 double-race wins amongst his 33 race wins. Clement Desalle won a single race and Cairoli won the remaining six races as KTM won every GP. Herlings has re-written the script this year, coming in leaner and fitter but with a maturity that allowed a more tactical approach. The young Herlings wanted to beat everyone by two minutes and lost a couple of MX2 titles as a consequence of bad decision making. This year he's learned to accept the odd second (and one third) place when necessary and kept his eyes on the bigger prize. Some predicted he would self-destruct and when he crashed whilst practicing, breaking his collar bone, it seemed that they might be right. But Herlings proved his toughness and desire, missing just one round, still kept the points lead and only lost a single race in the final nine rounds after his injury. Every rider in the top twenty believes they can win, indeed most have won in MX2 or MXGP which is what makes this era so good, but for those guys its going to be a long winter if they want to win again. Herlings has raised the bar and I wouldn't be surprised to see the first perfect season in MXGP in 2019 unless the others can find at least three seconds a lap, every lap. Herlings had one more job to do; beat Eli Tomac at Red Bud in the MXON.

Roger's riders

▲ *Ben Watson, Shaun Simpson & Petar Petrov (R)*

◄ *Alex Snow*

▲ *Ben Watson*

◄ *Conrad Mewse*

▲ *Connor Mullan, Cain McElveen & Ryan Mawhinney*

Gordon Grockard ▶
(photo; Honda)

▲ *Elliot Banks-Browne*

◄ *Graeme Irwin*

Jack Bintcliffe ▶
(photo Jack Bintcliffe)

Livin' the Dream

◄ Jake Nicholls

James Dunn ►

▲ James Cottrell

◄ Jordan Booker

▲ Josiah Natzke

◄ Kevin Strijbos (R)

▲ Mark Jones Adam Mckee James Noble

Mel Pocock ►

Livin' the Dream

◄ Natalie Kane

▲ Oli Benton
(photo Desmond Langley)

◄ Nathan Watson

Shaun ►
Simpson

▲ Scott Probert

◄ Stephen Sword

▲ Steven Clarke

Tom Church ►

▲ Todd Kellett
photo Haggis Hartman

Chapter 26 - MXON - the Motocross of Nations, Graeme almost leads the Irish team, Lyng

The Motocross of Nations is the biggest race of the year, the jewel in the F.I.M. crown. Known as the Olympics of motocross, three-man teams represent their country with each rider racing twice. Team and rider rivalries are put to one side as national pride is at stake. You would think that such a prestigious event would be a 'no-expense-spared' affair but that's the irony; national federations have to cover the costs of sending their riders, mechanics and necessary logistics rather than the riders' teams. That means spending the income from licence fees to fund the national team so federations' budgets are always going to be tight and inevitably the riders' sponsors end up subsidising the national teams to some extent. The race was in America this year in an attempt to encourage the Yanks to play but the consequence is that for most of the riders based in Europe the costs are huge. Denmark and Slovenia announced immediately that they would not send a team due to the cost. It's understandable as they only have one top class rider each anyway but it meant two of Europe's brightest talents, Thomas Kier Olsen and Tim Gajser, wouldn't be there. Other countries resorted to crowd funding, appealing for donations to help with the costs, including Ireland who had selected Graeme Irwin as their team leader.

Roger was happy to make the necessary arrangements and support the race, but the Irish federation would get a bill. How much does it cost to send a team? Team GB manager Mark Chamberlain gave an interview in

August and said it needed fifty to sixty thousand pounds to do it properly (but I was told his budget was less than half that amount). I think that's probably excessive but the cost of sending bikes, tools, riders, mechanics plus hotels and hiring the logistical support in America certainly adds up.

Team selection is often controversial. When Chamberlain picked Tommy Searle to ride a 250 over Ben Watson last year the internet went wild, it seemed like everyone had an opinion and needed to share it. This year the French federation snubbed Marvin Musquin despite him winning the AMA National at Red Bud, venue of this year's event. When France's first choice, Romain Febvre, was injured they asked Musquin who immediately declined the request despite his French teammates, Ferrandis and Paulin, trying to persuade him. A grateful Jordi Tixier accepted the call-up and promptly announced his new team. A report on racerxonline.com (racerhead -38) claimed that Paulin had threatened to pull out as he doesn't get on with Tixier. Politics and egos aren't confined to the French but they certainly do them well. Mark Chamberlain has got it quite easy by comparison!

The Irish team wasn't without controversy. Martin Barr riding a 250 in his fourteenth consecutive 'nations and Graeme on a 450 were obvious choices but the third rider, Stuart Edmonds, had been injured all year although he assured everyone that he would be fit and ready. The difficulty for a small nation like Ireland is finding a viable alternative. The issue was complicated further when the unlucky Edmonds re-broke his arm at the start of September, immediately ruling him out as he was replaced by Richard Bird. A fund-raising event at Desertmartin before the Assen MXGP had generated almost £5000 towards Team Ireland's expenses so hats off to the Irish fans for their passion and commitment. I asked Graeme what it means to him to be leading the team. *"It's a great honour obviously. I absolutely love getting selected to ride for my country. I want to go and get us into the 'A' final and I honestly believe if we all bring our A game we can be top ten. I'm really looking forward to racing in America, I've only ever practiced there. I look at the AMA Nationals and always thought it would be really cool to race some of their tracks. The atmosphere at Red*

Bud looks amazing. I think it will be a great race and I want a European team to win because that will raise the respect for MXGP"

The British team was announced quite late, at the end of August. Ben Watson was a no-brainer for the 250, he had shone all year in MX2. Max Anstie was the highest placed Brit in the MXGP championship, and after he won both races at last year's 'nations it was unthinkable to leave him out; he was selected for the open class. The third rider was the headache for Chamberlain. Tommy Searle and Shaun Simpson had both expressed their desire to be picked and Jake Nicholls had also made a strong case, leading the British championship since round two and racing the AMA National at Red Bud as a wild card where he finished tenth overall. Chamberlain attended the Swiss MXGP to talk to the teams. It's not as simple as just picking the riders; the teams have got to be willing to provide the bikes and support necessary. Ice One Husqvarna's price to support Anstie was more than the budget for the whole team (allegedly) but after some negotiation it came down to an affordable level. Kemea Yamaha were on board with Ben Watson and with support from Steve Dixon and Kawasaki in America, Tommy Searle would ride the open bike for team GB. Predictably, the announcement on Facebook was met with plenty of comments, a large percentage critical of Searle's selection and some very personal attacks. Watson and Anstie both posted statuses to say how proud they were to represent team GB while Searle stayed quiet, confirming to me at Imola that he was excited to be racing the 450 for his country but avoided social media because of all the crap and negativity, and just focused on himself doing a good job. Jake Nicholls posted a statement saying that he felt he had earned a place on the team while Adam Sterry and Shaun Simpson were also disappointed not to be selected. Simpson's results had improved and justified his selection but he was leaving the Wilvo Yamaha team and relationships had started to break down when Chamberlain was picking the team although they had agreed to support him if he were selected. With the Dixon team fully behind Searle he got the nod, but on the plus side Britain actually had six top riders all worthy of selection; what a lovely problem to have!

BC had prepared Graeme's spare race bike and was excited to be going. *"I went in 2003 as a fan, and every year since but this is my first time as a mechanic. I've been with Billy Mac but only as a man friend. I love it. I love the build-up; Herlings versus Tomac. I want the MXGP guys to win. I'm half Irish on my Dad's side too."*

There was enough in the crate to build another bike. Spare engine, spare suspension, sub-frame, radiators, everything except a frame and fuel tank. It was crated up along with Martin Barr's and Richard Bird's bikes before the final MXGP at Imola. Revo team owner Mark Yates (Martin Barr's sponsor) had stepped up to support the Irish team by arranging the shipping and with the Revo and Hitachi workshops in the same building it was easy to go together (and keep the costs down). Lee Tolan had arranged to hire the 'Team Seven' race truck at a cost of $3,500 for the Ireland Team to use in Red Bud. The plans were in place; flights, hotels and hire cars arranged for BC and Ian to fly out on the Tuesday and start re-assembling the bike.

When disaster struck Graeme at Imola it threw the Irish team plans into disarray. They had a reserve rider, Gary Gibson, but because of the tight budget no plans had been made for him to travel to America. The Kawasaki mounted Gibson was immediately contacted but despite frantic efforts, it was impossible to get his bike shipped in time and there was nothing available to borrow or buy in America. But the MXON isn't like any other race and within 24 hours agreement was reached; all Gibson's sponsors would release him and he would ride Graeme's Hitachi/ASA KTM UK with BC as his mechanic. They had even arranged a test track for Gibson to use on Friday so that he could at least get some time on the bike before the race. Graeme's bitter disappointment felt like winning the lottery for Gary, getting the call to represent your country with a fully prepared MXGP bike and MXGP mechanic. He had represented Ireland in 2013 but with Hitachi/ASA support it was even more special this time. BC arrived in the states on Tuesday but a hold up getting the bikes cleared through customs meant he couldn't start assembling the bike until late on Thursday. Gary had an hour on the bike on Friday morning but with heavy rain it was of limited use. He said *"Graeme is taller and heavier than me. We moved the handlebars back and softened the suspension."* It was a start but even after coming home in fourteenth in the qualifying race on Saturday, he said he was still not at home on the bike, it's very different to the Kawasaki.

The Ireland team are renowned for winning the 'B' final, in effect the LCQ to get into the main event but this time they qualified directly, Gary's result being the best of the team. BC made some further changes to soften the suspension and it was all systems go for the main races.

The mud made it a topsy-turvy race. Holland were clearly the fastest with Coldenhoff winning both his races and Herlings going 1-2, but when the doctor prevented Vlaanderen going out for his second race because of blood in his eye after a DNF in his first race, it left the door open for France to win their fifth straight Peter Chamberlain Trophy. All the recriminations about team selection evaporated as Paulin and Tixier embraced after their race when the result dawned on them.

The luck of the Irish eluded them this time but fourteenth overall was a very credible result. Everyone loves the underdog and what Team Ireland achieved was fantastic. Without insulting Richard Bird and Gary, this was the 'B' team (only Martin Barr was on the first-pick squad) but all three rose to the occasion to finish fourteenth overall. Gary looked like he belonged in the race and his results would have been better if he hadn't stopped for goggles twice in the first race.

To add insult to injury, Graeme's wife was at Red Bud along with her family, the long-planned trip was supposed to be so they could watch their son-in-law race. Lee Tolan was also there to support Graeme and discuss plans for next year. With Graeme in hospital back home in Northern Ireland it took the shine off what should have been a great finale.

For BC, it was a quick power wash to remove the worst of the Red Bud mud then back to Chicago to re-crate the bike for the return flight. Although Graeme was out of the championship there was still a championship for Conrad to win for the team.

Lyng. The British championship story requires a creative ending.

When the ACU decided to reschedule the cancelled first round of the championship (Lyng) to the 14th of October I thought it was a bad decision for a number of reasons. The season is over! It ended the previous week with the MXON. Winter weather has started, the nights are drawing in and everyone has had enough after twenty MXGPs and seven British championship rounds. To compound the issue Foxhills was also cancelled due to the weather so the ACU were between a rock and a hard place; they needed to run the last round (Lyng) and some teams were demanding that they reschedule the Foxhills event. With Weston beach race on the 21st of October the next available date was the 28th, the day when British summer time ends and it's dark by tea time. The other suggestion was to make the Lyng event a two-dayer with effectively two meetings at the same venue on Saturday and Sunday.

However the conundrum was resolved it left me with a problem; it would be impossible to include the final rounds of the Maxxis British championship in this book because of the print deadline. The schedule had been organised and the manuscript would be finished after the MXON which all worked perfectly until the Lyng date got postponed. The publishers had been as flexible as possible but it was a mammoth task to get the book turned around after the MXON in time to launch at the Dirt Bike Show and any further delay made it impossible.

The focus of the book has been life in the MXGP paddock and the business of running a Grand Prix team, and while the British championships would have been included in the story if they had stuck to the original dates, it's not a deal breaker, so we took the decision to stay with the original plan rather than miss the launch date at the Dirt Bike Show. Therefore, the only way out was to write two endings for the MX2 championship and leave you to pick the ending that is applicable. If you're reading this book you are almost certainly a motocross fan so you already know who won the British championships (or you can quickly check the results at www.mxgb. co.uk), so enjoy the ending(s) and the 'fake news' (or what could have been). In the MX1 championship one thing was certain; Graeme wouldn't win although the exact positions in the final standings were up for grabs. For the sake of full disclosure, the rest of this chapter was written ten days before the final round but I'm confident that ending #1 and ending #3 will turn out to be true!

MX2 British championship Ending #1. Conrad clinches the title.

In a nail-biting end to the season that has been an emotional roller-coaster, Conrad won his first British championship at the rescheduled Lyng event. Facing stiff competition all year from Josh Gilbert and Mel Pocock, Conrad was the most consistent on home soil despite a bad day in Duns and an injury at Hawkstone. When the penultimate round at Foxhills (his 'home track') was cancelled he took a slim fourteen-point lead into the final round at Lyng and knew that barring disaster the championship was his. Two safe rides were enough to get the job done and deliver Conrad's first MX2 British Championship, bring the team's tally to twelve British championships and remain Britain's most successful MXGP team!

MX2 British championship Ending #2. Conrad snatches defeat from the jaws of victory.

Despite being the fastest man in MX2 all season, injuries and bad luck have cost Conrad the championship. A disastrous day in Duns cost him dearly as his points lead was slashed before a hand injury at Hawkstone ended his second race and eroded the points lead further. Despite doing everything possible to recover, he had lost the championship momentum and when the penultimate round at Foxhills (his 'home track') was cancelled he took a slim fourteen-point lead into the final round at Lyng. Anything can happen in motocross and without lady luck on his side his points advantage slipped way; close but no cigar.

Despite not adding to their British championship tally of 11 titles this year, Hitachi/ASA KTM UK continue to be Britain's most successful MXGP team.

MX1 British championship Ending #3. This much we know, Graeme is side-lined.

Graeme started strongly, winning the first round but a serious injury at Blaxhall, bad luck in Duns with a DNF and the second race cancelled followed by a back injury at Hawkstone meant it was an up-hill battle all year. When the penultimate round at Foxhills was cancelled it left Graeme mathematically eliminated from the title but second place was still possible. Even second place became moot when he crashed at the final MXGP race in Italy, dislocating his wrist. Gracious in defeat, he would hand over his number 1 plate to a new champion. Jake Nicholls had been the red plate holder since round 2 and the most consistent rider but tragedy struck the luckless Nicholls with a broken leg two weeks before Lyng, the same weekend that Graeme broke his wrist at Imola. It left the door open for Bobryshev, Searle and Banks-Browne to fight it out for the championship podium with Graeme and Nicholls side-lined from the final event.

Just for fun, here is my prediction. Searle takes two wins and jumps to third. Bobryshev take two second places and leap-frogs Nicholls to win the championship, Nicholls is still second. Banks-Browne gets two third places and tying with Searle in championship points but loses on the tie-break so gets fourth. Graeme drops to fifth as Searle and Banks-Browne move up.

And it's still not over!

KTM UK decided not to exhibit at the Dirt Bike Show in November, the traditional launch of the next year's bikes opting instead to use the Weston Beach race on October 20th/21st as the platform for the new model launch. A big presence with race trucks and display trucks was part of their plan coupled with a few big KTM names in the race that included Graeme and Conrad, both scheduled to race specially prepared XC model machines with big tanks. With his arm in plaster Graeme was ruled out of Weston and he still had the "Fastest Irwin Challenge" to compete in (I detailed that event in chapter 19) to settle the long running family argument. That too would be put on hold while his wrist healed. It would've been great to include these races in the book but they will have to go in the sequel.

Ian, BC and Vas had work to do, rebuilding all the bikes with stock parts ready for sale and clearing out the workshop. The race truck would return to Lommel to be emptied out and prepared for sale with the tractor unit going back to M.A.N.

The 2019 bikes should arrive in December so that Graeme, Conrad and Bas can get some hours in before pre-season testing in Spain starts in January, and amongst all of that the mechanics and riders will try to fit in a long overdue holiday and Christmas! Although we talk about the 'off-season', there really is only a couple of weeks before the whole team cranks up again, preparing for the next season.

Epilogue

Whatever the outcome of the British championship it's still been a great year for the team and everyone who's a part of it. Obviously results are a big part of the sport but they are not the only measure of success. It's been a very challenging year for the team at the GPs where the results haven't matched early season aspirations but those knocks are all part of racing and you've got to be able to handle the setbacks and carry on. This book was about the business of running a team and the stories of the people involved; Roger has delivered another year in the MXGP paddock for his sponsors and partners, while Lee came in and did the same at the British championships, both improving the paddock presence and presentation of the team.

Graeme and Conrad had some growing pains and some tough times; both showed the speed to match their expectations at home and abroad but injuries and inconsistency had hurt both their championship aspirations. For Conrad it was a year of personal growth as he matures into manhood, and I know he's learned a lot from the experiences this year that will stand him in good stead. Graeme faced his own challenges, stepping up to compete at world championship level during the most talent packed era in our sport. It was never going to be easy especially with the injuries and bad luck he had to overcome but by the end of the season he had found his feet in the class and belonged amongst some very fast company. Equally important in my opinion is the way that Graeme and Conrad have conducted themselves; both are very likeable, friendly and gracious with their fans, consummate professionals who are a credit to the team and their sponsors.

Behind the scenes Roger, Ian, BC, Vas, Minty, Jakke, Shaun, Steve F, Justin, Jamie, Howard, Ali, Paul, Brooke, Cliff, Steve M, Lee et al have worked away, sometimes late into the night, in various capacities to support Graeme and Conrad. Going into 2019 Roger will again field a strong squad as Bas Vaessen joins Conrad in MX2 and Graeme in MXGP, building on this season to have an even more impressive paddock presence while they battle with the factory teams on track.

I said at the beginning that I didn't want this book to be a 'politically correct press release' that pretended everything was perfect. It's not always pretty but it's the challenges, the adversity and the people that make the story interesting and the outcome worthwhile. I've also covered some of the wider aspects of life in the MXGP paddock for context, to give a more complete picture of the business of running an MXGP team and the difficulties of competing at the highest level.

Thank you for buying my book, I hope you've been entertained and enlightened, and that you're living out your dream, whatever that may be.

MXGP & British Championship tables for Graeme & Conrad

Graeme's MXGP stats

Graeme Irwin	Argentina	Holland (Valkenswaard)	Spain	Italy Trentino	Portugal	Total
Positions	16th – 20th	19th – 21st	16th – 24th	21st – 19th	DNF – 23rd	
Points	5-1	2-0	5-0	0-2	0-0	15 pts
Ch'p pos	18th	23rd	22nd	21st	24th	

	Russia	Latvia	Germany	Britain	France	
Positions	19th - DNF	DNS*	DNS*	19th – 21st	23rd – 21st	
Points	2-0	- -	- -	2 - 0	0 - 0	19 pts
Ch'p pos	24th	25th	25th	24th	26th	

	Italy (Ottobiano)	Indonesia	Asia	Czech Republic	Belgium	
Positions	18th – 16th	DNS #	DNS #	21st – 20th	15th – 14th	
Points	3 – 5	- -	- -	0 - 1	6 - 7	41 pts
Ch'p pos	26th	26th	27th	27th	24th	

	Switzerland	Bulgaria	Turkey	Holland (Assen)	Italy (Imola)	Final
Positions	DNF**-DNS	DNS ##	DNS ##	20 - 17	20-DNF++	
Points	0 - 0	- -	- -	1 - 4	1 - 0	47 pts
Ch'p pos	25th	26th	26th	26th	26th	26th

KEY
DNS = did not start.#
*Injured (burns)
** Injured (rock in the mouth)
Team did not attend the MXGP's in Bulgaria & Turkey

Team did not attend the MXGP's in Indonesia & Asia
DNF = did not finish
++ dislocated wrist

Graeme's Maxxis ACU British championship stats

Graeme Irwin	~~Lyng~~	Culham	Canada Heights	Blaxhall	Desert Martin	Duns	Hawk stone	~~Fox hills~~	Lyng	Total
Position		1 - 3	11 - 3	4 - 7	2 - 4	29 - #	2 - 3		DNS	
Points	P	25+20= 45	10+20= 30	18+14= 32	22+18= 40	0+#= 0	22+20= 42	C	0 + 0 =0	189
Ch'p position		1	3	3	3	3	3			TBC

P = Postponed due to the weather
# = second race cancelled
C = Cancelled due to the weather
DNF = did not finish

C = Cancelled due to the weather
DNS = did not start, broken wristP = Postponed due to the weather
*= Penalised 5 positions for jumping under waved yellow flags
** = Injured hand

Conrad's MX2 stats

Conrad Mewse	Argentina	Holland (Valkenswaard)	Spain	Italy (Trentino)	Portugal	Total
Position	6th – 19th	5th – 4th	4th – 9th	20th – 4th	DNF – 21st	
Points	15 – 2	16 – 18	18 – 12	1 – 18	0 – 0	100 pts
Ch'p pos	13th	6th	5th	5th	7th	
	Russia	Latvia	Germany	Britain	France	
Position	15th – 19th	8th – 16th	23rd – 22nd	14th – 22nd	7th – 9th	
Points	6 – 2	13 – 5	0 – 0	7 – 0	14 – 12	159 pts
Ch'p pos	8th	10th	13th	13th	13th	
	Italy (Ottobiano)	Indonesia	Asia	Czech Republic	Belgium	
Position	8th – DNF	DNS #	DNS #	DNS *	6th – 8th	
Points	13 – 0	- -	- -	- -	15 – 13	200 pts
Ch'p pos	13th	13th	13th	14th	12th	
	Switzerland	Bulgaria	Turkey	Holland (Assen)	Italy (Imola)	Final
Position	DNS **	DNS ** ##	DNS **##	9 – 16	24th – 18th	
Points	- -	- -	- -	12 – 5	0 – 3	220 pts
Ch'p pos	13th	13th	13th	12th	12th	12th

KEY

DNS = did not start

= Team did not attend the MXGP's in Indonesia and Asia   * = Injured leg

** = Injured hand   ## = Team did not attend the MXGP's in Bulgaria & Turkey

Conrad's Maxxis ACU British championship stats

Conrad Mewse	~~Lyng~~	Culham	Canada Heights	Blaxhall	Desert Martin	Duns	Hawk stone	~~Fox hills~~	Lyng	Total
Position		1-1	1-1	8*-1	1 - 1	14 - 2	1-DNF**			
Points	P	25+25= 50	25+25= 50	13+25= 38	25+25= 50	7+22= 29	25+0= 25	C		
Ch'p position		1	1	1	1	1	1			TBC

P = Postponed due to the weather   C = Cancelled due to the weather

*= Penalised 5 positions for jumping under waved yellow flags   DNF = did not finish

** = Injured hand

And finally, some 'thank you's'

No book is complete without sharing some love at the end, so here goes; Roger Magee. Thank you for sharing your story and supporting this project. This book wouldn't have been possible if you hadn't been bold enough for a 'warts 'n' all' story.

Graeme Irwin, Conrad Mewse, Ian Browne, Bryan Connolly, Vaclav Lavicka. Thank you for giving me your time, answering all my questions and filling in the blanks. It would've been a boring book without your honesty and openness.

A big thank you to all the people that gave me their time and trust for an interview. Your thoughts and anecdotes have been the glue tying the story together; Lee Tolan, Shaun Osmond, Paul (Minty) Whitehouse, Riece Bellamy, Steve Fry, Howard Smith, Ali Rowlands, Jamie Dobb, Justin Morris, Steve Mewse, Lisa Leyland, Samanta Gelli, David Luongo, Brooke Irwin, Milly Sears, Jill Cairoli, Joan Magee, Jakke van Beal, Paul Keates, Max Anstie and Shaun Simpson.

The photographers; Ray Archer, Ian Cairns and Haggis Hartman. They say a picture is worth a thousand words, so thank you for saving me a lot of typing and providing some great images.

Proof reading and feedback was provided by Roger and Alistair; thank-you. If there's any spelling mistakes you're getting the blame!

And finally, a very big thank you to the sponsors who (with a nudge from Roger) generously backed this book and assisted with the production costs: Hitachi Construction Machinery, Milwaukee Tools, BOTT cabinets, Steve Benton Transport and ASA Scaffolding.